Growing with Children

HUMAN DEVELOPMENT BOOKS

Joseph and Laurie Braga, *general editors*

HUMAN DEVELOPMENT BOOKS is a series designed to bridge the gap between theoretical research in the behavioral sciences and practical application by readers. Each book in the series deals with an issue important to the growth and development of human beings, as individuals and in interaction with one another. At a time when the pressures and complexities of the world are making increased demands on people's ability to cope, there is a need for tools that can help individuals take a more active role in solving their own problems and in living life more fully. Such information is not easily found or read by those without previous experience or familiarity with the vocabulary of a particular behavioral field. The books in this series were designed and written to meet that purpose.

Drs. Joseph and Laurie Braga, both developmental psychologists, are now on the faculty of the Department of Psychiatry at the University of Miami Medical School. Joseph Braga was formerly on the faculty of the Division of Human Development and Learning, The University of Illinois, Chicago. The Bragas are co-authors of *Child Development and Early Childhood Education: a Guide for Parents and Teachers,* published by the City of Chicago.

GROWING
with CHILDREN

the early childhood years

Joseph and Laurie Braga

Prentice-Hall, Inc.   A SPECTRUM BOOK   Englewood Cliffs, New Jersey

Library of Congress Cataloging in Publication Data

BRAGA, JOSEPH, comp.
  Growing with children.

  (Human development books)
  Bibliography: p.
  1. Children—Growth. 2. Children—Care and hygiene.
3. Children—Management. I. Braga, Laurie, joint comp.
II. Title.
R J131.B69   649'.1'019   74-7315
ISBN 0-13-366260-8
ISBN 0-13-366237-3 (pbk.)

10 9 8 7 6 5 4 3 2 1

PRENTICE-HALL INTERNATIONAL, INC. (*London*)
PRENTICE-HALL OF AUSTRALIA PTY., LTD. (*Sydney*)
PRENTICE-HALL OF CANADA, LTD. (*Toronto*)
PRENTICE-HALL OF INDIA PRIVATE LIMITED (*New Delhi*)
PRENTICE-HALL OF JAPAN, INC. (*Tokyo*)

WE DEDICATE THIS BOOK TO
each other,
our son Tommy,
and
all kindred spirits
who are friends of children

To illustrate or support points made in their own writing, the authors have inserted a number of pertinent readings, cartoons, poems, and other selections, including the following: *The Miracle of a Mother's Touch* by Ashley Montagu; *Infant Crying and Maternal Responsiveness: Discussion* by Sylvia M. Vell and Mary D. Salter-Ainsworth; *What to Do When Baby's Crying Gets Trying* by Niles Newton; *Experience and Environment: Discussion and Conclusions* by Burton L. White; *Defense and Growth* by Abraham H. Maslow; *The Little Elf* by John Kendrick Bangs; *The Beginnings of the Self: The Problem of the Nurturing Environment* by Ira J. Gordon; *Down with Sexist Upbringing* by Letty Cottin Pogrebin; *A Tree Grows in Brooklyn* by Betty Smith; *Piaget for Early Education* by Constance Kamii and Rheta DeVries; *Punishment* by Robert Sears, Eleanor Maccoby, and Harry Levin; *Making Sense of Discipline* by Hettie James; *Children Learn What They Live* by Dorothy Law Nolte; *The Essential Ingredient* by Ruth Hartley.

Contents

To the Reader

This book is for you. From its conception to its completion, we have tried to think of you, to direct ourselves to you personally, and to make you a part of our writing. Many times throughout the book, we will ask you questions—ask you to consciously relate what you're reading to your own personal experience. There's a reason for our doing that; it is more than a device to get you involved in what you're reading. The reason is to get you to be consciously aware of what you do unconsciously most of the time.

All people filter and interpret what they experience in terms of their own personal beliefs, opinions, values, and past experience, but usually without conscious awareness that they are doing it. Have you ever looked through a book underlined by someone you knew and noticed that a reading of their underlining gave you an interesting insight into what they believed? Have you ever heard the same story told by two friends and been amazed at the different things each chose to report or at the differences in their interpretations of the same incident? Have you had the experience of judging friends' motives for doing something in a manner entirely different from their judgment of the same thing? All of these things illustrate how people filter in terms of their own viewpoint.

The way you view the world is related more to who you are than to some objective reality; what you attend to, what you hear, what you see, etc., and how you interpret what you attend to, is related to how you see the world in relation to your own self-concept. One of the purposes of this book is to try to get you to become more aware of these influences on your own behavior. For, as we will repeatedly emphasize, one of the most powerful influences you will have on children is through the models that your behavior provides them.

In addition, it is important to understand how your view of reality is related to your self-concept so that you can be more thoughtful in your guidance of children in their development of their own self-concepts. As you will read in Chapter V, it happens very early. "Gardner Murphy has indicated that the self-picture [self-concept] is fairly well integrated by the third year of life. Once it has developed, it becomes the evaluator, selector, judger, and organizer of future experience, and the child's behavior may be seen as organized to enhance and maintain his view." * How children see and feel about themselves will profoundly affect how they approach and respond to the world. Thus, the development of a child's self-concept is central to his or her** growth in every other area.

The focus of this book is on the development in children of a positive self-concept, one that will enable them to feel secure in their ability to be successful in their interactions, now and in the future. We will discuss the process of development of feelings about the self-in-relation-to-others in the context of (1) children's developmental needs, (2) your responses to those needs, and (3) your own personal feelings and past experiences. We stress, as our title implies, that you must grow *with* your children if you want them to grow to be all that they can

---

* Ira J. Gordon, "The Beginnings of the Self: The Problem of the Nurturing Environment," *Phi Delta Kappan,* (March 1969).

** An unusual aspect of this book that you will no doubt notice is our use of pronouns. Our language is so structured that the masculine singular pronoun is always used to stand for both sexes. In many books you will find an apology by the authors and an explanation that they know children come in two sexes, but that it is necessary to use "he" for clarity. We have given this much thought and have come up with an alternative: Wherever possible, we have used "they"; when it was not practical because it would lead to confusion, we have alternated between the use of "he" and the use of "she." If you notice yourself feeling a bit startled or uncomfortable each time you see "she" used to stand for both male and female children, let it be a reminder to you of how important language really is in forming impressions. It is hard to know, since we're so used to it, how the exclusive use of the masculine pronoun affects the self-concept of the growing female child; but it's an interesting question to ponder.

be. We hope that the insights gained from better understanding of how children grow may help you not only to
guide them in their growth, but also to continue your
own growth as a person.

Joe and Laurie Braga

1

Children,
Their Development,
and You

Most people reading this book will, at some time in their lives, have children. We direct much of this book to you in anticipation of that time. Some of you already have or care for children. For you, many of the thoughts and ideas we share will have even more meaning because you've experienced them already. We will often address the reader as "you," realizing that you may be a parent, other relative, a teacher, or simply a friend of young children. When we speak of "your child," we mean just that. We all, as adults who are concerned about children, take a personal responsibility for every child whose life we touch in the important early years.

We will discuss the role of the parent, and in particular, the role of the mother in the child's life a great deal. The reason for this is that, as our society is presently structured, parents, and especially mothers, are the persons who spend the most amount of time with very young children. But the ideas contained here have meaning for all of you, whether or not you ever *have* or care for children, because you all once *were* children. Understanding how children grow can help you understand yourself better and give you insight into your own growth as you rediscover the child within yourself.

How Do You Feel About Children?

What kinds of feelings do you have when you think of children? About being around them? About having ones of your own? About your own childhood experiences? Do you enjoy being with children, or do you find them a bother? How many children do you number among your friends? Did you like children when you were a child, or did you prefer the company of adults? What age children do you prefer? Why? How does it make you feel if someone calls your behavior "childish"?

How much can you remember of your own childhood? What kinds of memories do you have? Can you find any pattern to them? Can you think of any reasons why you might remember those things out of all your childhood experiences? How did you feel about adults when you were a child? Think about the adults you really liked and those you didn't like. Can you remember why? Do you remember times when your feelings were hurt by adults? Can you recall the reasons? Do you remember times of great happiness and contentment? Can you recall the source of your happiness?

How important do you think childrearing is? What kinds of things do you think people should know about children in order to be good parents? Who would you be more likely to trust to give you advice about your childen—a child psychologist? A teacher of young children? Your neighbor who has three kids? Your pediatrician? Yourself? Your children?

We hope that before you get into the rest of the book, you'll really give these questions some thought. Most of them have no right or wrong answers, no good or bad answers; the only valid answers are those that come from within you—what *you* really think and feel about them. You might want to jot down a few notes now about how you would answer the questions posed, and then look at them again when you're through with the book. See if you've gained any insights that changed your thinking or that, perhaps, jogged your memory about your own childhood experiences, attitudes, and feelings.

We begin this book by asking you questions for two reasons: (1) If you are to learn anything of value to you from reading this book, it will be because you actively participate in it. If you simply read the words, passively, you will get little out of it. We would like you to use it as a springboard for your own thoughts about the issues that are raised. For example, if you react very positively or very negatively to something that you read, try to figure out why. What you bring to the process of learning, whether from a book, a movie, a class, or a conversation, is at least as important as the material that is presented to you. (2) We were all children once, and we have memories of our own childhoods that affect the way we as adults feel about and respond to children with whom we interact. It is very important that you identify and try to understand those feelings, if at all possible, *before* you have any children of your own or have any responsibilities for, or significant interactions with, other people's children.

Adults are very important to children. Objectively, this is inevitable; children are totally dependent on adults for their welfare. Therefore, your impact on children is very great, especially if you have any sort of power over their lives (whether as parent, teacher, or in some other role). Knowing this, it is essential that you examine your responses to children so that you can treat those in your care with all the concern and respect that they deserve as human beings. We offer you a phrase that we hope will be in your thoughts whenever you interact with children: *"First, do no harm."* Beyond that, do whatever you can to contribute to (and not interfere with) those children's growth and happiness.

Childhood is a short time, but we carry our childhood experiences, feelings, attitudes, and problems with us throughout the rest of our lives. Some children are fortunate enough to spend their early years *growing* in all ways that they should, and they emerge from childhood feeling good about themselves and ready to meet the challenges of new stages in life. Too many people, however, leave their childhood years with unresolved issues of growth, with self-doubt and a lack of confidence in their ability to successfully deal with the problems and issues of adulthood. They spend the rest of their lives working out issues ("Am I a good, competent, worthy person? Do others care for me? Do they respect me?) that should have been settled, at least in their basic form, in early childhood.

In the readings and commentary in this book, you will find descriptions of what we know now to be stages of growth that every child, given the kinds of support and stimulation for growth that he needs, should experience in his early years. In addition to helping you to be an effective guide in the growth of children, we hope the ideas we will share in this book may give you some insights into your own growth. Clearly, we do not have all the answers to successful childrearing. But we have more now than our parents and their parents and their parents before them. Thus, it is not unusual that many of us as adults carry into our adulthood aspects of ourselves that never grew as they should have. Understanding the processes of growth in their optimal form may help you discover those parts of you that didn't grow; and on discovering them, you may be able, for yourself, to begin to accomplish that growth. This, then, is what we intend by our title, *Growing with Children.*

SHOULD YOU HAVE CHILDREN? [1]

As we become more and more aware of the importance of children's early years in shaping their lives, the corresponding importance of the

[1] This may seem a moot question to those of our readers who already have children. But we ask you to bear with the discussion because it contains thoughts for you too. Yours is the ultimate challenge—to grow with your children so that you may all be as happy and productive as possible.

role of parents in children's growth becomes obvious. Parents do not merely pass on a biological inheritance to their children; through their treatment of them, and equally important, through the models they provide, parents give their children patterns of behavior that will influence how they will relate to others, how they will view and approach the world, and, most importantly, how they will feel about themselves.

This book is about children. But it is also about you—how your growth relates to your own childhood and to your effectiveness in guiding the children in your care to become happy and productive people. An important stage in the growth of every psychologically healthy adult human being is the making of a commitment to the further growth of the human race. For many people, this commitment is expressed by a decision to combine resources with a partner of the opposite sex in the production of a child. For others, these same energies may be put into productive activity in some area of human need. Erikson[2] has termed this stage "generativity," by which he means a concern for establishing and guiding the next generation. He stresses that this is an important stage in the growth of the healthy personality that does not necessarily have any relation to having or even wanting children; in fact, he states, many young parents bringing their children to child guidance centers have not developed this parental sense.

At this stage of human history, we are no longer obliged to accept the responsibility of parenthood either (1) before we, ourselves, have grown as human beings sufficiently to freely choose and embrace that responsibility, or (2) as the only alternative avenue for expressing our creative, productive human energies. The purpose of having children, especially at a time when overpopulation is a continuing threat, must be to create productive world citizens capable of developing beyond the confines of self-interest. It is, therefore, with this and the recent freedom from our biological destiny in mind that we ask the question: Should you have children?

In considering the characteristics of healthy growth and in particular those qualities required in a parent in order to foster it in a child, we ask you to make an honest evaluation of your own capacity to be that kind of parent. Every person has his/her own particular *style* of child-rearing, and no one can or should tell you *how* to raise your children. What we *can* do is provide some of the tools and describe some of the methods of raising children that have proved successful. Thus, when we ask that you ask yourself whether or not you should have children, we are asking you to examine your motives and needs, not your style.

2 Erik H. Erikson, *Childhood and Society*, 2nd ed. (New York: W. W. Norton & Company, Inc., 1963), pp. 266–67.

Your own growth should be sufficient that when you have children you can serve their needs rather than the reverse.

Perhaps the first question you should ask yourself when considering having a child is whether there are qualities in you that you do not like and would not like to see passed on to your child. As we implied before, one of the most powerful means by which children learn is through modeling their own behavior after that which they see in their parents. If you are not prepared to change those qualities in yourself that you would not want to see in your offspring, you should wait until you have been able to do so. It is very common for people to dislike most in others behaviors that they are not happy with in themselves (often not even realizing that they share those behaviors). It would be very unfair to a child to "teach" her, through your behavior, those kinds of behaviors and then to punish her for possessing them.

Next, we ask you to consider the kind of life commitment that having a child implies. Babies grow into children, children grow into adolescents, and adolescents grow into young adults. Having a child is a very serious and long-term responsibility that does not end for many years. It requires a willingness and ability to compromise one's own needs and desires for someone else and to relinquish certain aspects of freedom that are not possible at this time, in this society, when one becomes a parent. For those who freely choose the responsibility of having and raising children, it is a highly creative, productive, and rewarding act—perhaps more than any other thing a person could possibly do. Producing a happy, healthy human being is a more creative act with more far-reaching consequences than producing fine paintings, great symphonies or any other traditional "creative" product.

Every child born is a renewal of hope for humankind; and children who fulfill their human promise will, as adults, have an impact on the future of the world, both through their own acts and through the children they may have, far greater than anything you could possibly do in your life span by yourself. That, then, is the purpose of having children—to further the growth (in quality, that is, not in number) of the human race. A decision to have children should carry with it a respect for the role you have chosen and for the important responsibilities that you incur as a parent.

It may seem, because of the emphasis we have put on the responsibilities that parenthood demands, that we are suggesting that a person must choose that role over all others. This question is particularly relevant for mothers, who traditionally have assumed the bulk of parental responsibility. In fact, some of the more successful mothers in White's study, which you will read about in Chapter 3, also held down part-time jobs. The time demands on a parent are obviously great in a child's infancy. But as a child gets older, the amount of time a parent needs to spend with his/her child decreases; it is the *quality* of the parent-child interaction that is important, not the *quantity* of time that they spend together.

Although many fathers have not, in the past, participated enough in the childrearing function, it was less because of time than because of role problems (i.e., childrearing was considered "woman's work"). No one ever questions a father's ability to handle both a job and fatherhood. The same should be true for mothers (if they so choose). As important as motherhood is, living a life that is 100 percent oriented to care and responsibility for a child can be very limiting and thus lead to less than optimal effectiveness as a parent. Mothers, like fathers, need and should have other avenues of self-expression of their own choosing in addition to childrearing.

The point is that effective parenting does not mean that you must devote your entire being to it; it requires that you give fully of yourself to your children while you are interacting with them, but there should be time in parents' lives for things other than children. One way to insure this is true is for both parents to participate equally, in a partnership, in the childrearing process. This will not only free the mother's time, but it should also contribute to a more complete, democratic, and cooperative relationship between the parents which will, in turn, provide a good model to their children. This, then, is another question that potential parents should enquire of themselves: Do we both freely choose this responsibility, and if so, do we both agree to share it equally? [3] "Mothering" is an acknowledged requirement for a child's healthy growth; but, as the cartoons below humorously illustrate, men can be "mothers" too.

[3] In a home where there are two parents childrearing should be a mutual process, shared by both parents, not a responsibility relegated solely to the woman because of tradition. However, the reality of the current status of families is that there are increasing numbers of families that have only one parent, either by necessity or by choice. Although it is very possible to raise happy, healthy children in such a situation, because our society does not yet provide sufficient supports for the single parent, it is a very demanding job. The search for self is the search for life's work, and an important aspect of any parent's life work should be the raising of his/her children to happy and productive adulthood. The additional challenge meeting the single parent thus also provides enormous potential for self-growth through creative investment of self in the raising of children.

Mothering Is Not a Job "For Women Only" . . .

Joseph and Laurie Braga

The message in the cartoons reproduced below is as pertinent today as it was in the early thirties when they were drawn. Men are perfectly capable of being effective child caregivers; but the "rules" of the culture and consequent attitudes of people in the culture tend to exclude men from the mothering role. Men must be allowed and encouraged to be more than fathers (a role that has traditionally been very confining to men's participation in their children's upbringing); they must be allowed and encouraged to be "mothers" too.

Cartoons and titles by Elzie Chrisler Segar. Popeye daily comic strips: 8-8-33 and 8-11-33. Copyright © 1933, King Features Syndicate, Inc. Reprinted by permission.

... But the Culture Can Make It Difficult for Men to Be Mothers

We suggested before that an understanding of the developmental processes of young children might help you to have some insight into your own growth processes. An important benefit of this kind of introspection should be the rediscovery of the child within you—remembering what it felt like, what things made you happy, what kinds of treatment bothered you, what was important to you, and so on. As adults, we tend too often to view children only from our own perspectives. Even for those periods, such as the first couple of years, when you can't really remember what it was like, if you can try sometimes to look at and experience the world as if you were the same age as your children, you will find it will give you an empathy with them that will be very helpful in trying to meet their needs.

Finally, rediscovering the child within you can be like a renewal for you—a reaffirmation of your selfhood. For you will find not only aspects of you that need growth and nurturance; you will discover also those parts of yourself that are most profoundly and basically *you*. And the best thing you can do both for yourself and for your child is to really get to know and like yourself. "Belief in self is the tap-root of every great life." [4] There is no greater strength that you could pass on to your child.

GUIDELINES FOR HELPING CHILDREN TO GROW

There are many things to know about how children grow and develop so that you can be most effective in facilitating their growth. We will try, throughout the book, to provide you with some general guidelines to meet their needs. The first, and the ones that really encompass all others, have to do with the question of what children's needs *are*. In the remainder of the chapter, we will discuss several very helpful guidelines to answering that question: (1) children's needs change as they grow; the kind of care a baby needs, for example, is very different from the care needed by a two-year-old; (2) children's needs change in a predictable and logical pattern, and growth proceeds as each new need is met; (3) children "tell" us, by their behavior, what their needs are; they are our best guides to what they need. We just need to learn to be attuned to their behavioral messages.

Children's needs change as they grow

Tiny infants' needs are basically physiological (e.g., they need to eat, sleep, breathe, maintain a regular body temperature, and eliminate wastes) and social—they need to establish a mutually gratifying relationship with a warm, loving, responsive human being. As they grow, children's physical needs become less urgent and therefore less central to their lives, their social needs become more specified and more varied, and they develop needs that are directly oriented toward self-growth.

The kind of care and treatment that Carla needs at a year and a half is very different from that needed by Rachel at five, and both of them need different things than a tiny infant. The fact that children's needs change as they grow may seem like a fairly obvious fact, but its implications for childrearing are very important and often not understood. You probably know someone who is great with babies but not at all effective with older children, or someone who is very good with children once they can talk and reason, but terrible with very young children.

[4] Helen Wilmans, 1885; from a personal collection of old news and literary items.

The reason for this apparent discrepancy is that children's needs change. The first step in effective parenting, then, is understanding what children's needs are at *all* the different stages of their development. Understanding the child's needs, you then have a better chance of meeting them successfully. Without understanding what their needs are, you may misunderstand children's behavioral cues and thus respond to them in inappropriate ways.

There are many, many specific, individual needs that a person can experience—so many that we could neither identify them all nor suggest specific ways of satisfying all of them. And each individual child will have his own specific set of needs—of things that are very important to his growth and well-being. However, there is a very logical and systematic organization to all these varied needs that enables us to provide some guidelines for dealing effectively with them. There are basic needs that are shared by all people, and knowledge of what they are and how they relate to children's development may help you to be more effective in guiding their growth. The basic needs can be classified into five groupings: (1) physiological; (2) safety; (3) belongingness and love; (4) esteem; and (5) self-actualization.[5]

Maslow formulated the "hierarchy of needs" as a construct through which we can view the growth of human beings toward psychological health and self-actualization. The basic premise is that we may view the path of growth as parallel to movement to increasingly higher need states, and that a person will advance to higher levels of need through the satisfaction of preceding needs. The real significance of this formulation (which is one aspect of an entire theory of personality) is that it looks at human beings as inherently growth-oriented. This is in direct contrast to past, philosophically based views of human beings (and especially children) as needing to learn to fight and resist the pull of their natural "bad-animal" instincts. The growth-oriented view of human beings says essentially that people will continue throughout their life span to move steadily in the direction of growth as long as their environment and experiences permit and support their growth; in contrast, the "bad-animal" view of human nature asserts that growth can occur only through overcoming the natural impulses that are essentially negative.

It should be stressed that Maslow's orientation toward human

[5] See Abraham Maslow, *Motivation and Personality*, 2nd ed. (New York: Harper & Row, Publishers, Inc., 1970), Chapter 5. The ideas contained in the following pages, pertaining to the changing needs of the child, are an adaptation of Maslow's formulation. Although Maslow refers to different periods in early childhood to illustrate different levels of needs, his construct is intended to cover the full life span. If you find these ideas thought-provoking, we would encourage you to read this as well as other books by Maslow.

growth, though in contradiction to many popularly held views, is strongly supported by research evidence from many different fields of study. The reading by Bell and Ainsworth in Chapter 2, for example, reports research that solidly challenges the previously held assumption that to pick up crying babies reinforces their crying. In fact, they found that babies use crying to communicate a need, and the more promptly and consistently their crying is responded to, the less they will cry in the future as they learn other means of communication. The reading by White in Chapter 3 illustrates the importance of structuring the environment and responding to "runabout" children in such a way as to meet their needs for safety, love, and esteem, thus fostering their growth of autonomy.

The point is that if the infant and young child's needs are met as they arise, they will be replaced by higher-level needs. The child will keep moving forward in a positive, productive direction if "old" needs have been relatively satisfied. Sometimes a child's way of expressing a need may be viewed as an undesirable behavior. For example, children in the "terrible two" stage show their need to assert themselves as persons, sometimes by being defiant, stubborn, and self-assertive (e.g., "Me do it") to a degree that is totally out of line with their real capabilities. But, they *need* to assert their wills, and they will only relax and become reasonable if allowed to do so. Parents often become anxious that response to a "negative" behavior will make that behavior a permanent part of the child's behavioral repertoire. In response to this anxiety, they may ignore the child's needs, thereby causing the behavior to become extended just as they feared. A need and the behavior expressing that need is prolonged when it is prevented from being satisfied.

A satisfied need loses its insistent quality, and the "desperate" kind of behavior that may sometimes express the need will disappear. When children's needs have been satisfied, they can then move on to new levels of growth, taking the satisfaction of lower needs for granted. It is essential to remember that *children grow*. We don't worry, when children begin creeping around on hands and knees, that they will do so forever; we assume that when they are able to walk, they will. The behavioral realm is more emotionally laden, and lack of certainty of what is normally expected behavior sometimes causes parents to worry that they will be reinforcing bad habits in children by catering to their needs. But, as you will see, one of children's higher needs is toward competence, independence, and autonomy, in the direction of becoming self-directed and responsible human beings. However, there are many needs along the way that must be met before they get to that point. As long as they are met appropriately, children will continue to move forward in the direction of growth.

We will discuss the relationship between the various levels of needs in particular as they relate to growth in the child under six years, but you should remember that the same principles apply to your own growth, whatever your age. Through an understanding of basic human needs, you can learn not only to meet your children's needs appropriately and thus keep them on the path of growth but also to recognize and perhaps cope better with your own needs.

A final note about needs—you may wonder whether children whose needs are consistently satisfied will become spoiled, always expecting the world to revolve around them. As we have intimated, this is not a justified fear. It is the child whose needs are *not* met with consistency who exhibits the behaviors we usually refer to as "spoiled" (e.g., overly demanding, whiny, dependent, not responsible for his own behavior, etc.). Because he has not received care that has been consistently responsive to what he needs at the time, he has not learned to count on their satisfaction and is, therefore, unreasonably demanding, as if constantly testing. For example, it is perfectly reasonable for tiny infants to demand immediate attention whenever they call; it is not at all reasonable for three- or four-year-olds to do so. If their needs for such attention are satisfied when it is realistically needed, children probably will not be overdemanding when their actual need for constant attention decreases. (Of course, there are other reasons, such as satisfying a child's every desire at the expense of everyone else's needs, why a child might become excessively demanding.)

WHAT DO CHILDREN NEED? Children need flexible, responsive care— care that is appropriate to their changing needs. You must be very tuned-in to them, watching them carefully to see what they need and then responding to their needs at the time. Because children's needs change as they grow, your treatment of them must also change. The treatment that children should have can, perhaps, be summed up by saying:

> Expect from children what they are able to give; give to them what they need.

Tiny infants are motivated (i.e., moved to act) first by *physiological needs*. They need to eat, sleep, breathe, maintain a regular body temperature, eliminate wastes, and so on. These are a baby's most obvious needs and are ordinarily met without problems. In the past, even the satisfaction of some of these needs in an appropriate way was in question, however, because mothers were advised (in an attempt to be "scientific" and systematic about child care) to feed their babies on a schedule rather than in response to the baby's actual needs. It is fairly well-acknowledged now that forcing a baby to conform to an arbitrary schedule is not a good idea; babies have their own individual schedules which, left to work themselves out, will usually become very regular in a short period of time. Babies should be fed when they're hungry, both for physiological and for psychological reasons.

In addition, infants are motivated by *safety needs.* (But, important as they are, they only become needs when a baby's physical needs are taken care of; if the baby couldn't breathe or weren't fed, his safety needs would make no difference.) Safety is more than being free from danger and physical harm; it is also existing in a consistently responsive environment, one from which the baby can learn to predict events because they become routine and familiar. Babies need the security of a safe, predictable world that they can count on. When they first enter this world, everything is very confusing. Through experiencing the same things over and over again, a baby begins to recognize some organization—"When I cry, someone comes"; "When I'm hungry, I am fed"; "When I'm lonely, someone keeps me company." Obviously, the tiny infant can't think these things, but the connections *are* being made.

In Chapter 2, the readings and commentary stress the importance of close physical contact and gentle, tender handling and of responding promptly to the baby's signals. These also are both related to the baby's needs for safety. We usually refer to the former (i.e., physical contact) as love because it *is* an expression of love from the baby's caregiver; but although tiny infants feel the love expressed to them and need it in order to grow, they do not recognize it as love. Tiny infants don't even know the difference between themselves and the rest of the world. They don't yet know how to love someone else because they don't know there is someone else. Infants' needs are for protection, security, and care they can count on from loving, responsive adults.

Safety needs remain important throughout early childhood and especially the first two years in the sense that children need a consistent, predictable environment in which to grow and learn. This is similar to what Erikson means by developing a sense of trust.[6] But for children whose physical and safety needs have been consistently met up to that point, at around six to nine months, *love needs* begin to emerge. As they begin to make the connections between their acts and the responses to them (e.g., "When I call, someone comes"), babies also begin to recognize the source of their satisfaction; they begin to apply some organization to that familiar touch, voice, smell, and of course, face, and to realize that they all go together in one person. At the same time, through repeated experiments (e.g., feeling the difference between suck-

---

[6] An excellent adaptation of Erikson's conceptualization of eight stages in the growth of human beings can be found in Helen Witmer and Ruth Kotinsky, eds., *Personality in the Making* (New York: Harper and Brothers, Publishers, 1952), Chapter 1. This is the report of the Mid-Century White House Conference on Children and Youth.

ing their mother's nipple and their own fingers), babies begin to get some idea that they are separate from the person who cares for them. When these things happen (usually some time between six and nine months), love is experienced for the first time.

Fraiberg[7] aptly describes the behavior of infants at this stage as very similar to that of a person of any age in that first intense period of a new love relationship; the baby's behavior is strongly motivated by a need to love and be loved. She may be very demanding and reluctant to spend any time apart from her "love." Incidentally, it is typical, at this time and for a few months, for babies to show a strong dependency on their love object (their mother or other primary caregiver) and a slight anxiety reaction to strange people and situations. However, it is precisely the attachment that babies have to their mothers that enables them to overcome their fear of strange situations; as long as she is near, they will be able to explore, using her as a secure home base. "Stranger anxiety" is perfectly normal; it is a baby's way of expressing that she now knows the difference between who and what she knows and who and what she doesn't know.

Of course, the appropriate response is to meet babies' love needs. As soon as they are secure that their love relationship is something that they can count on, they will be less dependent and less clingy; they will be willing to venture forth in adventures with the world around them, with only an occasional check to make sure Mom (or Dad) is within calling distance. On the other hand, if you respond to a baby's needs for reassurance of your love by rejecting his attempts to stay in close physical contact, by not picking him up when he reaches out to you, by leaving him with a strange babysitter, etc., his dependency will not go away; it will get worse, and he will not feel safe enough to begin to freely explore the world around him.

Satisfaction of the children's love and belonging needs is very important in the period between ten and eighteen months, as described in Chapter 3. During this time, children begin to be able to move about, to do things for themselves, and to assert their will with behavior and words. Because of these changes in the child, the environment becomes a less totally gratifying place: prohibitions and restrictions usually begin to be imposed on what they can do and where they can go. It is essential at this time, then, that children feel secure about their caregivers' love for them—that it is never threatened, either by any behavior on their part or by any restriction on your part. It is inevitable that you and your child will have times when neither of you likes the other's behavior. It is very important, beginning in this period, to

---

[7] Selma Fraiberg, *The Magic Years* (New York: Charles Scribner's Sons, 1959), pp. 47–48.

reassure children in behavior and words, that you *always* love *them* even though you may sometimes get mad at what they do, and that when you say no to something, it's not from lack of love.

Children in this period need to feel secure, valued, and loved; they need a secure home base from which they can venture forth and meet the world and to which they can retreat when they feel the need. The effective caregiver in this stage provides a nonthreatening, loving, safe haven that is organized and predictable in physical structure and behavioral expectations. Thus, the child's safety and love needs are consistently met, and the child has the freedom to grow. Children who experience this period as a time of overrestriction (expressed through an increasing number of "no's" or through actual physical restriction) or as a time of inconsistency of response from their caregivers (sometimes loving and supportive, sometimes punitive and restrictive) cannot feel safe enough to grow. They will instead abdicate their own needs for forward growth in exchange for seeking the safety of their caregivers' approval and affection. The selection by Maslow in Chapter 4 explains this phenomenon.

Toward the end of this period, an important thing happens to children—they begin to be aware that they are persons like other persons. Much of the obstinacy and negativity that characterizes what is popularly known as "the terrible twos" is a result of children's need to proclaim themselves as persons in their own right. We can see a similar stance in the beginnings of the various liberation movements and in the births of new nations—you must be able to shout, "I am a person, deserving of the same rights, dignity, and freedom of thought, feeling, and action as any other person" before you accept that you are but one person among a world of persons. So for young children, their first assertion of personhood may be a bit stormy before they can arrive at the realization of their common humanity, a learning that will take a bit longer to achieve.

Children are most strongly motivated at this stage, then, by *esteem needs*[8] (that is, of course, assuming that their other needs have been sufficiently satisfied to this point to have enabled them to reach this level of growth). They need to be able to feel that they have some control of their own actions, and that they are worthy persons. They need to be able to respect themselves and to expect others to respect them also. But this is a time of conflict. For just as children begin to become self-conscious about their competence, they coincidentally begin to be treated in such a way as to demonstrate to them their lack of it. That is, in our Western culture, the time that children begin to become aware

8 It is interesting to note, by the way, that although we share physiological, safety, and love needs with lower animals, the need for esteem (and for self-actualization) is uniquely human.

of themselves as persons is also the same time that they usually begin to be trained (e.g., to use the toilet, to feed themselves without mess, to respect others' property, etc.).

So children lose their pseudo-competence (the ability to command the services of their caregivers to do their bidding, a demand parents are willing to fulfill for a baby but usually not for a child over two) and in exchange, discover that their actual competence is meager in contrast to that of their caregivers. And the more demands that are put upon children at this time, the less competent they will feel.

Ausubel [9] sees this period (around two years) as one of crisis for children, in which the only way they can resolve their needs for esteem is to align themselves with their parents, becoming a "satellite" to them and thus deriving esteem from their association with them. In turn, parents must demonstrate unquestionably that they value their children as people, for themselves, without regard for what they do or do not do. Caregivers' respect for their children's personhood must not be contingent on their behaviors, but rather solely on their identity as human beings and as their children whom they love without reservation or evaluation.

Erikson[10] sees the period between one and three years (a time span overlapping somewhat with the one to which we have been referring) as a struggle between autonomy and shame and doubt. The same issues we have been discussing are involved—children are becoming sufficiently more competent that they can begin to act on the environment and assert themselves as persons. The ways in which children's parents respond to their efforts at independence will make the difference in whether they are able to achieve a healthy balance between dependence and independence (because they *are* realistically still dependent on their parents) or whether they become full of self-doubt and shame and therefore overly dependent on others to control them or defiantly shameless, acting in a delinquent manner whenever they are not watched.

Children's needs for self-esteem and the esteem of others (particularly their parents) require that they be treated in such a way as to encourage their independence while providing support and guidance when they need it. They will acquire a stable sense of esteem only through demonstration of *real* instances of competence. Thus, they should be helped to achieve competence in whatever areas possible, and at the same time, they should not be forced to do things that are beyond their capability and that would prove frustrating. For example, many children around eighteen months to two years begin to be interested in helping to put things in their place; this is both a think-

9 David Ausubel and Edmund Sullivan, *Theories and Problems of Child Development*, 2nd ed. (New York: Grune and Stratton, 1970), pp. 260–72.

10 In Witmer and Kotinsky, *Personality in the Making*, pp. 11–15.

ing skill—knowing what things belong where, what things go together, etc.—and a means toward growth of responsibility, a quality that will lead to self-esteem. If your child does show this interest, it should be encouraged, even if it takes longer to put things away than if you did it yourself.

Toilet-training has been the focus of many psychologists' explanation of the trials of this stage, since it is too often a source of struggle between parent and child. Here is a clear example of an area in which children should not be pushed. Children who are moving steadily and securely in a direction of growth will almost train themselves, given some guidance and encouragement. Toilet-training, like feeding oneself, dressing oneself, and other self-help activities, is an achievement that the healthy, secure child *wants* to accomplish because it will provide feelings of competence and self-worth; it will make a child more autonomous, and promote development of self-esteem.

As we have said, children's first attempts to establish for themselves a sense of esteem are usually negativistic—they seek their own identities through opposition to their caregivers, demanding the right to choose for themselves, to do for themselves, and in general, to proclaim themselves as persons. But the behaviors that children typically exhibit in their quest for esteem change as they grow. The negativistic behaviors do not last if children are supported in their efforts to gain some independence and, at the same time, helped to accept, without too much frustration or loss of face, that there are some things that they are not yet sufficiently competent to accomplish on their own.

If children emerge from this negativistic period feeling that their parents are friends and allies in their growth, then they will begin to align themselves with their caregivers—i.e., try to do things that will win them their parents' praise and nurturance, to model some of their behaviors after things they see their caregivers do, etc. The first instances of this imitative behavior can usually be seen sometime around age two—children may like to dust and clean and wash dishes, or they may pretend to smoke a pipe or cigarettes like their parents. By three to four years, this kind of simple imitative play has bloomed into elaborate role-playing, like "trying on" different behavioral repertoires of people children have seen or learned about.

While this behavior is still satisfying children's needs for esteem, for defining and delineating their personhood, it is also more than that. Once a child has established that she is, in fact, a person, her next task is to decide what kind of a person she is. Beginning about age four to five,[11] *self-actualization needs* begin to emerge in children whose lower needs have been relatively well-satisfied. Children who have been

[11] The ages are only approximates; so much depends on children's experiences that the older they get, the harder it is to specify ages for emergence of new levels of need.

growing in healthy, productive directions up to this point have enough of an identity as persons that they begin to need avenues through which they can try out and express that selfhood, thus further defining who they are.

Self-actualizing is a lifetime process that *should* begin in early childhood [12] and that does not end (for the psychologically healthy person who is functioning at that level) until the last breath is taken. It is the process of becoming most fundamentally *you*, and at the same time, more fully and profoundly human. Self-actualization, then, is the ultimate human goal, and those persons who approach that condition (i.e., those persons who are self-actualizing) are viewed by Maslow as prototypes of the species in its most highly evolved state. This, then, should be our ultimate goal in raising children—to guide them well enough in the early years that they are able to responsibly guide their own continuing growth and development throughout their lives, so that they may become as fully human, as self-actualized, as they are capable of becoming.

What children need in order to pursue their self-actualizing needs is, first, the satisfaction of all preceding needs (since, if any of them are seriously threatened, children will have to divert their energies to meeting those needs). In many parts of the world, and even in many parts of our own society, it is impossible for a child ever to reach this level, because needs as basic as eating and being free from physical harm cannot be satisfied. Tragically, those segments of our society that have the potential to become self-actualizing, and thus, reciprocally, to effect positive change in those less fortunate segments, are too often stuck at lower levels, such as satisfaction of love and esteem needs.

We refer you again to the title of this book as an important focus of the childrearing function—you *must* grow with your children in order to be able to guide their growth so that they may become self-actualizing. For if you, yourself (like most of us in the world today) are still working out your own safety, love, and/or esteem needs, you will be that much less capable of guiding your children to becoming self-actualizing persons. We all have enduring needs left over from our

12 Maslow used older subjects in his studies of self-actualizing people, and he concluded that self-actualization of the sort that he found in these people was not possible in our society for young, developing people. While this may be true, we feel that the seeds of self-actualization are sown in early childhood, and that psychologically healthy children may begin to pursue self-actualizing needs (if their lower needs have been met) by age four to five. In describing the tendency toward self-actualization, Maslow states that it is "the desire to become more and more what one is, to become everything that one is capable of becoming" (p. 92, *Motivation and Personality*). We acknowledge that this is a lifelong process, but we feel that this description closely corresponds to the process of intrinsic motivation described in Chapter 7, which is said to begin by four to five years.

own childhoods that get in the way of our becoming all that we can be. But growth is a continuous process, and knowledge and understanding of what basic needs are motivating your behavior is the first step toward meeting those needs enough for you to begin to overcome any obstacles to your personal growth. And, as we have said before, that is the best thing you can do for your children, both through freeing more of your own energy to give to them and, most importantly, through providing them with a positive identification model.

How do you know what children need?

You know what children need by being very attuned to their behavioral messages and by having some knowledge of what is developmentally appropriate at different times (to help guide your observation, not to measure your children's behavior against). You need to learn to "read" your children's behavior, to know what their behavior is "telling" you they need. Your children are your very best guide to meeting their needs appropriately—they communicate their needs to you by the way they act and the way they respond to what is happening to them.

For example, tiny infants cry to communicate their needs; they do not cry without cause. It is up to you, through a process of informed trial and error, to discover what they are signaling and thus to satisfy their needs. You will know when you have found the cause of a child's problem when she stops crying or fretting; as long as she continues, you've not discovered what she needs. In Chapter 2, the reading by Bell and Ainsworth and the one by Newton will provide additional insight into the reasons and causes of crying and appropriate responses to it.

Preschool children also tell you, through their behavior (and perhaps through their words if you ask the right questions) what they need. For example, if you are trying to teach Peter to do something and it takes a very long time and you have trouble keeping his attention to the task, he is telling you that he's not yet ready to learn that task; a task that is developmentally appropriate for a child is learned quickly and easily. Preschool children tell you what they're ready to learn by what they already know how to do—they will learn something new only if it is just slightly different from and harder than what they already know. We will discuss this further in Chapter 7.

An important part of being an effective child caregiver, then, is being a good observer—your eyes and ears and whole being should be alert to the messages that your children are sending through their behavior. As we have said before, you should try to put yourself in your children's shoes, to really *feel* how they are feeling, to see the world through their eyes, hear it through their ears, and so on. It is a necessary and built-in part of the parent-child relationship that an effective mutual signaling system be set up between you. Children send signals that you, as a human being and as their parent, are geared to receive if you are open to them. Dr. Spock offered American parents the adage to relax and enjoy their babies; we add to that: relax, enjoy, and be receptive and responsive to your child's behavioral cues.

Following is a reading that will give you some guidelines to recognition of your children's needs at various points in their development. It is an overview of development in the child from birth to six, organized by year (e.g., Birth to One Year, etc.). It will provide you with some clues as to what behaviors you are likely to see at different times. We have included it because it helps sometimes to improve your observational skills when you have some ideas of what you're looking for. We stress, however, that you should not use these age norms as a standard against which to measure your child's behavior. It is only a guide to your observation, and the ages are averages, not indices of when your child should be expected to show a particular behavior. Children have individual rates of growth, and your best guide to understanding their behavior is always the child, not information in this or any other book on child development.

The Child from Birth to Six Years: An Overview by Age Level

Joseph and Laurie Braga

This selection will provide you with some concept of the general age ranges within which children normally develop different abilities. It will also highlight some of the more prominent aspects of a child's development at different stages. The purpose of this age summary is to help you gain a mental picture of what kinds of behaviors are typical at what times as well as of the changes of behaviors over time. This will help provide a focus to your observation of your children's behavioral messages and thus, hopefully, improve your effectiveness in meeting their needs. The ages should be viewed only as a general guide to the child's level of development, not as a yardstick against which to measure any individual child's behavior. The age levels noted are averages. They represent only signposts of developmental trends. No individual child is expected to achieve these steps of growth at exactly the ages given in this reading. A particular child might be ahead in some areas and behind in others. This is normal. So, for example, the picture of the two-year-old that is given in the reading will describe many children in some ways but probably no child in every way. Use the developmental information given in the selection as a context for viewing the other readings and commentary—a general guide against which you can check the other information that is offered about children's developmental needs and characteristics.

BIRTH TO ONE YEAR

In the first year of their lives, infants grow more and at a more rapid rate than at any other time of their lives. When they enter the world they are helpless. They cannot care for themselves; they have no voluntary control over their bodies, they cannot move around; they can't even roll over. They even have some difficulty at first with eating and digesting food, breathing, and maintaining an even body temperature.

By the end of the year, most infants move around quite effectively; they can reach smoothly and accurately for and grasp things, pick things up deftly between their thumb and forefinger, drink from a cup and hold it themselves with two hands, and eat from a spoon (but not efficiently by themselves for another year). They can chew and digest semi-solid or chopped foods. They can understand some words and may even say a few themselves. They recognize familiar people and things and know that even when things are not in sight, they still exist. And they begin to learn about themselves—that they are persons separate from the world of people and things around them.

In the first six months of life, most infants develop muscular control over the upper portion of their bodies—eyes, head, neck, shoulders, arms, and upper torso. They learn to follow moving objects with their eyes, then eyes and head, and to reach for and grasp stable objects (leading with the shoulders now more than with the hand). They also learn to sit with support. But it is in the second half of their first year that infants usually accomplish the most dramatic motor achievements, the ones which make them mobile. From six to twelve months, most infants master unsupported sitting, rolling completely from stomach to back and back to stomach, standing with help, pulling up to standing, creeping on all fours, and even walking with a little help. Even though they are not achieved until the latter part of the first year, the motor achievements just listed have their origins in muscular control and coordination developed previously.

Communication between infants and their caregivers begins with the baby's first cries for food, comfort, or company. But those early cries aren't conscious and deliberate, and they're not very efficient. Over the period of their first year, most infants develop more varied, efficient, and deliberate means of communicating. They learn early to smile back to a smiling face and look into the person's eyes. They develop a repertoire of noises and speech-like sounds with the rhythm and tonal qualities of real speech, and with facial expressions and gestures to accompany their sound-making. By a year, a few "real" words may be included in many infants' vocalizing.

The first year of infants' lives is marked by growth in their ability to make some sense out of the world around them—to apply some organization to all the information coming into their sensory channels (eyes, ears, skin, mouth, and nose). When babies are born, all their sensory receivers are in good working order. But they need experience before any of the information coming into these receiving stations makes any sense. Through their first year, building on their initial wired-in reflex responses to the world, infants learn increasingly more varied and integrated actions on their world.

Through their own action schemes, children selectively react to, act on, and organize sensory input. For example, in the first month as their eye muscles strengthen, most infants look at anything that happens to be around, without any real regard; then by three to four months, they look to see—they look at what interests them. What interests infants, and, therefore, what they attend to visually, changes through the first year with growth in their memory and in their motor skills. At first it's the familiar—infants' own hands and other people's faces. Then it's something similar to the familiar.

By the end of the first year, children respond to things slightly different from what they are familiar with by reacting to the new thing in the way they would react to the familiar thing. They are learning to organize sensory input into "chunks" based on how it relates to what they have already experienced. Gradually those chunks become integrated and internalized so that infants consolidate their knowing. They learn that things stay the same from day to day and that they can be known in various ways; they begin to construct a consistent reality for themselves.

When they're born babies don't even know that there's a "me" that's separate from the rest of the world of people and things. Slowly, through experience, infants begin to define themselves as persons in relation to other persons (a process that will continue through their lives). Infants develop feelings about themselves based on the feedback they receive from others. If the world around them is positively responsive to them, children will feel good about themselves. If the world is unresponsive or unreliable, they will feel incompetent and fearful. And they will carry those feelings into their future; they will learn to anticipate the kind of responses they have become used to receiving and will adapt their behavior accordingly.

ONE TO TWO YEARS

From one to two years, children refine previously acquired skills and develop new ones. They learn to walk, improve their balance and coordination in an upright posture, and learn more difficult walking-related motor acts such as trotting, running, climbing, and going up and down stairs. They gain voluntary control of their hands for controlled letting go now, in addition to their previously acquired skill of grasping and holding. So dropping and throwing become favorite pastimes (they usually begin toward the end of the first year). Children learn about gravity, also, from these "experiments." In addition, they learn better control of tools such as a cup, a spoon, and a crayon. By the end of the year, most children will have gained enough control of their sphincter muscles, both for holding in and for letting go, that they can be toilet trained.

Children's ability to discriminate the sounds and the meaning of the language spoken around them improves as does their ability to imitate and produce speech sounds themselves. Because of their preoccupation with motor learning, children may make very slow progress in language development in the first part of the year. Toward the latter half of the year, however, they will make fast gains in vocabulary (from an average of ten or twenty words at eighteen months to over two hundred at two years) and will begin speaking in short phrases. Most children, in this period, go from a few words mixed in with a lot of jargon to mostly all real words. In the second year of their lives, children's memories increase—for things, people, places, and ideas. They not only recognize the familiar now, but they begin to show the ability to recall and reproduce recent memories of words, actions, behaviors, and experiences. In solving new problems, children now bring to bear old experience. They try out different known procedures of action in the new situation and begin, toward the end of the year, to develop new procedures through combining and changing old ones. Children are beginning to have representations of real things in their heads (memories of pictures, sounds, feelings, etc.) that help them to think about something without its being physically present.

Between one and two years, also, children begin to develop a sense of themselves as persons. They begin to respond to and call themselves by their names; to claim possessions as "mine," and to recognize their mirror images. By two, they may even begin to want to hear stories about themselves. In this period, children are still very attached to and realistically dependent on their caregivers. But the skills they are learning enable them to become increasingly self-reliant in contrast to the helplessness of much of their first year. They are learning to feed themselves; help undress and dress themselves; control their bowels and bladder; eat solid, nonsimplified foods; and of course, get around well on two feet. In addition they are learning the power of words, on their own and others' behavior.

Two to Three Years

The two- to three-year-old is undergoing some important changes. In a sense, this is a period of transition—from the babyhood of the first two years to the early childhood or preschool period of the next few years. Before two, children are very motor-minded; they not only expend a great deal of energy learning control and coordination of their bodies' movement, but they "think" primarily with their bodies. Gradually in those infant years, children began to develop internal memory images of some of the things and people around them as well as of their own behaviors. By two, most children have not only internalized images of their world, but they can begin to act on the world through the manipulation of those images in their heads. They are no longer bound to the immediate context of their experience; they can think about things that aren't right there in front of them.

From two to three, children develop more efficient ways of representing their experience. They translate what they have learned before through direct sensory-motor experience into different shortcut codes. For example, most children expand their understanding and use of language in this period.

Many two-year-olds accompany their activities with talking. But the talking doesn't direct the actions. The actions lead, and the words seem to arise from the experience as if the children were trying to give their actions a name, to translate them into an efficient, mentally manipulable form. By three, most children's behavior is more under the control of language. They are able, for example, to begin or end an activity according to verbal directions. Between two and three years, children are learning their language; so that by three they will be able to use it to learn other things. But for the two- to three-year-old, actions are still more a reality than are words.

The average number of words in the vocabularies of two-year-olds is two hundred fifty and of three-year-olds, nine hundred. This increase in number is indicative of the growth in language skills at this age; but more important are the changes in the kinds of words used, the kinds of sentence structures used, and the purpose and function of language in this period. Most two-year-olds speak, to a great extent, in telegraphic sentences, leaving out all but the essential words. Also, their repertoire of language probably includes several stereotyped one-word "phrases" to which they attach a whole variety of subjects, e.g., "*See* cookie, boy, dog, man. . . ." By three, most children's language includes a greater range of types of words and sentences, their sentences are more complete, and the structure of their sentences is becoming more like those of adult speakers.

The further refinement of motor skills does not, of course, stop with infancy. Most children from two to three are gaining total mastery of the upright posture. At two they can run, but not well; by three they are beginning to learn running maneuvers such as stops and starts, turning corners, and avoiding obstacles. At two most children can climb stairs, but they take it one tread at a time, bringing both feet together at each tread. By three, most children alternate feet going up stairs, and also in riding a tricycle. Between two and three most children also learn to jump with both feet, walk on tiptoe, balance briefly on one foot, kick a ball, and throw a ball into a basket.

All of these larger motor skills require, also, more complex thinking about spatial relationships than most children show before this time. In order to accomplish many of these acts, children must be aware of their position in space in relation to other things as well as the position in space of things in relation to each other. And, to make it even harder, the children must understand these relationships when either they or the things are in motion.

The development of more refined fine motor skills contributes to children's growing independence. They are learning increasing numbers of self-help skills such as undressing themselves (and helping with the dressing), going to the toilet on their own and washing themselves (though still not very well), feeding themselves very adequately, using a spoon and cup well without spilling and a fork to spear chunks of food. Fine motor skills improve also, with practice, for such tasks as cutting with scissors, drawing, and manipulating puzzles. From two to three children really enjoy art activities such as drawing, painting, modeling with clay, snipping paper and pasting, and so on. They enjoy the process of using their hands and a few simple tools more than they care about producing anything. They're not very interested in the things they make; they're more interested in the making.

From two to three, children also are changing their relationships with other people. Whereas through age two, most children are more responsive to adults than to other children, by three they are beginning to play together. The two-year-old might play side by side with another child, but even though they might be playing at the same activity, they will not do it together. So the two-year-old engages in role-playing and make-believe behavior, but she plays all the parts herself. By three, if she has had some experience with other children, a child will join forces with one or two others to play together at the same activity.

The period between two and three years is perhaps best known as "the terrible twos." Some people who study children have suggested that in this period, children's behavior is characterized by rigidity and inflexibility. They want things just so and no other way; they don't like change, can't wait, won't give in; they often do just the opposite of what they're told. Although this kind of behavior can occur, and when it does occur, it can be annoying, it should not be thought of as *bad* behavior. There's a very good reason for it.

Children at this age have just begun to figure out things about the world they live in. They're beginning to have "ideas" about the way things are. But their ideas aren't yet secure. Therefore, they don't feel comfortable with a lot of change; that makes it harder to be sure about things. Also, children are beginning to gain command over many new skills, most notably understanding and using speech. Much of their behavior is the result of their checking out the power of their new skills. For example, if you say "come here" and your child walks in the other direction, she's showing that she understood you well enough to do just the opposite—quite an accomplishment.

Finally, this is an age when children's "eyes are bigger than their stomachs," in terms of trying to do things. They can't do everything they try to do, and that's frustrating. They have not yet learned to find reasonable solutions to feelings of frustration. At this age, they still just become enraged. Patience and sympathy will see them through this period until they become more secure and more in command of their own emotions.

THREE TO FOUR YEARS

Three begins the "age of reason." To three- to four-year-olds, everything is simple and logical and has a reason for being. And if they don't know the reason, they will ask. They are discovering (if their experience so far supports it) that adults are resources to them; adults' advice, help, or knowledge can be sought when the child has determined that the task is beyond him or that he cannot answer for himself a question he has. At three, many children ask questions to which they may already have an answer. This is probably a way to check themselves and, perhaps, the adult too. By four, if their questions have been answered, children will pose them now more to seek information.

Three- to four-year-olds join human society. They no longer always try to bend people to their whims. They are willing to bend themselves. They learn to share, to take turns, to play cooperatively with other children. As they become more aware of other people, they also become more aware of themselves. Children at this age are very interested in what they were like "when they were little." They learn to tell what sex they and other people are (although because this knowledge is based on superficial characteristics such as clothes, hair, jobs, and mannerisms, it may be quite fluid for children at this age; they may think it possible to switch sexes if they'd like).

Children from three to four are very interested in sociodramatic play. This is a way they have (1) to act out relationships they're involved in, often taking other roles than their own, and (2) later, to try out different role behaviors they've seen in other people, including roles they've never had any personal experience with. In addition to allowing children the opportunity to work out some of their own role relationships through play, sociodramatic play is an avenue for them to expand their thinking skills. It helps them, through sharing ideas about role definitions with other children, to see things from other points of view and to broaden their own scope. In addition, it is a way that they can manipulate the order of things in their own way, to fit their own point of view.

Children's endeavors to both learn the existing organization of things and to apply their own is seen also in their manipulations of objects. In this age period, children are very interested in taking things apart to see how they work and in putting things together. Most children are still interested in the process involved in an activity more than they are in the product. But in the year from three to four, they may become more concerned with using materials to make something (e.g., a picture, the letters of their name, a prop for dramatic play).

The child's motor skills are becoming so good by this age that he can begin to use them in his new learning priorities; they have become a part of his behavioral repertoire. By four most children have good balance and coordination. Walking is automatic, and running is accomplished with ease, with quick stops and starts, changing speeds, turning corners, and so on. They can jump, and they can skip with one foot. Fine motor coordination is being used effectively in the manipulation of tools in this age period. For example, by four many children are beginning to use crayons, pencils, and scissors to make some thing whereas before, they were learning how to use them.

Self-help skills improve in the year from three to four, making children increasingly able to care for some of their own needs, including feeding themselves except for cutting; dressing and undressing themselves; toileting themselves; washing their own face and hands; and brushing their own teeth. Supervision is needed, but most children learn to do these things for themselves. These and other developing skills help to make children more independent and more responsible to themselves for their own actions. And the reciprocal outcome of their growing independence from others to meet all their needs is that children become more aware of and concerned about others.

From three to four, language begins to be used as a tool to help children find out about things in their world, through questioning, labeling, and thus classifying not only things but groups of things (e.g., animals, fruit) and as part of their sociodramatic play. Vocabulary is expanded, and various complex sentence constructions are added to the child's repertoire. In addition, the child's speech becomes more articulate, more easily understood.

Four to Five Years

From four to five, most children become more organized, focused, and conventional in their thinking. They learn to follow an idea, problem, or task to its conclusion, staying with it even from one day to the next until it is successfully completed. Five-year-olds are concerned about order and completion. They can think of an idea and then carry it out, whereas at the beginning of the year they might flow quickly from one idea to the next. Their thinking is becoming more defined, and their memory for events, situations, strategies in problem-solving, etc. is improving.

The growth in independence increases from four to five. The things they did at four to care for themselves, children do more easily and with less supervision at five. By five, many children are very helpful around the house, washing or drying dishes, setting the table, etc. From four to five, children should be beginning to internalize social rules and to rely on their own judgment of their behavior. They are becoming more aware of themselves in relation to others, and will pursue learning tasks because the task makes them more like an admired person who possesses attributes similar to and valued by them. They continue to participate in sociodramatic play as a way to define their own self-concept as they explore a range of different roles.

Four- to five-year-olds' large motor skills are sufficiently advanced that their play can include a variety of stunts and simple gymnastics as well as some simple organized games such as "Mother May I?", "Simon Says," and "Statues." They can hop, jump, skip, run, climb, twist, and so on. These games are a way to practice motor skills as well as to learn to cooperate with others, fit actions to verbal instructions, and to retain and follow a simple set of rules. Fine motor skills become more refined and in control. Some children may be interested in learning to write; and most children's drawing is more controlled and adapted to a mental plan or image. Their pencil grasp is improving, and scissors are used effectively for cutting out things.

Language is used in this period increasingly as a substitute for action. Children can "pretend" to do something just by verbally saying they did it; e.g., "Let's pretend I'm the mother and you're the baby and I just gave you a spanking." Children are learning to seek verbal solutions to problems to which they used to react bodily and with heightened emotions. From four to five, children continue to expand their vocabulary, extend the length of their sentences, increase the complexity of their sentence structure, and use language more and more as a way to learn about things in their world. Questions are becoming more information-seeking, and interest in books and stories more reality-based. Finally, language is not only a part of their play, but it can serve as the basis of play itself. Playing with rhyming and silly words can be a fun game for the child of this age.

Four-year-olds already understand that the things in their world have an order, that they can put them back in that order once they have taken them apart, and that many things can be compared or related to each other in an orderly way. Between four and five years they are free to explore more complicated ways of ordering more and more objects in their world, according to their physical attributes (including how they look, feel, etc. and what you can do to them or with them), their positions in time and space, and/or how they are defined or described by other people.

FIVE TO SIX YEARS

The period from five to six years is another period of transition for children, similar in ways to that which they experienced from two to three years. At five, most children seem well in control. They can care for many of their own needs; they identify themselves with more competent adults and older children; they use language articulately and meaningfully; they are in control of their body movements, and so on. But, following the typical course of development, this period of self-containment and relative competence in coping with the world is followed by one of apparent disintegration. Six-year-olds are, in fact, more cognitively competent than five-year-olds, but they may seem less so. Whereas at five they seemed to accept their role in life, by six many children are not at peace with themselves and others. They may be argumentative, subject to abrupt mood swings and changes of mind and opinion, and so on.

What has happened between five and six years to produce this kind of change is a growth in children's social intelligence which, until they work out the problems that this new awareness brings them, is more a liability than an asset. At the beginning of the year, most children are not consciously concerned about defining themselves as persons; they just accept themselves without too much question. Through the year, children typically become increasingly sensitive to their role in relation to other people.

In the same way as when they were two to three, new demands are being put on children from five to six, and the demands may be more than they can handle comfortably. Thus, at a time when they are becoming more consciously aware of themselves as persons, children see themselves as incompetent in comparison with adults, and they are realistically so. But their inability to always cope with the demands of adults reinforces their feelings of incompetence. In defense of their own position and in fear of progressing into the increasingly demanding adult world, children may behave in a way that might seem less mature than before.

This change in behavior that occurs in the sixth year is not serious except for the moment. Children have simply become self-conscious and therefore overly harsh on themselves. They may have internalized too well the discipline they have received, punishing themselves now for the smallest error or even for one in thought but not in action. If children are treated with concern and understanding and demands are lessened to a comfortable level, if they are not forced to do things which cause them pain, fear, or anxiety, this stage will pass and most children will once again be able to function competently, at their own level, and happily.

Children are once again in the process of reorganizing their thought processes. Language is becoming more distinct from the things, actions, and events it is used to describe. It is becoming more of a reality in itself rather than the inseparable part of what it describes that it was for the younger child. When the child first began to learn words, they were more to her than a way of representing experience; they *were* the things they described. That's why the child had trouble understanding how someone else could have *her* name or how the same thing could have two names (e.g., coat and jacket).

From five to six years, children are becoming less literal about both their understanding and use of language. A symptom of this is the name-calling behavior of many children in this stage and the retort "Sticks and stones can break my bones, but words will never hurt me."

In general, the child at this stage is very good in using language. By the end of this year, most children are using all types of sentences and kinds of words found in the language of their culture. They can use language to describe things, to argue, to tease and joke, to lie and make believe.

Through their experiences with objects, children learn to compare sizes, shapes, colors, and textures. They learn concepts of numbers and the relations of parts and wholes by such activities as working with puzzles, blocks, etc. They learn about volume and conservation through such experiences as play with sand and pails and with water and containers. They continue to practice classification of objects through what they can do with them, what they look like, and so on. In line with their developing flexibility with language, children's classification skills are becoming both more consistent and more flexible; they can begin to order things along more than one dimension (e.g., according to *both* color and size), but still one after the other, not at the same time.

The knowledge of order children have at five to six is greater than that of younger children. They can tell when part of something is missing; they can compare things; they can begin to use what they have learned about order so that they can take something apart and remember how to put it together again correctly. (Before, they could take things apart and put things together, but not necessarily the same things.) Five- to six-year-olds are able to organize their own thoughts, too, so that they can tell long stories; so that they can correct their own errors; and so that they can begin to reason with ideas based on past experience, rather than having to try everything out with real objects.

Children's growing knowledge of order is also illustrated by the fact that they become more able, between five and six years, to play games with simple rules. In their own behavior, they are beginning to follow the rules of their culture; so, for example, girls and boys are beginning to separate in their play choices into more "socially approved" role behavior. But though they may be more aware of the rules of the adult world than before, by six, children may rebel against adult rules if they don't coincide with their own ideas about the way things should be. There is a tendency, in this period, for children to become increasingly concerned about their relationships with other children and more rejecting of adult control.

In summary, five- to six-year-olds are continuing to expand their learning and development of skills. But because they are on the threshold of a new role in life, because more demands are being put on them, and because physiologically they are in a period of change, their behavior may seem to be becoming less organized throughout the year. But this is a period of transition. By seven, most children should once again be in a stage of equilibrium and integration.

2

Infancy:
What Does a Baby Need
to Grow?

The first thing that a baby needs is consistent, responsive, and loving care. Babies need to be fed when they're hungry, changed when they're wet or soiled, comforted when they're distressed, entertained when they want company, etc. And they need to be able to really count on another human being to meet their needs as they arise, consistently and promptly. Young babies cannot wait. First, their needs are urgent; for example, when they're hungry, it's because their stomachs are empty, not just because they have an appetite as is usually the case for us as adults. Second, they don't understand waiting because they have no memory. As babies grow, they will learn to wait as their need for food becomes less urgent and because they will know that when they're hungry, someone will feed them; but in the first months, they know only the pain in their empty bellies.

Thus, one of the important lessons babies must learn in their first months is that there is someone they can count on to meet their needs. As they learn this basic lesson in trust, and as their physical needs become less insistent, they will become less demanding (in proportion to their actual needs). It is the baby who is never able to establish a basic sense of trust that his needs will be met who continues to test his caregivers' responsiveness by demands that are in excess of his real needs.

Human infants are born with a set of inborn responses such as clinging, sucking, "following" with the eyes, crying, and smiling that enable them to survive as long as their needs are met by a person who is attuned and responsive to them. These wired-in responses act as part of the system of communication that must be developed between caregiver and child in order to insure survival and growth. Babies' first responses are to human stimulation (e.g., to the human face, voice, and touch) over any other kind of stimulation, and their behaviors (e.g., crying, following a person with their eyes, fixing their eyes on their caregivers' face, and smiling) in turn are geared toward provoking a response in their human caregivers. These facts support the premise that a mutually responsive social interaction is a necessary condition for a child's growth.

Although the establishment of an effective system of communication seems to be innate to the human species, because we are thinking beings, it is possible to thwart that natural inclination. For example, it is logical that crying is an important and necessary behavior in young infants that enables them to bring their caregiver to them in times of need, and the natural response of a caregiver is to stop the crying by going to the baby. But we are still suffering the effects of advice given to mothers over fifty years ago that childrearing should be objective and intelligent, not emotional and sentimental, and thus that to answer children's cries and needs for tenderness would merely spoil them.

If there is one thing that we have learned about child development in the past years, it is that we can trust babies' behavioral cues to tell us what they need. To impose a rigid schedule on a baby, to accept others' advice over the baby's own responses, is both unfair and wrong. For example, eating should be a satisfying and enjoyable experience for the baby (and mother); they should both be relaxed and comfortable. If, instead, the baby is crying and her body is rigid or flailing, there is something wrong with the feeding situation. Well-meaning mothers have been known to force solids into their six-week-old infants, withholding the bottle until the child complied, while the baby cried desperately and tried to refuse the solids.[1] This would not happen if parents were taught that their own babies are far superior guides to how they should be treated than their next door neighbor or even many "how-to" books on childrearing. We are focusing on the feeding situation for a very important reason: It is the center of the young in-

---

[1] Sylvia Brody, Sidney Axelrad, and Marjorie Adams Krimsley, *Mother-Infant Interaction* (New York: Infant Development Research Project, Distributed by New York University Film Library, 1967). This is a film demonstrating the different types of maternal behavior in the feeding situation found by Brody et al. in a study of more than 100 mother-infant pairs. Although the study followed the mother-child pairs over the period of the infants' first year, the film concentrates on typical styles of interaction when the babies were six weeks old. Mothers' behaviors at this early stage were found to be predictive of their future interactions and to have a significant impact on their children's growth in all areas (including motor behavior, emotional stability and responsiveness, and cognitive style). The mothers' feeding behaviors were classified on a scale with three measures: empathy, control, and efficiency. The most effective interactions were those in which mothers were high and consistent in empathy with their babies, moderate and appropriate in their control (letting their infants' behaviors lead their responses to them), and high in efficiency. These mothers were relaxed and responsive to their babies and very attuned to their needs. Feeding was a pleasurable time for both, involving close body contact, touching, and other forms of affectionate nonverbal and verbal communication.

fant's waking life, and thus sets the tone of the total caregiver-child relationship. "If a mother is inefficient or anxious, or dependent on inappropriate habits or traditions to guide her, the quality of her response to her baby's needs may be sharply impaired." [2] In feeding, as in other caregiving situations, you should follow the baby's cues—let his behavior tell you what he needs. In a choice between what you have been told is correct management and the baby's response, always trust the baby's behavioral cues.

For example, following the advice of their mothers or a neighbor, many mothers begin too early to give their babies solid foods. In the example given above of the crying, flailing six-week-old protesting the substitution of solids for her bottle, there is a message. The baby was telling her mother that she needed the nutrition of milk and the experience of sucking, not mashed bananas. There does come a time when babies need the introduction of some foods with vitamin C (a nutrient lacking in milk).[3] Conveniently, this occurs at the same time that babies become capable of handling well-mashed or puréed foods. You will know they're ready when a small amount of simplified food placed on the front of the tongue can be taken to the back of the mouth and swallowed. In the first months, babies have a reflex that will force solid food back out unless it's put far back on their tongues. By three months, this reflex is gone, and they are ready to begin eating a few puréed or well-mashed solid foods. They tell you they're ready also by the fact that they begin to drool and bite at about this time.

When babies' teeth begin to erupt, usually between six and nine months, they are ready to handle some chopped foods and foods such as toast, baked potatoes, and egg. They show readiness for these coarser foods by putting everything into their mouths and biting on it and by their ability to swallow small lumps. Babies also tell you, through their behavior, how much food is enough. Although they eat very often when they're tiny, babies' appetites may be much smaller than you imagined, and of course, like all of us, they vary. So follow your baby's lead to know when, what, and how much she needs to eat.

Another important part of feeding and of the entire caregiver-child relationship is close body contact and touching. The importance of touch to the child's healthy development in all areas cannot be over-

---

2 Ibid.

3 The best source of information about the nutritional needs of infants and young children that we have found is: Marian Breckenridge and Margaret Murphy, *Growth and Development of the Young Child,* 8th ed. (Philadelphia: W. B. Saunder Company, 1969), Chapter 5. The information is presented in a simple and readable form but in all the detail you may have looked for and failed to find before. The authors explain nutrition in the context of the child's changing needs for and ability to handle different kinds of foods—they give you the whys as well as the whats.

emphasized. The reading by Dr. Ashley Montagu in this chapter communicates this eloquently. Parents know they should love their babies. But young infants do not understand the abstractness of that concept. Rather, they need concrete illustration that they are loved: close and tender physical contact is the first way that love is communicated.

When being fed, babies should be held close, with very little distance between them and their caregiver. This is automatic in a nursing situation, but not necessarily so when a baby is bottle-fed. Although nursing is recommended for many reasons (e.g., for nutritional reasons, to give the baby important antibodies against disease, to insure close contact between baby and mother), it should not be chosen through pressure. A woman must feel comfortable and relaxed with the concept and the actual process; if she is not, that will be communicated to her baby.

However, if a mother decides not to nurse, then she should try in all ways to replicate the nursing relationship in her bottle-feeding. For example, she should switch her baby from one side to the other as she would when nursing; this is important to babies' visual development and to the development of the muscles they use to turn their heads. She should always hold her baby; babies should not be left to lie alone in a crib or infant seat with a bottle propped up next to them. Babies *need* the experience of being lovingly held, often, when eating and at other times. A parent should not neglect the importance of skin-to-skin contact because the baby is not nursing. If not always in the feeding situation, there should be ample other opportunities for caregiver and baby to be physically "in touch." This is true for fathers and their children as well as for mothers. And the one real advantage of the bottle is that it can give fathers more of a chance to be intimately involved in the feeding interaction. A close relationship between father and child is important for both people.

Baby Doesn't Live by Bread Alone

As we explained earlier, we have stressed the feeding interaction because it is so central to babies' early lives, and many aspects of the total caregiver-child relationship have their origins in the feeding interaction. But after the first months, eating begins to take up less time and energy, and babies' other needs have prominence.

In the next chapter, we discuss the changes that occur in the caregiver-child relationship and in children's growth in all areas when they become self-moving. In the remaining pages of our commentary in this chapter, we would like to talk about your role in your children's growth before they become mobile.

Babies need stimulation in order to grow. When they are born, all their sensory collectors (i.e., eyes, ears, nose, tongue, skin) are in good working order; but babies need to practice using them and to experience sorting out and fitting together the pieces of their puzzle world before all the information coming into their sensory collectors makes any sense. Babies are not empty receptacles to be filled up by information, and they are not sponges that absorb the information around them. They are active scientists, making experiments on the world around them, slowly constructing their concepts about the way things are. They are active participants in their own learning even before they can move around on their own. But they need your help.

Before babies can get about by themselves, they need to have stimulation brought to them, and to be brought themselves to stimulation. By stimulation we do *not* mean that you should bombard your child with toys and special "learning materials." For the first weeks, too much stimulation (including too many people and too many things going on) is upsetting to a baby. Gradually, babies begin to want and seek out different kinds of stimulation. But, as in all areas, let your children be your guide. Provide them with stimulation to match their growing abilities.

For example, the first parts of babies' bodies to come under control are the muscles controlling their eye movements and those controlling their heads. They will appreciate things to look at, changing in position relative to the mobility of their head and eyes.[4] When they begin to reach out and bat at things, there should be something nearby to bat at; when they begin to touch and grasp, there should be things to touch and grasp.

But much more important to babies than things are people. We are frequently asked by parents who have just completed one of the far too many "how to make your baby smarter" books whether there's any hope for their children, since they haven't done all those games and activities or given all those learning materials to their babies. What most of these books neglect to tell parents is that there is no toy, no learning material, and no special teaching game more interesting and better stimulation than honest, spontaneous, loving interaction between them and their children. If you enjoy your children and find experiencing the world through their eyes and ears (and other senses)

---

[4] Ruth Hartley and Robert Goldenson's *The Complete Book of Children's Plays,* rev. ed. (New York: Thomas Y. Crowell Company, 1963) is an excellent developmentally based source of learning activities and materials for children from birth through adolescence. In addition, our book, *Child Development and Early Childhood Education* (Chicago: Office of the Mayor and Model Cities—Chicago Committee on Urban Opportunity, 1973), contains explanations of young children's development and appropriate stimulation to enhance their development and learning at different stages, from birth to five years.

an adventure, and if you're very responsive to their needs, then just living will be a constant source of learning for your children.

Studies have been made over the past forty to fifty years, but particularly in the last ten to fifteen, of what kinds of stimulation are most interesting (and thus the best source of learning) to babies. Rather than go into the details of the findings, we will point to two important conclusions resulting from them: (1) babies differentiate, from birth, between pleasant and unpleasant stimulation (e.g., sweet vs. bitter tastes, gentle vs. harsh sounds) and (2) many of the qualities of stimuli that greatly attract babies are contained in people (e.g., they are complex sights with sharp contrast, they move, they make noise, etc.). We may derive from these two statements, then, an adage: You are your baby's most important learning material; remember that in your interactions, and try to make them as pleasurable as possible.

Babies *should* have interesting things in their environment to play with in whatever way they can at the particular stage that they're in. (Toys should invite active involvement, not passive observation.) Even more important, because they're stuck wherever they're put until they become self-moving, babies should be taken to the world; just walking around the house with you, in a carrier at your chest or on your back, can be an adventure. Finally, stimulation from you—your touching, handling, talking, singing, romping, and so on, and your consistent, loving care—is the most important of all.

The readings that follow were chosen because they deal with some of the more persistent concerns parents seem to have in relation to caring for infants in the first year of life. The first reading, a selection by Dr. Ashley Montagu, stresses the importance of touching for the infant's development. The second reading, by Drs. Silvia Bell and Mary Ainsworth, deals with the relationship between an infant's crying and his mother's responsiveness, reporting research with results that challenge the old belief that to respond to a baby's crying will cause him to cry more. Finally, the third reading, an article by Dr. Niles Newton, gives some tips on effective means of dealing with a baby's crying.

The Miracle of a Mother's Touch

Ashley Montagu

This selection discusses the critical importance of skin stimulation to a baby's survival and growth. It is through the skin that children first experience the feelings of love communicated by their caregivers through secure holding, gentle stroking, tender caressing, and rhythmic rocking. And it is this early physical handling that forms the basis of a child's future love relationships, both with sexual partners and with his/her own children. Through secure and gentle handling, babies are comforted and made to feel secure and loved. In contrast, a lack of touching or rough, rigid handling will make children nervous and insecure. Touch is our most basic language—we can disguise our feelings through language, but not through touch. Through the communication of touch, babies experience the feelings that their caregivers have for them. A baby who is loved, who is "told" this through close body contact and skin stimulation (by mother and father), will grow to love in similar ways; for it is through being loved that one learns to love.

Do you know the lift of spirit one gets from a loving caress, an enfolding bear hug, a consoling hand?

Few of us are strangers to the enrichment, the special nourishment of another's touch.

But suppose I asked if you know what absolute essentials a human being must have to live. Would you think of mentioning touch, along with food, shelter, air and water?

Most people aren't aware that the need for touching *is* basic—utterly necessary for survival. In fact, a baby's need for it is so compelling that if skin stimulation were denied entirely, he would die.

During the nineteenth century, more than half the infants in institutions in the United States died during the first year of life from a disease called marasmus, from a Greek word meaning "wasting away." As late as the second decade of the twentieth century, the death rate for infants under a year of age in such institutions was nearly 100 percent! The reason: they were deprived of adequate handling, caressing, rocking and so on. Today, we have greater understanding

Ashley Montagu, "The Miracle of a Mother's Touch," *Woman's Day*, July, 1971, pp. 72, 96, 98. Adapted from the book *Touching: The Human Significance of the Skin* (New York: Columbia University Press, 1971). © 1971 by Ashley Montagu. Reprinted by permission of the author.

of a baby's critical need for body contact, but that understanding is still not great enough.

Physiologically, the differences between those who have been handled lovingly from birth onward and those who have not are measurable in changes in nerves, glands, muscles, body chemistry and skin.

Emotionally, the difference can be measured in the ability to love. We learn to love not by instruction but by being loved. To be tender, loving and caring, human beings must be tenderly loved and cared for in their earliest years—held in the arms of their mothers, caressed, cuddled and comforted from the moment they are born.

The influence of the skin and skin contact on human emotion is enormous. My approach to understanding it has been from the outside in, from the skin to the mind. I wanted to discover what kind of skin stimulation is necessary for the development of mental and physical health, and what happens if we aren't given enough body contact.

MOTHERING AMONG ANIMALS

Studies of animals of our own kind, the mammals, provide fascinating insights to the benefits of skin stimulation. The way the young of all mammals snuggle and cuddle against the body of the mother or the bodies of litter-mates or of any other animal available strongly suggests that skin stimulation is an important biological need for both physical and behavioral development. Domestic or wild, almost every animal enjoys being stroked or otherwise having its skin pleasurably stimulated.

For example, in a series of experiments supervised by Dr. John Benjamin of the Child Research Council, Denver, Colorado, one group of twenty laboratory rats was caressed and cuddled by the investigators, while the other group, supplied with exactly the same kinds and amounts of food and living conditions, was treated coldly. "It sounds silly," Dr. Benjamin remarked, "but the petted rats learned faster and grew faster." It's not silly at all. Gentled rats show greater liveliness, curiosity and problem-solving ability than ungentled rats. They also tend to be more dominant, calmer and better at learning and retention.

The constant licking that mother cats and many other mammals give their young not only signifies maternal affection, but is essential in helping the processes of elimination get started. Newborn laboratory animals such as mice and rabbits who had been separated from their mothers died from the lack of this licking until researchers began swabbing them regularly with moist cotton. Chihuahua puppies have a high mortality rate because, according to breeders, their mothers often make no attempt to lick them. Workers at Cornell University's Behavior Farm in Ithaca, New York, found that with no licking at all, many newborn lambs failed to stand up after birth and subsequently died.

Touch communication plays a major role among monkeys—they're essentially contact animals. The young are carried on their mothers' bodies for long periods of time. There is much clinging, riding and contact with other members of the group. Young animals, and often adults, tend to sit and even sleep together in close contact.

In a series of studies, Professor Harry Harlow of the University of Wisconsin found that laboratory-raised baby monkeys who were deprived of their mothers could barely survive cage life until a mother substitute was developed—a terry-cloth-covered cone shape with a lightbulb behind it to radiate heat.

Professor Harlow was also able to trace back the histories of several female monkeys who were complete failures as mothers. He found that they had never known a real monkey mother of their own, never had the opportunity as babies to develop a normal infant-mother relationship.

A human mother's response to her newborn also depends in an important way on her own early experience as an infant and child.

How Mothering Affects Us

Body contact with our mothers provides our first contact with the world. Through a mother's body we are enfolded in a new dimension of experience—the experience of the world of the other. This bodily contact with the other provides our essential sense of comfort, security and warmth, and increases our aptitude for new experiences.

As recently as the 1930's and later, American mothers were being warned by the "Dr. Spock" of the time that rocking a baby in a cradle was a "vicious and unnecessary practice"; they were also advised not to pick up their babies when they cried, to feed them by the clock and to avoid spoiling them with too much handling. This unsentimental, mechanistic approach was not only adopted by millions of conscientious mothers, but greatly influenced psychology and profoundly affected pediatric thinking and practice.

Today we know that a child whose mother hasn't handled him enough fails to develop into a whole human being, for she hasn't communicated that he is loved. From her stroking and carrying and caressing and cuddling and cooing—her loving gestures—he learns to stroke and caress and cuddle and coo to others. In this sense, love is sexual in the healthiest meaning of the word. It implies involvement, concern, responsibility, tenderness and awareness of the needs and vulnerabilities of others. All this is communicated to an infant through his skin in the early months of his life. All this is communicated through a mother's touch.

LOVING BEGINS WITH LABOR

The newborn elephant and fallow deer are able to run with the herd shortly after they are born. By the age of six weeks, the infant seal has been taught to navigate his water world. But human babies are born in a state so immature that they need eight or ten months to learn to crawl and another four to six months to walk and talk. Like the little kangaroo or opossum, the human baby really hasn't completed his gestation period when he is born—but he doesn't have the wonderful advantage of a maternal pouch, a sheltering "womb with a view" that these marsupial infants have access to.

Because the human baby is born in such a precariously immature state, he needs very special touch conditioning to prepare him for functioning in the postnatal world. This is provided by the massive contractions of his mother's uterus on his body during his birth.

A mother experiences labor for an average of fourteen hours with her firstborn, eight hours with subsequent babies. The stimulation the baby receives from the contractions of her uterus tone up his sustaining systems—respiratory, circulatory, digestive, eliminative, nervous and endocrine—for the functions they will be called upon to perform after birth.

Since the baby is usually in a head-down position in the narrowest part of the womb prior to birth, stimulation of his face, nose, lips and the remainder of his head is very considerable. It actually corresponds to the licking of the muzzle and oral regions, described earlier, that other animals give their young. These uterine contractions of labor constitute the beginning caressing of the baby in the right way —a caressing that should be continued in very special ways in the period immediately following birth and for a substantial period of time afterward.

WELCOME TO THE "BOSOM OF THE FAMILY"

During the birth process, mother and infant have had a somewhat trying time. At birth, each clearly requires the reassurance of the other's presence.* For a mother, the reassurance lies in the sight of her baby—his first cry, his closeness to her body. For the baby, it consists in the contact with and warmth of his mother's body, the support in her cradled arms, the caressing he receives and the suckling at her breasts—his welcome into the "bosom of the family."

These are words, but they refer to very real psychological and physiological conditions. As a baby nurses, not only the stimulation of contact with his mother's body, but especially the stimulation of his face, lips, nose, tongue and mouth during suckling are important in improving his ability to breathe and get more oxygen into his blood. At the same time, he is ingesting colostrum from his mother's breasts, the best of all substances he could possibly have. The colostrum lasts only two days and, among other things, acts as a laxative that puts his elimination process into operation. It also encourages the growth of desirable bacteria and discourages undesirable bacteria in his gastrointestinal tract. The colostrum and the transitional and permanent milk that gradually come into his mother's breasts are perfectly timed and adjusted to the physiological development of the baby's digestive system.

Much else could be said on the advantages of breast-feeding for both mother and child. Its aim, of course, is to give the baby something rather more than an adequate diet: to provide him, in sum, with an emotional environment of security and love in which his whole being can thrive. Breast-feeding alone will not secure this. It is the mother's total relatedness to her child that makes breast-feeding significant. The breast-feeding relationship establishes the foundation for all of his future social human relationships. The communications he receives through the warmth of his mother's skin constitute his first socializing experience.

LET THE CRADLE ROCK

In America, the cradle was banished to the attic in the early 1900's when the notion became fashionable that fondling and rocking a baby endangered his development as an unspoiled independent person. It has never made a real comeback, and I occasionally speculate on a possible connection in the aptly named "rock" music of our day, sometimes plaintive and beautiful as a lullaby, sometimes strident and

* As Dr. Montagu communicates in *The Direction of Human Development* (New York: Harper & Row, 1970), the routine practice in hospitals of separating mother and baby following birth is detrimental to both of them and to their relationship. They need each other at this time.

percussive. It's danced to with swaying, rocking, rolling motions, and the lyrics, addressed to parents or the older generation in general, only too often say "You don't understand me," "Where were you when I needed you?" or words to that effect. Perhaps this music and dancing represent both an unconscious protest against an earlier lack of cradling and rocking and a compensation for it.

To get to my point, having spent the whole of his preceding life snugly ensconced in his mother's womb, a baby would certainly feel more comfortable cozily tucked into a cradle than abandoned to a large crib in which he lies, either on his front or his back, exposed to the dull and uninteresting flat white surface of either the sheet or the ceiling, with only the prison bars at the side of his crib to break the monotony of this bleak, one-dimensional landscape.

Since a baby assures himself that all is well largely through the messages he receives from his skin, the support he receives in the enveloping environment of a cradle—in contrast to the amorphousness of a big crib—is very reassuring. The cradle provides something of a replication, a continuation, of the life he led so long in the womb, and this is good and comforting. When the baby feels uncomfortable or insecure he may whimper, and if his mother or anyone else rocks the cradle this will have a soothing effect. Rocking reassures the baby, for in his mother's womb he was naturally rocked by the normal motions of her body. To be comfortable means to be comforted, and for the infant this comfort is largely derived from the signals he receives from his skin. The greatest of all comforts is to be cradled in his mother's arms or supported on her back in a baby carrier.*

The benefits of rocking, whether in arms, cradle or chair, are considerable. When the baby is too warm, the rocking has a cooling effect, hastening evaporation from his skin. When he is too cold, the rocking helps warm him. The warming has a hypnotic effect on him and is soothing to his nervous system. Above all, the rocking motion produces a gentle stimulation of almost every area of his skin, which has physiological benefits of every kind.

MOTHERING AND THE CAPACITY TO LOVE

Cuddling, nursing and rocking play a very effective and important role in a child's sexual development. A mother who loves must enfold the child she loves. She must draw the child to her in a close embrace

---

* Author's note: Even better are the carriers that hold the baby snugly against the mother's breast.

and, whether male or female, this is what the child will want as an adult—and be able to demonstrate to anyone he or she loves. (In many of its elements the sexual relationship reproduces the loving-mother-child relationship.) Children who haven't been held and fondled enough will hunger for such attention as adolescents and adults. If they have been warded off during childhood they remain isolated, demanding full gratification for themselves and showing small capacity for reciprocity.

Women often complain of the clumsiness, crassness and incompetence of men in their sexual approaches and in sexual intercourse itself. This, as well as a lack of skill in foreplay and a failure to understand its importance, almost certainly reflects the lack of tactile experience that many men suffer in childhood. When a man handles women —and children—roughly, you can be sure that he has been failed in early body contact, for it is difficult to conceive of anyone who has been tenderly loved and caressed in infancy not learning to approach a woman or child with special tenderness. The very word "tenderness" implies softness, delicacy of touch, caring for. The gorilla, that gentle creature, is the most frequently slandered animal when women describe the approaches of the kind of man (and there are many) who seems to regard sex as a tension releaser rather than a profoundly meaningful act of communication in a deeply involved human relationship.

You may well ask, if men can be so marked by lack of early tactual experience, how are women affected? The answer to that question: by more or less frigidity, or by a nymphomania that abnormally craves tactual sensations. But I must emphasize that such conditions are not entirely the result of tactual deprivations in early life, although they may, in part, be so.

Tactile demonstrations of affection between mother and daughter are not as inhibited as they are between mother and son. Many mothers begin early to reject demonstrations of love by their sons in the mistaken fear that unless they do they will cause their sons to become too deeply attached to them.

Many fathers reject their sons' embraces because as one father, a physician, remarked to me, "I don't want him to become a homosexual." The very thought of any such demonstrations between father and son makes most American fathers squirm. A boy putting his arm across the shoulders of another boy is cause for real alarm. It simply isn't done. The appalling ignorance revealed in such attitudes is very damaging and serves to reinforce a boy's inability to relate tactually to another human being. Yet a significant measure of the individual's healthy development is the extent to which he or she is freely able to embrace another and enjoy the embraces of others . . . to get, in a very real sense, into touch with others.

THE IMPORTANCE OF FATHERING

If in our culture we could learn to understand the importance of fathers as well as mothers giving their babies adequate tactile satisfaction, we would be taking a considerable step toward the improvement of human relations. But the father, in civilized societies, is to a large extent deprived of the possibility of such direct, reciprocal, pleasure-giving exchanges. The reason is "image."

To begin with, a boy has a much harder time than a girl growing up and separating himself from the loving mother and identifying himself with a father with whom he is nowhere as deeply involved as he remains with his mother. This often puts strain on him. The switch in identification he is called upon to make results in a conflict. He usually tries to resolve this by, in part, rejecting his mother and relegating her to an inferior status. Antifeminism in men can be regarded as a defense against the strong unconscious trend toward mother-worship. Yet when a man's defenses are down, when he is dying, his last word, like his first, is likely to be "mother." This resurgence of feeling comes because he has never really repudiated his mother— he has simply been forced to disengage himself from her.

So only one thing exists to prevent a father from bathing his child, from drying it, fondling it, caressing it, cuddling it, changing its diapers and cleaning it, from holding it, rocking it, carrying, playing with it and continuing to give it a good deal of tactile stimulation. That simple barrier is the ancient and outmoded tradition that such conduct is feminine and therefore unbecoming to a man.

Fortunately, this tradition is rapidly breaking down. Increasingly I see young fathers involved with their children very much more deeply and in all sorts of "feminine" ways that only a generation or so ago were considered beneath the dignity of a "real" man. Dignity, as Laurence Sterne pointed out, is usually a mysterious carriage of the body calculated to conceal the infirmities of the mind.

"THE HUMAN TOUCH"

The *Oxford English Dictionary* says that touch is "the most general of the bodily senses, diffused through all parts of the skin, but (in man) specially developed in the tips of the fingers and lips."

For a time, a baby's lips represent his only means of judgment. Through his lips he grasps not only body-building substances, but reality. That is why, as soon as he is able, he puts things to his lips in order to judge them, and continues to do so long after he has arrived at other means of perception and judgment. These other means arrive, ultimately, through the tips of his fingers and the palm of his hand, a hand that has rested upon his mother's palpable and reassuring breast. At birth, all the baby's other senses are so undeveloped that they convey very little information of value to him. He depends on his sense of touch: lips and generalized body contact, then fingertips to hand.

During the middle 1960's many people began rediscovering something of the importance of the skin in encounter, marathon and sensitivity-training groups. These groups, usually consisting of adults or older adolescents, put principal emphasis on touching. But the reputable ones are concerned with much more than physical pleasures. What they seek is a greater behavioral aliveness to their own and others' presence, and relatedness to the environment; they seek to put people who have become disassociated back in touch with the world they live in and their fellow man. The idea is a good one, even though it comes late in the day for many participants. To be "in touch" means to be in communication. Man's primary and basic means of communication comes in the experiences he undergoes as a baby in contact with his mother's body. These experiences represent his first language, his first entering into touch with another human being, the origin of "the human touch."

Infant Crying and Maternal Responsiveness: Discussion

Silvia M. Bell and Mary D. Salter Ainsworth

This selection is the discussion section of a report of research investigating the relationship between babies' crying in the first year of life

Adapted from Silvia Bell and Mary Ainsworth, "Infant Crying and Maternal Responsiveness," discussion section, *Child Development,* 43 (1972), 1185–89, Copyright © 1972 by the Society for Research in Child Development, Inc.

and their mothers' responsiveness to them. Bell and Ainsworth's find-ings contradict the popular advice to parents that picking up a crying child will increase his crying. In fact, they found, mothers who re-sponded consistently and promptly to their babies' signals (crying and noncrying) in the first months of life were rewarded by a decrease in frequency and duration of crying in later months. In contrast, mothers who were unresponsive to their tiny infants' crying had babies who cried more later on. Other related findings: babies whose mothers were responsive to their signals developed more effective and varied means of communication other than crying as they grew, whereas babies with unresponsive mothers seemed to lack noncrying means of communi-cation. Close physical contact—picking a baby up to hold and rock her or to feed her—was the most frequent and most effective means of stopping a baby from crying; just talking to or interacting with the baby without physical contact was least effective. The most important factor in reducing crying was the promptness with which a mother answered her baby's signals. Maternal responsiveness also has an ob-servable impact on babies' development of a sense of confidence that they can, through their actions, control what happens to them. Re-sponsive mothers encourage children's development of competence, not only in eliciting help from others but also in learning to act on their own without needing others to do so much for them.

Our data suggest that, in the first ¼ year, crying is a signal that promotes proximity and contact with the mother by activating her behavior. Tiny babies tend to cry more frequently when out of visual, auditory, and physical contact with others and to be soothed most effectively by close physical contact. Mothers, in turn, tend to pick their crying babies up more frequently than they intervene in any other way. Thus infant and maternal behavior are basically well adapted to each other. . . .

Crying is the earliest of a repertoire of proximity-promoting, sig-naling behaviors. Maternal response to the crying signal tends to ter-minate an episode of crying. Reasonably consistent promptness of re-sponse tends to decrease an infant's readiness to use crying as a signal, this effect following not immediately but by the second quarter of the first year. Concomitant with this decrease, there is a development of other social signals and, later, communications which also become focused on the mother as a major attachment figure. Although the data reported here did not deal directly with maternal responsiveness to signals other than crying, our observations yield the unequivocal impression that mothers who promptly heed an infant's cries are sensi-tively responsive to other signals as well. Mother and infant form an interactional dyad: the more responsive she is the less likely he is to cry and the more likely he is to develop more varied modes of communication.

It is useful to view these findings in the light of an ethologically oriented paradigm advanced by Ainsworth (1967, 1969, and in press, a and b; Ainsworth & Bell, 1970) and Bowlby (1958, 1969).* A basic assumption of this approach is that species-characteristic behaviors, including attachment behaviors such as crying, have become part of the genetically programmed repertoire of the species through performing a significant survival-promoting function for individual, population, and/or species in the environment in which the species evolved —and indeed continue to perform such a function in the present environments occupied by the species. Bowlby has argued that the biological function of infant-mother attachment, and of both infant attachment behaviors and reciprocal maternal behaviors, is protection from danger; and in the original environment of evolutionary adaptedness it was likely that predators were the most conspicuous danger. Attachment behaviors protect an infant by bringing him close to his mother, who can defend him from danger or help him escape from it. In a species in which an infant is as helpless as the human, attachment behavior could not effectively perform its protective function were it not dovetailed with reciprocal maternal behavior, activated either by the infant's signals or directly by danger or by both in combination. Infant and maternal behaviors are adapted to each other, and thus the environment to which an infant's attachment behaviors are adapted includes a mother who responds to his signals without undue delay.

From what is known of ground-living nonhuman primates and present-day human communities of hunters and gatherers, it is believed that in the original environment of evolutionary adaptedness mother and infant, usually with companions, moved about frequently through open country where predators presented an ever-possible danger. In a wide variety of mammalian species that currently occupy such environments, the victims of predation tend to be limited to the very young, the very old, and those disabled through illness or injury —especially when they become separated from their companions. Under such circumstances it is of obvious survival advantage for an infant who has somehow lost proximity to his mother to emit a vocal signal perceptible across a distance; it is equally of advantage for his mother to respond to such a signal promptly. Since a vocal signal might also attract a predator, it is of advantage also that it be terminated promptly once infant and mother are together again, but at

* Bell and Ainsworth's bibliography follows this extract.

the same time it seems adaptive for an infant to continue and perhaps intensify his signals should his mother not respond quickly. Nevertheless it is advantageous for an infant to learn to reserve crying for the more alarming situations he encounters, and to use other modes of communication, provided, of course, that his mother is close enough to perceive them.

Our argument is thus that babies are programmed to cry when out of contact or otherwise distressed, behaving as though it were a matter of life or death, even though such behavior may not be necessary to ensure protection under the conditions that commonly (although not invariably) prevail in the present-day Western world. Although mothers may be influenced by a realistic perception of the improbability of danger, a baby's behavior is nevertheless adapted to the prototype of a responsive mother.

Many contemporary mothers are promptly responsive to infant crying, but many are not. Some are deliberately unresponsive, in the belief that to respond will make a baby demanding, dependent, and "spoiled." Our data suggest the contrary—that *those infants who are conspicuous for fussing and crying after the first few months of life, and who fit the stereotype of the "spoiled child," are those whose mothers have ignored their cries or have delayed long in responding to them.**

Other aspects of our analysis of mother-infant interaction in the first year (Ainsworth, Bell, & Stayton, in press) confirm the conclusion that *maternal responsiveness promotes desirable behavior rather than "spoiling" a child. Infants whose mothers have given them relatively much tender and affectionate holding in the earliest months of life are content with surprisingly little physical contact by the end of the first year; although they enjoy being held, when put down they are happy to move off into independent exploratory play. In contrast, those held for relatively brief periods during the early months tend to be ambivalent about contact by the end of the first year; they do not respond positively when held, but yet protest when put down and do not turn readily to independent activity.*

When in the familiar home environment, those babies who tolerate without distress mother's leaving the room briefly tend to have mothers who have been responsive to crying and other signals, while those who more frequently cry when she leaves and do not want to let her out of sight tend to have mothers who have been unresponsive. Finally Stayton, Hogan, and Ainsworth (1971) found that *disciplinary practices, such as frequent commands and physical interventions intended to restrict and modify a baby's behavior, do not foster infant obedi-*

---

* Note: Italics are the editors'.

ence. Those infants who can be controlled by their mothers across a distance and who comply with maternal commands are those whose signals have been promptly and sensitively heeded by their mothers. In short, *those infants in our sample who are fussy, demanding, and difficult to control are those whose mothers have been unresponsive to signals and generally insensitive or interfering in their efforts to mold their babies to their routines, wishes, and expectations.*

It has commonly been assumed that what terminates crying—picking up, feeding, etc.—constitutes a reward which necessarily reinforces the behavior. Furthermore, according to popular belief, crying should decrease through maternal failure to respond contingently to it. Such an "extinction" mechanism may operate under conditions of extreme lack of contingent responsiveness, as, for example, in typical institutional environments where babies soon become quiet and cry little and also become apathetic and retarded in overall development (Provence & Lipton, 1962; Schaffer & Callender, 1959). There is no evidence of an extinction process in our sample of home-reared infants. It has sometimes been suggested that the crying of babies with unresponsive mothers does not decrease because it has been partially or intermittently reinforced, thus making it resistant to extinction. Such an explanation cannot account for individual differences in our sample, since all infants experienced intermittent interventions; not even the most responsive mother can over time respond to all cries promptly. Our findings clearly indicate that the processes implicit in a decrease of crying must be more complex than these popular extrapolations from learning theory would suggest.

In the first part of the first year, crying may be viewed as a fixed-action pattern, activated by a variety of conditions in which intra-organismic components are often conspicuous but which include environmental components as well. Crying is terminated by various other conditions, but it seems most likely to remain deactivated for long periods if the terminating conditions substantially alter the activating conditions. *A responsive mother, our data suggest, not only provides the conditions that terminate a cry, thus reducing its duration, but also is likely to provide conditions that tend to prevent crying from being activated or reactivated.* Thus, for example, we found that mothers who are sensitively responsive to infant signals in regard to the onset, termination, and pacing of feeding in the first quarter have babies who cry less than the infants of mothers who are relatively unresponsive (Ainsworth & Bell, 1969). From other findings (Ainsworth et al., in press) we may also infer that tiny infants who have relatively long periods of physical contact in nonroutine contexts would less frequently than other infants have crying activated by being alone and out of contact. Thus, infants whose mothers are responsive to their signals have less occasion to cry—not only in the first few months but throughout infancy.

Nevertheless, in the latter part of the first year, crying loses some of its fixed-action quality in that it can be directed specifically toward the mother and thus can be used intentionally as a means to an end, as a mode of communication. According to Piaget's (1952) observations, it is not until about 8 months of age that a baby can differentiate means from ends and flexibly use a variety of "schemata" as means with intent to achieve an end. It is our hypothesis that *in responding to a baby's signaling behavior a mother provides feedback, which, since it is contingent upon his signals, fosters the development of flexible, means-end communicative behavior. The child of a responsive mother comes to anticipate her responsiveness.* Although some of his communications may be cries, the predictability of his mother's responsiveness tends to reduce the intensity of the conditions that might otherwise activate a cry, if only because he does not feel alone and out of contact. Thus a mother who is responsive to the signals implicit in a wide range of her baby's behavior creates an atmosphere in which he can signal through varied means less urgent than crying.

An infant whose mother's responsiveness helps him to achieve his ends develops confidence in his own ability to control what happens to him. It seems likely that toward the end of his first year he begins to distinguish between what he can effect directly through his own actions and what he can accomplish through eliciting his mother's cooperation. Although before this his confidence rests in part on a magical control of others, nonetheless it fosters increased initiative in the acquisition of other means-ends activities through which he can achieve his own goals without requesting the intervention of adults. Even before a baby can differentiate between means and ends, there is an inverse relation between crying and competence. A baby who is unable to roll over from a supine to a prone position may fuss when his efforts to do so are in vain; when he is yet unable to reach out and grasp an attractive object he may "cry for it"; when he has mastered rolling over, reaching, and grasping, he has fewer occasions to cry. There is no reason to suppose that to turn him over or to give him the attractive object will deter the development of these basic abilities. *A baby is so eager to explore his world and to practice his developing manipulative and locomotor skills that there is no basis for fear that to respond to his signals will hamper the development of competence and self-reliance.*

Thus two central concepts have been brought to bear on an understanding of the processes implicit in the decrease of crying and the relations of the decrement to maternal responsiveness. First, *crying is not viewed as a behavior to be reinforced or extinguished in isolation from other signaling behaviors, but as one manifestation of an emergent communicative system. Second, a baby, although helpless and dependent at the beginning, not only learns to affect the behavior of others in his environment through his signals and communications, but is also biased from the beginning toward the development of abilities that will make him increasingly competent and self-reliant so that he is increasingly able to act on his own behalf without requiring others to do so much for him.* Maternal responsiveness to signals fosters the development of communication. It does not interfere with the early development of increased competence, and through giving a child confidence, it positively encourages the later development of means-ends activities.

References

AINSWORTH, M. D. S. *Infancy in Uganda: infant care and the growth of love.* Baltimore: Johns Hopkins University Press, 1967.

AINSWORTH, M. D. S. Object relations, dependency, and attachment: a theoretical review of the infant-mother relationship. *Child Development,* 1969, *40,* 969–1025.

AINSWORTH, M. D. S. The development of infant-mother attachment. In B. M. Caldwell & H. N. Ricciuti (Eds.), *Review of child development research.* Vol. *3* Chicago: University of Chicago Press, in press (a).

AINSWORTH, M. D. S. Attachment and dependency: a comparison. In J. L. Gewirtz (Ed.), *Attachment and dependence.* New York: Academic Press, in press (b).

AINSWORTH, M. D. S., & BELL, S. M. Some contemporary patterns of mother-infant interaction in the feeding situation. In A. Ambrose (Ed.), *Stimulation in early infancy.* London: Academic Press, 1969. Pp. 133–170.

AINSWORTH, M. D. S., & BELL, S. M. Attachment, exploration and separation: illustrated by the behavior of one-year-olds in a strange situation. *Child Development,* 1970, *41,* 49–67.

AINSWORTH, M. D. S.; BELL, S. M.; & STAYTON, D. J. Individual differences in the development of some attachment behaviors. *Merrill Palmer Quarterly,* in press.

BOWLBY, J. The nature of the child's tie to his mother. *International Journal of Psychoanalysis,* 1958, *39,* 350–373.

BOWLBY, J. *Attachment and loss.* Vol. *1. Attachment.* London: Hogarth (New York: Basic), 1969.

PIAGET, J. *The origins of intelligence in children.* 1936. 2d ed. New York: International Universities Press, 1952.

PROVENCE, S., & LIPTON, R. C. *Infants in institutions.* New York: International Universities Press, 1962.

SCHAFFER, H. R., & CALLENDER, W. M. Psychological effects of hospitalization in infancy. *Pediatrics*, 1959, *24*, 528–539.

STAYTON, D. J.; HOGAN, R.; & AINSWORTH, M. D. S. Infant obedience and maternal behavior: the origins of socialization reconsidered. *Child Development*, 1971, *42*, 1057–1069.

What to Do When Baby's Crying Gets Trying

Niles Newton

The previous selection suggested that you should respond to your baby's crying and that the more differentially responsive you are— trying to figure out what the child wants rather than performing some stereotyped action (e.g., always just checking his diapers or offering a bottle)—the more likely you are to promote the development of other means of communication than crying. This selection gives you some pointers on some of the possible reasons babies might persist in crying and some of the strategies that you might find successful in terminating their crying. You may be able to think of other ways of comforting a baby that are not mentioned here. The important thing to remember is that babies cry for a reason. It is up to you to discover the reason and respond appropriately as promptly as possible.

Your Baby is crying. He just has been fed and diapered, but still he is fussing. What do you do next to quiet him?

Your baby is asking for something. The key questions are: Is your baby in physical discomfort? Is he missing the constant contact, the rhythmic heartbeat sound, and the physical joggling he got in the womb? Could your baby be bored, wanting a greater variety of sights and sounds?

Physical discomforts are often the easiest to remedy. Here are some practical measures:

Some babies fuss while they are having a bowel movement. It sometimes helps to give an infant's feet something firm to push on to help the process. Try holding him up over your shoulder as you walk back

Niles Newton, "What to Do When Baby's Crying Gets Trying," Chicago *Tribune*, Tuesday, June 26, 1973. Reprinted by permission of the author.

and forth, and place your second hand on the sole of his feet so he can push against it.

Sometimes an air bubble in the tummy is uncomfortable and has prevented the baby from eating as much as he would like.

One easy way of bubbling or burping your baby is to lay him across your crossed knees, holding his abdomen with one hand while his head rests against your arm. With the other hand gently rub his back with an upward motion. After this another suck at bottle or breast may be appreciated.

Dirty and wet diapers do not bother many babies unless they have a sore bottom or have been trained by a meticulous mother to expect the constant dry feel. Mild soap and many rinses should be used on home-washed diapers, with enough changing to help forestall diaper rash.

If rash develops, try leaving off the diapers, soakers and plastic altogether. Free circulation of air helps skin healing and a baby usually loves it. When he needs to be socially acceptable, wrap a receiving blanket around his bottom but not between his legs.

Other physical discomforts may involve feeling too hot or cold or wanting more feeding even though some has been obtained. Sometimes you are more hungry than other times and babies are equally variable.

Another cause of fussing is what I like to call "missing the womb fuss." A baby finds it comforting to have some of the conditions he experienced for most of his life restored to him particularly during the first weeks after birth.

Before birth, your baby has heard the steady beat, beat, beat of your heart, which may make him appreciative of rhythmic sounds. Lullabies are used the world over, and radio, record players, and cassette tape recorder make it easy to supply sounds.

Your baby has also felt warmth and snugness in the womb so that wrapping blankets tightly around him, swaddling him, is sometimes comforting. If you are placing him on his side, put a rolled blanket behind his back since he cannot at first control his own wiggling and flopping and gets upset by his own unrestrained sprawling.

Rocking chairs and rocking baby beds to an infant have a long and honored tradition and are very effective. The rocking chair has an advantage since both mother and baby may be soothed at the same time.

Some mothers, especially those who are breastfeeding, go back to the ways of their great, great grandmothers when faced with a fussy baby at night. Many old medical textbooks emphasize the need for the baby to be comforted by sleeping with his mother.

One way of sleeping with a baby is to have your arm curled around him. Another very comforting way is to place the baby on your chest with his tummy against yours. Pat or rub him gently until he quiets down.

Another form of fussing is the "I want to be up and around" type of cry. Babies do get bored, and since they cannot move themselves to interesting sights and sounds, their only way of helping themselves is to fuss for attention.

Although this kind of fussing can happen at many times of the day, it is most usually in the late afternoon when mother is busy cooking supper and getting ready for father's return, and when other children are demanding extra attention.

One of the best solutions to this is a baby carrier that holds the baby against the mother's chest. The framed kind of carriers used on the back are not as comforting for a new baby who likes to be held close to his mother's heart, feeling her body very close to his.

Another way of giving variety and stimulation is to take a bath with your baby. It is restful for both mother and baby, and a baby usually loves the skin contact with his mother.

An air bath also sometimes delights a baby. With all his clothes off, he can have the fun of kicking totally unrestricted.

Fathers and neighbors and relatives can be a great help to a hurried mother by giving her a "half hour break" to regain her energy. While she takes a little rest and freshens up, others can take the baby on a tour of the home, talking to him and letting him see each room.

Taking the baby outdoors to see the bright sky and new objects sometimes works wonders and if extra soothing is required, a car ride may have remarkable quieting results.

3

The Runabout Child:
Ten to Eighteen Months[1]

The period beginning about ten months marks a time of significant change for the infant-child. For although she is still dependent on her caregivers for most of her needs, she now probably has enough control of her body to get about on her own and meet the world. Whereas in the first half-year of their lives babies needed to have the world brought to them or to be, themselves, brought to the world, in the second half-year of their lives they learn to reach out, then to venture out under their own power. By ten months, most infants can creep on hands and knees; they are never again to be safely planted wherever they are put down. Once mobile, children become adventurous explorers with all the world around them the subject of their explorations.

This is a very exciting time for children and a turning point in their relationship with their caregivers that has ramifications for their future as learning beings. Dr. Burton White and his colleagues[2] have identified the period between ten and eighteen months as a critical period for the development of the foundations of competence. This is a time when infants are trying out many of their new skills; the kinds of responses they get to their activities from their caregivers

[1] "Runabout" is a term borrowed from the British; they use it to refer to the toddler, the child from about fifteen months to two or two and a half years. Though ten-month-olds are really still babies and won't be actually "running" about for a while, nevertheless, they are beginning to get about on their own (on hands and knees), an achievement that we feel sufficiently distinguishes them from their younger selves that we prefer this division to that typically used.

[2] Burton L. White and Jean Carew Watts with Itty Chan Barnett, Barbara Taylor Kaban, Janice Rosen Marmor and Bernice Broyde Shapiro, *Experience and Environment*, vol. I (Englewood Cliffs, N.J.: Prentice-Hall, Inc., 1973). The inspiration for this chapter was the work of White et al., and our reading selection is the chapter from this book that discusses their study and its implications for childrearing practice.

will make a big difference in whether they become adventurous, self-confident, secure learners or cautious, insecure, hesitant learners.

In early infancy, children are totally dependent on their caregivers. They can't even change position on their own. Gradually, babies gain control of the muscles that enable them to move their bodies on purpose. This occurs roughly in a direction from head to "tail" and from the midline of the body to the extremities. In the first half of their first year, babies learn to control their eye muscles for focusing on near objects and following moving objects with their eyes; their neck muscles to move and support their head; their upper back to sit with support and to roll over; and their arms and hands to reach out and grasp nearby objects. These accomplishments enable babies to become more active participants in their world, but none of them gives them any independence from their caregivers.

In the second half of their first year, babies begin to develop the kinds of motor (movement) skills that can potentially lead to problems between them and their caregivers. They learn to sit alone, which is all right at first because they can't move from the spot on which they're placed. They continue to refine their skill with their hands and fingers. This can lead to trouble when they begin to grab everything in sight; and when they learn to drop and throw objects to the floor (a favorite game beginning at about ten months), even the most patient caregiver can become annoyed if he/she doesn't understand its developmental significance. Feeding can become a problem, since babies begin to grab the spoon and try to feed themselves at least a year before they learn how to do so at all competently. But most of all, when children begin to creep about on hands and knees, then stand, then cruise around holding onto furniture, then walk, climb, trot, and run, the stage is set for potential trouble if these new-found competencies are not dealt with appropriately.

How caregivers respond to this period of active motor involvement is important both to growth of a child's self-concept and to the child-caregiver relationship. If caregivers are supportive of children's attempts to "conquer the world," children will feel good about themselves and will see their caregivers as allies in their growth. On the other hand, if children's attempts at independence are met with resistance, they will begin to feel incompetent and insecure, and the battle lines will be drawn between them and their caregivers.

When children begin to move out under their own steam, unfortunately their newly acquired motor skills are not matched by an understanding of the importance of personal caution or property rights. It is up to the caregiver to prepare the environment so that it is safe both to and from the child. That means that as soon as babies become self-moving, the home must be "baby-proofed." Some parents think they are solving the problem by fencing off parts of the house, or worse still, by fencing in the baby, but neither of those techniques will promote the development of competence in the young child; children need the freedom to explore freely without constantly being hovered over or restricted. The only alternative is to accept the fact that part of the responsibility you assume when you accept the role of parent is to provide the conditions for your child's optimal development even if it means temporary inconvenience for you.

As children become more competent in this period between ten and eighteen months, they will also become more responsible in their behavior *if you allow them the freedom to grow* within necessary, but not unreasonable boundaries. For example, put covers over electric sockets and avoid having to yell at your children every time they want to put their fingers in a socket. Put breakables away or up high enough that they can't reach them. Don't expect self-control at this stage. Clear the environment of potential problems, and deal gently with any that occur in spite of your caution. Decide those few things (e.g., not touching hot stoves or radiators, not running in the street) that must be learned, and concentrate on those and forget the non-essentials for now.

Of all the times in the parent-child relationship, this is one of the more difficult and trying. A responsive caregiver is constantly "on call." This does not mean that you should be doing things for or with your children all the time; on the contrary, they need to learn to do things for and entertain themselves. But it does mean that you should be available when you're needed, to help out, redirect, make suggestions, and so forth. And you need to learn how to be omnipresent without hovering. It isn't safe to leave a young child alone for too long, but constant supervision of a child does not promote the development of competence. Children need to feel that you trust them (more perhaps than you actually do) in order to learn a sense of responsibility for their own actions, an essential component of growth.

There will be many things that children want to do in this stage that you might rather do for them or wish they wouldn't do, thinking that they can't do it efficiently or competently (e.g., feeding themselves, carrying around heavy things, climbing up onto high places). But try to remember the process you went through when you learned to drive a car or to do some similarly difficult task. It takes practice to learn any new skill, and children need your encouragement more than they need your help. They must be given the freedom to learn things themselves and not be overly restricted. Unreasonable restriction and over-protection are ways of telling children that you don't trust them. And if you don't trust them, how can they learn to trust themselves?

Don't arbitrarily impose restrictions on what children should be allowed to do, unless their behavior would harm themselves or someone else. Children need to feel the freedom to try things out on their own. If they sense fear or lack of confidence from you, it will inhibit their attempts to test themselves. It is very important that children learn to judge their own capabilities and limits. Sometimes this may mean an accident, but children will learn from that too, and no amount of protection will prevent all accidents.

Lest you misunderstand the point we have been trying to make about freedom: We are not suggesting that children be allowed to "run wild in the streets." And we are not talking about "permissive" childrearing. What we *are* talking about is allowing children as much freedom as they can responsibly handle and not keeping them dependent on you beyond the time that they should be. That means you need to know something about what is normal behavior at different ages so you don't interpret as "naughty" behavior that is simply the child's way of practicing newly emerging skills. It means continuing to be responsive to your children's signals of what they're ready for. And it means that you should spend at least as much time being concerned with your children's happy and healthy growth as with training them to be civilized members of society.

The emergence of motor abilities is not the only important thing that is happening to children in the time period between ten and eighteen months. As White explains in the selection that follows, the real significance of this period is the coincidence of major growth in a number of areas: children become able to move about on their own; they become able to understand and use language; and they begin to be aware of themselves as persons and to assert their will, often in defiant and negative ways. All these things coming together can be a great challenge to any caregiver. Dr. White and his colleagues have studied mothers who have met that challenge with great success.

Experience and Environment, Discussions and Conclusions

Burton L. White

In 1965, Dr. White began the Harvard Preschool Project. At that time, he and his colleagues began studying preschool-age children in an effort to discover what kinds of practices in a child's first six years promote the development of the ability to be successful and to profit from formal education at age six. After observing many young children, testing them, and talking to their teachers, they identified two groups of children, whom they designated as the "A" group and the "C" group. Those in the first group were competent in thinking and social skills; "they were able to cope in superior fashion with anything they met, day in and day out." In contrast, those in the latter group seemed to have a very difficult time coping both socially and intellectually.

As the study proceeded and the specific characteristics of competency were delineated (e.g., to use adults as resources; to lead and follow peers; to praise oneself and/or show pride in one's accomplishment; intellectual competence—the ability to sense dissonance or note discrepancies, the ability to anticipate consequences), it became obvious that the children they were studying were too old. Whatever environmental influences and experiences serve to promote competency in children apparently had their impact before age three; differences in basic competency existed at age three, there were striking similarities in clusters of competency among their "A" children who were three to six, and three-year-old "A" children were more competent, in many ways, than older "C" children. So the researchers took their work into homes, looking for that critical time when the differences between "A" and "C" children begin to appear. It was within this context that White and his colleagues discovered the significance of the ten- to eighteen-month time period for the development of competence in children; by eighteen months, differences in competency were apparent, whereas at ten months no outstanding differences could be identified.

Burton L. White et al., *Experience and Environment: Major Influences on the Development of the Young Child*, vol. I, © 1973. Reprinted by permission of Prentice-Hall, Inc., Englewood Cliffs, New Jersey.

The book from which the following selection is taken reports the history, techniques, and preliminary findings (the study was not to be completed for another two years after the book was written) of this important study. The chapter that we have included here provides a description of the significant developmental characteristics of children in the ten- to eighteen-month-old period that make this such a crucial stage. In addition, it describes in some detail the particular qualities and behaviors that distinguish "A" from "C" mothers, and gives some "best guesses about most effective child-rearing practices."

The critical period of development

Many people who study the development of children have made statements about the special importance of particular age ranges. In this regard, we are no different. Our study, even though incomplete at this writing, has convinced us of the special importance of the 10- to 18-month age range for the development of general competence. At this time of life, for most children, several extremely important developments seem to coalesce and force a test of each family's capacity to rear children. The primary burden in most cases falls upon the mother.

Let us first characterize children during the second and third years of life, to help set the stage for explaining why we believe so strongly in the unique importance of the 10- to 18-month period. We will then summarize what we think we are learning about desirable child-rearing practices.

THE CHILD AT ONE YEAR OF AGE

Most one-year-olds appear to resemble each other in a few interesting and fundamental ways. First of all, perhaps the hallmark of this age is curiosity. The one-year-old seems genuinely interested in exploring his world throughout the major portion of his day. Aside from mealtimes and the need to relieve various occasional physical discomforts, his consuming interest is in exploration. This fact is confirmed by our task data, especially in the predominance of the *explore, mastery,* and *gain information—visual* experiences. Unfortunately, not all situations are optimal for nurturing that curiosity, nor are the rules governing exploratory behavior equivalent across homes. Nonetheless, the one-year-old is primed for expending enormous amounts of energy exploring and learning about his world.

The curiosity of the one-year-old is aided by his newly acquired ability to cover space. Whereas, at 6 months of age, he was limited to the places his mother kept him (i.e., crib, high chair, playpen, changing-table, bath, carriage, etc.), he can now either crawl, cruise, or walk wherever he wishes, subject to his mother's approval and the physical layout of the home. Unfortunately, he is not yet very skillful with his body, nor very knowledgeable about danger or destruction. On the one hand, he is capable of enormous amounts of intellectual and social learning and development of motor skills such as walking, climbing, and especially the use of his hands. On the other hand, razor blades, broken glass, and electrical equipment are to him only additional opportunities for exploration. In addition, fragile objects that are precious to other people engender no special treatment from him. This combination of factors alone places considerable stress on most mothers. But there is more.

The one-year-old is poised for fundamental development in social and language development as well. During the first year of life, there is little to suggest that infants are self-conscious or particularly thoughtful creatures. During the second year, however, one can observe the emergence of a sense of self. Increasingly, the child seems to assimilate ideas of who he is. His name comes to produce an appropriate and a special response from him. Gradually, he begins to use the terms "me" and "mine." Also during that second year, he begins for the first time to seriously engage in interpersonal contests. As many have noted before, a sense of autonomy begins to manifest itself during this period.*

Along with a growing sense of self and independence, the child during the second year of life seems to be learning a great deal about his mother and her reactions. He studies her and approaches her often during this period and seems to develop a very strong attachment to her. Other human beings count, but not much compared to his mother, in most cases. Peers ordinarily spend very small amounts of time with him. Fathers may spend a bit more when we do not observe, but they still probably do not compare with the mother as centers of continuing interest (except in rare cases). During the second year, unlike any other time in his life, the child seems to develop in these directions in a manner that may produce a vigorous, secure, loving, and healthy social animal, or else may take other paths. By two, he may become a modest form of social tyrant whose major orientation

---

* For a graphic illustration, see our section on the ratio of compliance/noncompliance responses between one and three years of age. The one-year-old is largely compliant, as are most two- to three-year-olds. The 1½- to 2-year-old is considerably more likely to refuse a request than he was when younger or than he will be when he is older.

during his waking hours is clinging to and dominating his mother,* or he may learn that his mother is rather unpredictable—sometimes, someone to fear, while at other times, someone who will protect him.

Before 8 or 9 months of age, there is little reason to believe that infants understand words. By 36 months of age, they seem (in most cases) to be able to process most simple language. It is clear that a remarkable amount of language development is taking place beginning at about one year of age. . . . Certainly, no analysis of the effects of child-rearing practices during this age period should ignore this fact.

A further point on one-year-olds concerns the issue of physical maturity. At one, some children look and behave very much like the average 9- or 10-month-old, while others appear several months advanced. The fact that walking ability emerges at about this time helps accentuate differences in maturity at this age. We suspect that part of the reason one cannot predict future development from a one-year-old's behavior is this factor. The commonly seen, striking differences in physical maturity become much less marked by the time the child reaches two years of age, but at one they hinder prediction and also complicate the problem of effective child-rearing techniques.

THE CHILD AT TWO YEARS OF AGE

Data about the two-year-old (24 to 27 months) are slightly less interesting to us than data about the one-year-old. The reason is that it appears the two-year-old has already taken shape, to a degree that suggests that many basic formative experiences are already behind him. Our test data, like that of many other studies, indicate that children who are going to develop well or poorly (during the preschool period, at least) begin to reveal which course they are on at about the middle of the second year of life.

The two-year-old is usually just emerging from a rather dramatic phase, the aforementioned emergence of his sense of agency. This has been manifest in many ways, but perhaps the most dramatic is reflected in our compliance/noncompliance data. . . . As we discussed earlier, the one-year-old is generally an agreeable child, as are most three-year-olds, but sometime during the second year of life, our subjects begin asserting themselves, rejecting suggestions, ignoring commands, testing limits, and generally flexing their muscles. Some

* A major casualty of such a development is that normal intrinsic interest in exploring physical reality and mastering skills becomes subjugated to the social orientation. This division of interest may have profound importance.

mothers cope well with this normal phenomenon, others not so well. Not all children have left this stage behind at two, and in many cases, children seem to carry the related conflicts along for many years.

Two-year-olds usually maintain a high level of intrinsic curiosity, but not as uniformly high as among one-year-olds. They are much more sophisticated about social relations, although their prime area of knowledge concerns their own family. They seem to have developed a standard inventory of social-interaction patterns to use with the family, and are usually more shy with strangers than one-year-olds. Their language capacities have increased dramatically, such that most everyday simple language is usually understood, if not expressed. They may now exhibit the capacity for "pretend" or fantasy behavior, and you may see signs of a budding sense of humor. They are now slightly more interested in television but still spend (on the average) no more than about one-half hour a day really attending to the screen. Their body control is now much advanced over the one-year-old, and they have moved on to practicing advanced motor skills like tricycle and wagon riding and climbing. Their play with objects involves more practicing of skills than exploration of object qualities, but they have not yet ordinarily begun to *construct products,* such as drawings, puzzles, or playhouses. Their capacity for sustained conversation is very limited, although they will listen to language for fairly long periods. Finally, their direction of interest still shifts rapidly, with typical units of experience lasting only twenty to thirty seconds or so, with the exception of occasional long periods of viewing television.

THE SPECIAL IMPORTANCE OF THE 10- TO 18-MONTH PERIOD OF LIFE

At the beginning of this section we remarked that the 10- to 18-month period of life was of peculiar importance for the development of overall ability in children. In addition, we believe that families first reveal their level of capacity for child-rearing during this period. What follows is an explanation of why we think this way.

First of all, the development of the capacity for receptive language begins to become substantial at about 8 or 9 months of age. Our subjects developing *very well* (and those of other studies) first show fairly clear precocity, as compared with children developing poorly, at about 18 months. Variations in the language milieu prior to 8 months of age are far less likely to affect language and related development than are those occurring subsequently. Second, the emergence of locomotor ability in the form of crawling at about 9 or 10 months of age combines with several factors to place a great deal of stress on the primary caretaker. Locomobility plus intense curiosity, plus poor control of the body, plus ignorance of common dangers, plus ignorance of the value of things, plus ignorance concerning the rights of others, spells trouble. Third, sometime toward the end of the first year of life, two social developments of significance begin to undergo rapid development. Babies begin to reveal a growing awareness of themselves as agents, as beings with separate identities. The form of this identity appears to be shaped largely through social interactions with the primary caretaker. These interchanges also appear to shape the infant's basic orientation toward people in general. He typically reveals a very strong orienting tendency toward his mother and initiates very sizable numbers of overtures in her direction. He seems to be acquiring his basic style as a social animal. . . .

It seems to us that mothers are obliged to make at least three major sets of choices in regard to child-rearing practices during this period. The first choices become necessary when locomobility emerges (ordinarily in the form of crawling). The resultant potential for self-injury and for destructiveness, creation of clutter, and intrusion on the private domain of older siblings must be coped with by every family. The choices made vary widely and seem to link with subsequent developments in the child.

Some time late in the first year or into the second, mothers make a second important modification of their child-rearing practices. Sooner or later they become aware of their child's emerging capacity for language acquisition. Some choose to feed the growth of language by going out of their way to talk a great deal to their children. Some provide language input effectively by careful selection of suitable words and phrases and by exploiting the child's interest of the moment. Others provide a great deal of input but with considerably less skill and effectiveness. Other mothers show minimal attention to the language interests of their children or for other reasons provide negligible amounts of language input.

The third major shaping of fundamental child-rearing practices during this period appears to be triggered by the onset of negativism sometime after 14 or 15 months of age. The disappearance of the benign, easy-to-get-along-with 12-month-old is very disconcerting to many mothers. Negativistic behavior is usually experienced as stressful to some degree by all mothers. Styles of reaction to such behavior in children vary from the overpunitive all the way to the overacquiescent.

These three emerging phenomena—locomobility and its stressful consequences, language-learning ability, and negativism—force maternal reactions that become fairly fixed in most cases by the time the child is 18 months of age. It is this three-step creation of the early child-rearing styles that underlies our emphasis on the 10- to 18-month period of life.

Families, especially mothers, react to their particular infants in a variety of ways during the 10- to 18-month period. Certainly, few are prepared to react on the basis of training or even reliable advice. This to us constitutes a gross injustice to many children and their parents. How do those families who are currently doing a first-rate job function? What are the characteristics of successful caretakers (usually mothers)?

IMPORTANT CHARACTERISTICS OF PRIMARY CARETAKERS

The responsibility for child-rearing currently rests in the hands of the mother in American society. That situation may change if and when day care for infants becomes more prevalent. We believe the ideas we are espousing will be relevant to good infant day-care practices as well as to home rearing of children. What then can we say in a succinct fashion about optimal characteristics of mothers? We can divide the problem into a few major components.

Attitudes and values

The performance of a mother derives in part from her attitudes and values. It is also significantly affected by her resources, both material and psychological. We can single out at least the following areas of importance with respect to attitudes and values: life in general, young children, the formative role of infancy, possessions, housekeeping, and safety.

LIFE IN GENERAL. A woman who is seriously depressed or very angry or unhappy about life probably cannot do a good job of getting her young child off to a good start. None of our successful mothers has such attitudes toward life, while a few of our unsuccessful mothers do.

YOUNG CHILDREN. Some mothers don't seem to really enjoy their children during the one-to-three age range. They spend as little time as possible with them, and when they interact with them, they don't seem to get much pleasure from the experience. Some of our mothers who do poorly fall into this category, others of them do not; virtually all our successful mothers seem to derive a great deal of pleasure from their children during this age range.

THE FORMATIVE ROLE OF THE ONE- TO THREE-YEAR AGE RANGE. Mothers seem to vary considerably on this dimension. We doubt that many of our C mothers believe strongly that this period of life has profound significance for development. On the other hand, not all A mothers do either. It is our impression that many of our A mothers perform excellently without any measurable degree of commitment to this thesis. They seem to spontaneously grant their infants generous measures of attention and consideration, simply as a part of a natural way of life.

POSSESSIONS. There is a fair degree of incompatibility between a strong desire to preserve the contents of one's home and the normal tendency toward nonmalicious destructiveness in infants. The mother who is very concerned about her possessions is in for trouble. She has basically three routes to take. She can physically prevent her child from contacting many items in the home by the habitual use of playpens, cribs, and gates. We suspect this route produces frustration and stunting of curiosity in infants. She may allow the child the run of the house and attempt to prevent damage by stopping the child with words or actions when he appears about to break something. This route is often unsuccessful because of the child's limited understanding of words and normal development of negativism. At the very best, it results in a mother who is very frequently saying "No, don't touch that" to her child. Another practice is to allow the child to roam, and to accompany him in an attempt at constant supervision combined with gentle redirection. This route is very time- and energy-consuming, and few mothers can afford it.

HOUSEKEEPING. Very few of our A mothers are meticulous housekeepers. Most of them seem to have accepted the idea that an infant and a spotless home are incompatible. The problem is often aggravated by a husband who insists on a spotless home, in part because he doesn't realize how much work is entailed. The paths a mother of an infant may take to maintain a spotless home are similar to those for the preservation of possessions, and the pitfalls are similar.

SAFETY. We have already described the potential for self-injury that every infant has. The danger is very real. Again, mothers vary widely in how they deal with danger. And again, most of the ways that reduce the danger carry with them the real possibility of reducing the child's normal curiosity and development. About all our study tells us so far is that our A mothers are usually more inclined than our C mothers to take risks on this score with their one-year-olds. There is some research that suggests that children have more built-in controls than we give them credit for. The work on depth perception by Gibson and Walk (1960), for example, suggests that by the time children begin to crawl, they can skillfully discriminate depth and furthermore are inclined to avoid moving off safe positions and injuring themselves. There are certain African tribes that allow their infants access to sharp weapons and utensils, with no apparent serious injuries resulting. It is our impression that infants are generally far more careful about protecting themselves than we think. We do not mean to suggest that no caution need be exercised. Earlier, we alluded to the problems of razor blades, broken glass, and so on, but there is a middle ground in the treatment of the problem of safety, and some mothers are markedly overprotective to the point where they seem to interfere too much with good development.

MOTHERING, A VASTLY UNDERRATED OCCUPATION

We will begin with the bold statement that the mother's direct and indirect actions with regard to her one- to three-year-old child, especially during the second year of life, are, in our opinion, the most powerful formative factors in the development of a preschool-age child.

Further, we would guess that if a mother does a fine job in the preschool years, subsequent educators such as teachers will find their chances for effectiveness maximized. Finally, we would expect that much of the basic quality of the entire life of an individual is determined by the mother's actions during these two years. Obviously, we could be very wrong about these declarative statements. We make them as very strong hunches that we have become committed to, as a kind of net result of all our inquiries into early development.

Let us quickly add that we believe most women are capable of doing a fine job with their one- to three-year-old children. Our study has convinced us that a mother need not necessarily have even a high school diploma, let alone a college education. Nor does she need to have very substantial economic assets. In addition, it is clear that a good job can be accomplished without a father in the home. In all these statements we see considerable hope for future generations.

BEST GUESSES ABOUT MOST EFFECTIVE CHILD-REARING PRACTICES

Our A mothers talk a great deal to their children, and usually at a level the child can handle. They make them feel as though whatever they are doing is usually interesting. They provide access to many objects and diverse situations. They lead the child to believe that he can expect help and encouragement most, but *not all* the time. They demonstrate and explain things to the child, but mostly on the child's instigation rather than their own. They prohibit certain activities, and they do so consistently and firmly. They are secure enough to say "no" to the child from time to time without seeming to fear that the child will not love them. They are imaginative, so that they make interesting associations and suggestions to the child when opportunities present themselves. They very skillfully and naturally strengthen the child's intrinsic motivation to learn. They also give him a sense of task orientation, a notion that it is desirable to do things well and completely. They make the child feel secure.

Our most effective mothers do not devote the bulk of their day to rearing their young children. Most of them are far too busy to do so; several of them, in fact, have part-time jobs. What they seem to do, often without knowing exactly why, is to perform excellently the functions of designer and consultant. By that I mean they design a physical world, mainly in the home, that is beautifully suited to nurturing the burgeoning curiosity of the one- to three-year-old. It is full of small, manipulable, visually detailed objects, some of which were originally designed for young children (toys), others normally used for other purposes (plastic refrigerator containers, bottle caps, baby-food jars and covers, shoes, magazines, television and radio knobs, etc.). It contains things to climb, such as chairs, benches, sofas, and stairs. It has available materials to nurture more mature motor interests, such as tricycles, scooters, and structures with which to practice elementary gymnastics. It includes a rich variety of interesting things to look at, such as television, people, and the aforementioned types of physical objects.

In addition to being largely responsible for the type of environment the child has, this mother sets up guides for her child's behavior that seem to play a very important role in these processes. She is generally permissive and indulgent. The child is encouraged in the vast majority of his explorations. When the child confronts an interesting or difficult situation, he often turns to his mother for help. Although usually working at some chore, she is generally nearby. He then goes to her and usually, but *not always,* is *responded to* by his mother with help or shared enthusiasm, plus, occasionally, an interesting, naturally related idea. These ten- to thirty-second interchanges are usually oriented around the child's interest of the moment rather than toward some need or interest of the mother. At times, under these circumstances, the child will not receive immediate attention. These effective mothers do not always drop what they are doing to attend to his request, but rather if the time is obviously inconvenient, they say so, thereby probably giving the child a realistic, small taste of things to come.

These mothers very rarely spend five, ten, or twenty minutes teaching their one- or two-year-olds, but they get an enormous amount (in terms of frequency) of teaching in "on the fly," and usually at the child's instigation. Although they do volunteer comments opportunistically, they react mostly to overtures by the child.

These effective mothers seem to be people with high levels of energy. The work of a young mother without household help is, in spite of modern appliances, very time- and energy-consuming. Yet we have families subsisting at a welfare level of income, with as many as eight closely spaced children, that are doing every bit as good a job in child-rearing during the early years as the most advantaged homes. (A Russian-type "Hero of the People" award ought to go to such remarkable women.)

4

To Grow
Or Not to Grow

Unless there is some physical disability, nutritional deficiency, or very extreme experience deprivation, all children normally grow in the sense that they gain weight, get taller, and gain increasing control over the movement of their bodies. These are aspects of growth that are firmly established in the maturational code of human beings as biological organisms, and it takes severe forms of interference (such as those mentioned) to prevent growth of this kind. There are other aspects of growth, however, that are much more easily interfered with. Certainly in recent years, we have heard a great deal about experience deprivation and its potential effects on the growth of thinking skills. And children who are not encouraged to learn to use language for communication with others will be limited in their growth of language skills. But more devastating (perhaps because of its subtlety) and far more pervasive is the inhibition of growth in many aspects of socioemotional development that many children experience.

We have emphasized in preceding sections of the book the importance of appropriate responses to children's needs in order to promote their growth as persons. Our primary concern in this context has been for children's socioemotional development—i.e., their development of skills for coping with others while, at the same time, gaining increasing understanding of themselves as persons. Our reason for focusing on this area of development to such an extent is that it has such a profound impact on all other areas of a child's development. Children who feel good about themselves will be able to accomplish those things within their power to which they set their energies; in contrast, children who are filled with self-doubt will expend their energies defending their ego and will be inhibited in whatever they do by the fear and anxiety that accompanies a lack of belief in one's self.

In Chapter I, we referred to children's needs as motivators for their behavior—that is, their needs at any particular time have a major influence on what moves them to act as they do. We introduced Maslow's theory of motivation as a structure within which to view a child's changing needs and their impact on his growth. In the reading by Maslow in this chapter, the development of the child is looked at from the perspective of growth vs. safety needs.[1] That is, Maslow suggests that although human beings are naturally inclined toward growth, nevertheless, there are influences on children that can make growth appear to be a very frightening prospect and safety the only comfortable option for them to choose. At each new step of growth, there exists a potential counterforce toward maintenance of the status quo or regression to an earlier, more comfortable place. If growth appears frightening and safety reassuring because of its familiarity, then the child will not grow.

For example, it is a natural exercise of their growth needs for babies to attempt to grab everything within reach when they are developing the capacity for reaching and grasping. But for the caregiver with valuable possessions who has not prepared for this stage by removing untouchables from temptation, the baby's new talent will not be appreciated. If the caregiver's response is to reprimand the baby, to get angry at her for doing what comes naturally, then the seeds of self-doubt will begin to be planted. A routine occurrence of this kind of punitive approach to childrearing leaves a child with only one option: she is realistically dependent on her caregivers, and cannot, therefore choose to reject their expectations of her; she must, therefore, reject her own developmental needs and choose the safety of her caregivers' approval (and consequent care) over her own growth as a person.

Young children do not have to be forced or coaxed to grow. For physically and psychologically healthy children whose basic needs are met, growing is a way of life. They actively seek opportunities to learn new skills; their initial involvement in learning is motivated by what seems to be a drive toward mastery.[2] There is an inner mechanism

---

[1] Safety needs here are used in a broader sense than in the first chapter, to include all needs below the needs for self-esteem and self-actualization when threat to those needs causes regression to the level of the need that is threatened. In this context, then, love and esteem from others as well as safety needs are included as part of the broad category of safety needs. Safety refers to defense of the self from perceived or actual threat of harm. When loss of security, love, or esteem from others appears to be a consequence of pursuing growth needs (as for example, when child and caregiver are in constant conflict over the child's attempts to do things for himself, and the caregiver gets angry and impatient with the child's imcompetence while never enabling the child to get enough practice to become competent), then a child must, by necessity, make the safety choice of others' needs over his own. But, in doing this, the self is slowly sacrificed, since it is through growth that the self becomes actualized.

in children which, when activated by stimulation from the environment, causes them to move in a positive direction toward growth and self-reliance. They will continue to move in that direction as long as their needs for nourishment, safety, love, and respect are met, and if they have sufficient stimulation from the environment and opportunity for practicing their developing skills.

As each new skill emerges as a new goal to be attained, children begin again their attempts toward mastery. Inevitably, there will be frustrations and failures as they push themselves beyond their present capacity. They may even occasionally drop an emerging skill for a while and go back to a more familiar, already mastered skill (e.g., creeping on all fours instead of trying to walk) until they regain their bearings. But they *will* move forward and attain their goal; it seems that infants and young children have a built-in self-mover, at least to begin with, that pushes them on—to practice each new skill and to progress continuously to increasingly more advanced levels of development.[3]

From earliest infancy, children are moved from within by their own drives for growth and development of skills which will make them more competent and independent. For example, children actively seek practice and stimulation in order to learn to perfect a skill such as walking because it will enable them to be self-moving. But because they are dependent on others for relief of all but their growth needs, children's own inner needs for growth and self-reliance become secondary to their needs for food, security, attention, etc. from others when the satisfaction of these needs seems threatened.

For example, if Tash's efforts to work out his own identity through role-playing are consistently met with reactions such as "Don't be such a show-off"; "People will think you're stupid (strange, dumb, etc.)"; "You're always trying to get attention," he will begin to feel very humiliated. Even if their parents do care about them, if the message children receive is "We don't like the way you act," they will feel insecure in their parents' love and esteem for them (and will, therefore, be motivated primarily by a need to gain their parents' love and esteem). They will become overly self-conscious and will lose the

[2] Robert W. White, "Motivation Reconsidered: The Concept of Competence," *Psychological Review*, 66 (1959), 297–333.

[3] See Arthur Jersild, *Child Psychology* (Englewood Cliffs, N.J.: Prentice-Hall, Inc., 1968), pp. 15–18, for an excellent short review of motivation for mastery. See also Muriel Beadle, *A Child's Mind* (New York: Doubleday and Company, Inc., 1970), Chapter 9, for a very enjoyable anecdotal account of research on motivation that suggests learning, growing, and doing are best motivated by "the pleasure principle," curiosity, and a natural drive toward exploration of novel but nonthreatening environments.

capacity to make accurate judgments of their own actions because of overconcern with others' opinions of them.[4]

There are three discernible stages in the development of children's motivation to act. In the first stage, infants are inwardly motivated, but not consciously so; they have an inner drive to learn to master their environment, to express their developing competencies, but they have no idea of who they or anyone else are—they are not conscious of themselves as persons. In the second stage, children have become aware of other people and of themselves in relation to them. Thus, although they still have an inner drive toward self-growth, children also are becoming concerned about how their caregivers treat them and feel about them. So they become extrinsically motivated to please them—i.e., they become motivated by a desire to win the praise and nurturance of their caregivers.

The third stage is the resolution of the conflict that arises in the second stage: If children's own inner needs to grow and learn come into conflict with their safety needs—to be cared for and loved by their caregivers—they will choose safety over growth. Thus, they will be most influenced to act for extrinsic reasons—to win the approval or escape the disapproval of others. On the other hand, if children's caregivers are very supportive of their self-growth and realize that they need a guide, not a "trainer," they will continue to be mainly motivated to act for intrinsic reasons—to do things that fit with their growing idea of who they are and that helps them to become more autonomous and independent.

So, for example, when children begin to want to feed themselves, they do so because they have a desire to learn and to do for themselves—because it makes them more independent and more skilled. If this is in conflict with their caregiver's wishes and they are made to feel bad for trying to feed themselves because they make a mess, children will begin to learn that there's a difference between what they want, what feels right to them, and other people's views. It will cause fights for a while, but after a while the results are children who cannot trust their own judgment, who will even allow people to do things to them that are bad for them because they have so little faith in themselves and their own feelings about what's good for them.

We have given several examples of potential conflict areas between

---

[4] Unfortunately, because children don't always know how to express their needs directly since they do not consciously recognize what those needs are, they are likely to repeat those behaviors that earn them rebukes because they also gain them attention. Attention, even negative attention, is a powerful reinforcer of a child's behavior; a good rule to remember is that if you want to see a behavior again, pay attention to it.

children and caregivers that can lead the children to question their value as persons and thus threaten their development of a sense of esteem. However, it should be made clear that it is never an isolated incident that has such an effect on a child. Rather, it is the accumulation of a regular pattern of conflicts between parent and child that consistently end with the child as loser. There are necessarily going to be many instances in which the child's natural tendencies to explore will have to be thwarted (e.g., touching a hot stove, crossing a street in traffic), and we are certainly not advocating a parent-child relationship in which all the child's needs are met at the expense of the parent's needs. Rather, what we are suggesting, both through the readings and in our commentary, is that a child-centered approach to childrearing is more likely to promote optimal development than an adult-centered one; that is, you should be sensitive to your children's needs and follow their leads in treatment of them rather than imposing adult standards and expectations on them.

Failure to respond to children's needs has varying effects at different points in their development. Tiny infants whose needs are not met will not grow in any way; they will perish. Runabout children whose needs are not met will not grow in the attainment of competence and confidence in their ability to positively affect their own lives. The next stage in children's lives (beginning about eighteen months to two years) is extremely important for their growth as persons. For many children this is a turning point in their definition of self. This is often the time, referred to in the readings in this chapter by Maslow, when many children are forced to make a choice between their own selves and others'. And, as Maslow points out, it is always the child's own self that must necessarily lose out.

Children's primary needs in the period from two to four years (or somewhere within that range),[5] as we discussed in Chapter I, are to establish a sense of esteem—to define themselves as persons in such a way as to derive some feeling of worth. Most two-year-olds have just begun to realize that they are persons like other persons, and their first experiences in proclaiming their personhood are typically in opposition to others, principally their caregivers.[6] If caregivers re-

[5] If their needs up to that point have been consistently and appropriately met. There is a sequence to the kinds of things that motivate people to act. What stage in the sequence a person is at has some relationship to changes with age, but it has a great deal more to do with the person's experiences. Therefore, although it may be said that most children are "ready" for a stage at a certain age, this readiness depends on their personal experiences. Thus, some adults may still be operating at a low stage of motivation because of the level of their needs and their experiences in early childhood.

[6] You will recall that in the last chapter, the selection by White places at four-

spond to this behavior with understanding, then it will pass fairly quickly, and children will be able to explore who they are in a less explosive way; they will be able to continue to grow. If caregivers react to children's tantrums, stubbornness, and general negativity with counterforce and if they also take this time to try to drastically change the children's behaviors, "training" them to be members of civilized society, then children will be forced to stop growing.

In other words, the message that children receive from their caregivers in this period beginning at about two years will have a very strong impact on their growth.[7] If they receive a message that "We love you and value you as a person, and we are here to guide you in your growth," children will feel safe enough to continue to grow. On the other hand, if they receive a message that "We want you to be a certain kind of person and we will tell you what kind," then children will not be able to gain a secure enough sense of their *own* selfhood to feel safe enough to continue its growth. Rather, they will opt out for trying to meet the expectations that their caregivers have of them (if they care about them), or they will be largely unresponsive and perhaps defiant (if they have never developed a mutually rewarding relationship with their caregivers). Either way, children will put their energies into fighting the same battles at the same level of

---

teen to fifteen months the time when many children begin to assert their wills in a negativistic way. It is at this point that children are beginning to become aware of themselves, but their self-awareness is not yet accompanied by an awareness of others in relation to them; this is part of the lesson that begins with self-assertion in the second year—seeing how others respond to it. The period of negativism to which we refer here typically occurs around two and a half years, that period infamously known as the "terrible twos." Of course, as we have stressed, the actual age at which behaviors occur for any particular child depends on his particular experiences. The difference between these two negativistic periods is significant for our discussion. In the latter instance, children's self-in-relation-to-other awareness has increased, and a major task of this period is to establish a stable sense of self-in-relation-to-other: e.g., "How much do my will, desires, needs, opinions, etc. count in relation to the will, desires, needs, opinions of significant others?" Thus, the negativism of the two and a half-year-old is more self-conscious than that of his younger self.

7 Again, a reference to White's work as presented in the previous chapter seems appropriate. When White explains the importance of the period between ten and eighteen months for children's growth of competence and asserts that differences in competency are already apparent by two years, he is not claiming that it's all over by eighteen months or that important aspects of growth do not continue beyond that point. What his findings suggest, rather, is that patterns of behavior and especially of mother-child interaction seem to be fairly well structured by the end of this period. Thus, "A" mothers are likely to deal much more effectively with "the terrible twos" than are "C" mothers, and "A" children are likely to be less "terrible" in this period than are "C" children, since the former group have already established a rudimentary sense of their own competency.

growth, at maintaining the status quo for safety's sake—both at the expense of forward growth.[8]

As we have said before, we can trust children to "tell" us, through their behavior, what they need. We know now that the organism is programmed, given a full range of choices, to make the right ones—those that will promote growth. For example, studies done in the late Twenties[9] demonstrated that babies, given a cafeteria-style choice of foods over a period of time, chose a nutritionally balanced diet for themselves. We cannot generalize from this and similar studies that children will always choose correctly, because you must establish first that they have a full range of choices, which is rarely possible in a small-family situation. However, we can use such findings to acknowledge that natural growth tendencies are a reality and thus we can feel more secure in trusting children's behavioral messages to indicate accurately what their needs are.[10]

As a child becomes more conscious of other people, their desires and opinions, it is important to help her also to become more conscious of her own inner messages (what is referred to in the Maslow reading as the child's own "yes-feeling"—"This I like; that I don't for *sure*"). As Maslow points out, children are your best guide to what is best for them, and you are their best guide to growth within secure enough boundaries and at a slow enough pace that it is pursued with delight and without fear of loss of safety. Therefore, at all periods of their life, and in particular in this period beginning at about age two, it is very important that you be a partner in your children's growth, encouraging them to continue to move forward, to define who they are and what things feel right for them, and so forth. As children begin to work out their personhood, it is essential that they feel good about who they are and that they learn that they are persons who can assume increasing control of their own actions and thus have increasing power over their own lives.

We have chosen two selections to include in this chapter. The first, the reading by Maslow, explains further the influences of the forces

---

[8] But, you may say, "This doesn't make sense, because most children do grow." Yes, but as you will see in the Maslow selection, it may be a pseudo-growth—a denial of the child's true self and a substitution of a self molded to fit others' wishes and expectations.

[9] C. M. Davis, "Self-Selection of Diet by Newly Weaned Infants, American Journal of Disturbed Children, 36 (1928), 651–79.

[10] The more appropriately responsive you are to children's messages throughout their growth, the clearer their messages will be. Adults too, signal their needs through their behavior; but their messages are often unclear because of a failure to develop a productive feedback system through the years. Because of a loss of self, they lose the ability to recognize their own needs and thus their messages are often disguised, even to themselves.

of growth vs. safety on a child's development. The second is a short poem by John Kendrick Bangs which expresses a sentiment that has meaning for our entire book and especially for this chapter—accept children for who they are *right now.* Do not, in your concern that they continue to grow, push them so fast that growth becomes something to be feared.

Defense and Growth

Abraham H. Maslow

In Chapter I, we used Maslow's hierarchy of needs as a structure within which to view children's growth to increasingly higher levels of being. We suggested that Maslow's theory of personality was very important because it provided a growth-oriented view of human beings. In the selection that follows (a chapter from a book that explains the "psychology of health" which Maslow has offered as an alternative to the "psychology of sickness" traditionally adhered to), Maslow explains the forces that operate to keep a child (or any other person) from growing forward. He faults those who "see everything through brown-colored glasses" for failing to acknowledge the healthward possibilities in the human being, but he also warns against seeing only through rose-colored glasses and in so doing, ignoring the realities of sickness and failure to grow.

Only through understanding both the forces toward growth and those that prevent or inhibit growth can a parent (or other caregiver) effectively help a child to continue to move in the direction of growth and not be held back by the more compelling need for safety. Children are naturally, intrinsically motivated from within to grow—to explore, experiment, use their emerging skills, and become increasingly more competent. But the need for safety is more powerful than the need for growth when the former need is threatened. Thus, in order to enable growth to continue to occur, you must make sure you do not endanger children's psychological safety, forcing them to make the defensive rather than the growth choice.

From *Toward a Psychology of Being* by A. Maslow, © 1968. Reprinted by permission of Van Nostrand Reinhold Company.

Just how does growth take place? Why do children grow or not grow? How do they know in which direction to grow? How do they get off in the direction of pathology?

After all, the concepts of self-actualization, growth and self are all high-level abstractions. We need to get closer to actual processes, to raw data, to concrete, living happenings.

These are far goals. Healthily growing infants and children don't live for the sake of far goals or for the distant future; they are too busy enjoying themselves and spontaneously living for the moment. They are *living*, not *preparing* to live. How can they manage, just being, spontaneously, not *trying* to grow, seeking only to enjoy the present activity, nevertheless to move forward step by step? i.e., to grow in a healthy way? to discover their real selves? How can we reconcile the facts of Being with the facts of Becoming? Growth is not in the pure case a goal out ahead, nor is self-actualization, nor is the discovery of Self. In the child, it is not specifically purposed; rather it just happens. He doesn't so much search as find. The laws of deficiency-motivation and of purposeful coping do not hold for growth, for spontaneity, for creativeness.

The danger with a pure Being-psychology is that it may tend to be static, not accounting for the facts of movement, direction and growth. We tend to describe states of Being, of self-actualization as if they were Nirvana states of perfection. Once you're there, you're there, and it seems as if all you could do is to rest content in perfection.

The answer I find satisfactory is a simple one, namely, that growth takes place when the next step forward is subjectively more delightful, more joyous, more intrinsically satisfying than the previous gratification with which we have become familiar and even bored; that the only way we can ever know what is right for us is that it feels better subjectively than any alternative. The new experience validates *itself* rather than by any outside criterion. It is self-justifying, self-validating.

We don't do it because it is good for us, or because psychologists approve, or because somebody told us to, or because it will make us live longer, or because it is good for the species, or because it will bring external rewards, or because it is logical. We do it for the same reason that we choose one dessert over another. I have already described this as a basic mechanism for falling in love, or for choosing a friend, i.e., kissing one person gives more delight than kissing the other, being friends with *a* is more satisfying subjectively than being friends with *b*.

In this way, we learn what we are good at, what we really like or dislike, what our tastes and judgments and capacities are. In a word, this is the way in which we discover the Self and answer the ultimate questions Who am I? What am I?

The steps and the choices are taken out of pure spontaneity, from within outward. The healthy infant or child, just Being, as *part* of his Being, is randomly, and spontaneously curious, exploratory, wondering, interested. Even when he is non-purposeful, non-coping, expressive, spontaneous, not motivated by any deficiency of the ordinary sort, he tends to try out his powers, to reach out, to be absorbed, fascinated, interested, to play, to wonder, to manipulate the world. *Exploring, manipulating, experiencing,* being interested, choosing, delighting, *enjoying* can all be seen as attributes of pure Being, and yet lead to Becoming, though in a serendipitous way, fortuitously, unplanned, unanticipated. Spontaneous, creative experience can and does happen without expectations, plans, foresight, purpose, or goal.[1] It is only when the child sates himself, becomes bored, that he is ready to turn to other, perhaps "higher," delights.

Then arise the inevitable questions. What holds him back? What prevents growth? Wherein lies the conflict? What is the alternative to growth forward? Why is it so hard and painful for some to grow forward? Here we must become more fully aware of the fixative and regressive power of ungratified deficiency-needs, of the attractions of safety and security, of the functions of defense and protection against pain, fear, loss, and threat, of the need for courage in order to grow ahead.

Every human being has *both* sets of forces within him. One set clings to safety and defensiveness out of fear, tending to regress backward, hanging on to the past, *afraid* to grow away from the primitive communication with the mother's uterus and breast, *afraid* to take chances, *afraid* to jeopardize what he already has, *afraid* of independence, freedom and separateness. The other set of forces impels him forward toward wholeness of Self and uniqueness of Self, toward full functioning of all his capacities, toward confidence in the face of the external world at the same time that he can accept his deepest, real, unconscious Self.

I can put all this together in a schema, which though very simple, is also very powerful, both heuristically and theoretically. This basic dilemma or conflict between the defensive forces and the growth trends I conceive to be existential, imbedded in the deepest nature

---

1 "But paradoxically, the art experience cannot be effectively *used* for this purpose or any other. It must be a purposeless activity, as far as we understand 'purpose.' It can only be an experience in *being*—being a human organism doing what it must and what it is privileged to do—experiencing life keenly and wholly, expending energy and creating beauty in its own style—and the increased sensitivity, integrity, efficiency, and feeling of well-being are by-products" [3, p. 212]. [Maslow's bibliography follows this reprint.]

of the human being, now and forever into the future. If it is diagrammed like this:

Safety◄──────────────〈PERSON〉──────────────►Growth

then we can very easily classify the various mechanisms of growth in an uncomplicated way as

a. Enhancing the growthward vectors, e.g., making growth more attractive and delight producing.
b. Minimizing the fears of growth,
c. Minimizing the safetyward vectors, i.e., making it less attractive.
d. Maximizing the fears of safety, defensiveness, pathology and regression.

We can then add to our basic schema these four sets of valences:

Enhance the dangers   *Enhance the attractions*

Safety◄──────〈PERSON〉──────►Growth

Minimize the attractions   *Minimize the dangers*

Therefore we can consider the process of healthy growth to be a never ending series of free choice situations, confronting each individual at every point throughout his life, in which he must choose between the delights of safety and growth, dependence and independence, regression and progression, immaturity and maturity. Safety has both anxieties and delights; growth has both anxieties and delights. We grow forward when the delights of growth and anxieties of safety are greater than the anxieties of growth and the delights of safety.

So far it sounds like a truism. But it isn't to psychologists who are mostly trying to be objective, public, behavioristic. And it has taken many experiments with animals and much theorizing to convince the students of animal motivation that they must invoke what P. T. Young [4] called a hedonic factor, over and above need-reduction, in order to explain the results so far obtained in free-choice experimentation. For example, saccharin is not need-reducing in any way and yet white rats will choose it over plain water. Its (useless) taste *must* have something to do with it.

Furthermore, observe that subjective delight in the experience is something that we can attribute to *any* organism, e.g., it applies to the infant as well as the adult, to the animal as well as to the human.

The possibility that then opens for us is very enticing for the theorist. Perhaps all these high-level concepts of Self, Growth, Self-realization, and Psychological Health can fall into the same system of explanation with appetite experiments in animals, free choice observations in infant feeding and in occupational choice, and the rich studies of homeostasis [2].

Of course this formulation of growth-through-delight also commits us to the necessary postulation that what tastes good is also, in the growth sense, "better" for us. We rest here on the faith that if free choice is *really* free and if the chooser is not too sick or frightened to choose, he will choose wisely, in a healthy and growthward direction, more often than not.

For this postulation there is already much experimental support, but it is mostly at the animal level, and much more detailed research is necessary with free choice in humans. We must know much more than we do about the reasons for bad and unwise choices, at the constitutional level and at the level of psychodynamics.

There is another reason why my systematizing side likes this notion of growth-through-delight. It is that then I find it possible to tie it in nicely with dynamic theory, with *all* the dynamic theories of Freud, Adler, Jung, Schachtel, Horney, Fromm, Burrow, Reich, and Rank, as well as the theories of Rogers, Buhler, Combs, Angyal, Allport, Goldstein, Murray, Moustakas, Perls, Bugental, Assagioli, Frankl, Jourard, May, White and others.

I criticize the classical Freudians for tending (in the extreme instance) to pathologize everything and for not seeing clearly enough the healthward possibilities in the human being, for seeing everything through brown-colored glasses. But the growth school (in the extreme instance) is equally vulnerable, for they tend to see through rose-colored glasses and generally slide over the problems of pathology, of weakness, of *failure* to grow. One is like a theology of evil and sin exclusively; the other is like a theology without any evil at all, and is therefore equally incorrect and unrealistic.

One additional relationship between safety and growth must be specially mentioned. Apparently growth forward customarily takes place in little steps, and each step forward is made possible by the feeling of being safe, of operating out into the unknown from a safe home port, of daring because retreat is possible. We may use as a paradigm the toddler venturing away from his mother's knee into strange surroundings. Characteristically, he first clings to his mother as he explores the room with his eyes. Then he dares a little excursion, continually reassuring himself that the mother-security is intact. These excursions get more and more extensive. In this way, the child can explore a dangerous and unknown world. If suddenly the mother were to disappear, he would be thrown into anxiety, would cease to be interested in exploring the world, would wish only the return of safety, and might even lose his abilities, e.g., instead of daring to walk, he might creep.

I think we may safely generalize this example. Assured safety permits higher needs and impulses to emerge and to grow towards mastery. To endanger safety, means regression backward to the more basic foundation. What this means is that in the choice between giving up safety or giving up growth, safety will ordinarily win out. Safety needs are prepotent over growth needs. This means an expansion of our basic formula. In general, only a child who feels safe dares to grow forward healthily. His safety needs must be gratified. He can't be *pushed* ahead, because the ungratified safety needs will remain forever underground, always calling for satisfaction. The more safety needs are gratified, the less valence they have for the child, the less they will beckon, and lower his courage.

Now, how can we know when the child feels safe enough to dare to choose the new step ahead? Ultimately, the only way in which we can know is by *his* choices, which is to say only *he* can ever really know the right moment when the beckoning forces ahead overbalance the beckoning forces behind, and courage outweighs fear.

Ultimately the person, even the child, must choose for himself. Nobody can choose for him too often, for this itself enfeebles him, cutting his self-trust, and confusing his *ability* to perceive his own internal delight in the experience, his *own* impulses, judgments, and feelings, and to differentiate them from the interiorized standards of others.[2]

2 "From the moment the package is in his hands, he feels free to do what he wants with it. He opens it, speculates on what it is, recognizes what it is, expresses happiness or disappointment, notices the arrangement of the contents, finds a book of directions, feels the touch of the steel, the different weights of the parts, and their number, and so on. He does all this before he has attempted to do a thing with the set. Then comes the thrill of doing something with it. It may be only matching one single part with another. Thereby alone he gets a feeling of having done something, that he can do something, and that he is not helpless with that particular article. Whatever pattern is subsequently followed, whether his interest extends to the full utilization of the set and therefore toward further gaining a feeling of greater and greater accomplishment, or whether he completely discards it, his initial contact with the erector set has been meaningful.

"The results of active experiencing can be summarized approximately in the following way. There is physical, emotional, and intellectual self-involvement; there is a recognition and further exploration of one's abilities; there is initiation of activity or creativeness; there is finding out one's own pace and rhythm and the assumption of enough of a task for one's abilities at that particular time, which would include the avoidance of taking on too much; there is gain in skill which one can apply to other enterprises, and there is an opportunity each time that one has an

If this is all so, if the child himself must finally make the choice by which he grows forward, since only he can know his subjective delight experience, then how can we reconcile this ultimate necessity for trust in the inner individual with the necessity for help from the environment? For he does need help. Without help he will be too frightened to dare. How can we help him to grow? Equally important, how can we endanger his growth?

The opposite of the subjective experience of delight (trusting himself), so far as the child is concerned, is the opinion of other people (love, respect, approval, admiration, reward from others, trusting others rather than himself). Since others are so important and vital for the helpless baby and child, fear of losing them (as providers of safety, food, love, respect, etc.) is a primal, terrifying danger. Therefore, the child, faced with a difficult choice between his own delight experiences and the experience of approval from others, must generally choose approval from others, and then handle his delight by repression or letting it die, or not noticing it or controlling it by willpower. In general, along with this will develop a disapproval of the delight experience, or shame and embarrassment and secretiveness about it, with finally, the inability even to experience it.[3]

---

active part in something, no matter how small, to find out more and more what one is interested in.

"The above situation may be contrasted with another in which the person who brings home the erector set says to the child, 'Here is an erector set, let me open it for you.' He does so, and then points out all the things in the box, the book of directions, the various parts, etc., and, to top it off, he sets about building one of the complicated models, let us say, a crane. The child may be much interested in what he has seen being done, but let us focus on one aspect of what has really been happening. The child has had no opportunity to get himself involved with the erector set, with his body, his intelligence, or his feelings, he has had no opportunity to match himself up with something that is new for him, to find out what he is capable of or to gain further direction for his interests. The building of the crane for him may have brought in another factor. It may have left the child with an implied demand that he do likewise without his having had an opportunity to prepare himself for any such complicated task. The end becomes the object instead of the experience involved in the process of attaining the objective. Also, whatever he may subsequently do by himself will look small and mean compared to what had been made for him by someone else. He has not added to his total experience for coming up against something new for the next time. In other words, he has not grown from within but has had something superimposed from the outside. . . . Each bit of active experiencing is an opportunity toward finding out what he likes or dislikes, and more and more what he wants to make out of himself. It is an essential part of his progress toward the stage of maturity and self-direction" [5, p. 179].

[3] "How is it possible to lose a self? The treachery, unknown and unthinkable, begins with our secret psychic death in childhood—if and when we are not loved and are cut off from our spontaneous wishes. (Think: what is left?) But wait—victim might even 'outgrow' it—but it is a perfect double crime in which he him-it is not just this simple murder of a psyche. That might be written off, the tiny self also

The primal choice, the fork in the road, then, is between others' and one's own self. If the only way to maintain the self is to lose others, then the ordinary child will give up the self. This is true for the reason already mentioned, that safety is a most basic and prepotent need for children, more primarily necessary by far than independence and self-actualization. If adults force this choice upon him, of choosing between the loss of one (lower and stronger) vital necessity or another (higher and weaker) vital necessity, the child must choose safety even at the cost of giving up self and growth.

(In principle there is no need for forcing the child to make such a choice. People just *do* it often, out of their own sicknesses and out of ignorance. We know that it is not necessary because we have examples enough of children who are offered all these goods simultaneously, at no vital cost, who can have safety and love *and* respect too.)

Here we can learn important lessons from the therapy situation, the creative educative situation, creative art education and I believe also creative dance education. Here where the situation is set up variously as permissive, admiring, praising, accepting, safe, gratifying, reassuring, supporting, unthreatening, non-valuing, non-comparing, that is, where the person can feel completely safe and unthreatened,

---

gradually and unwittingly takes part. He has not been accepted for himself, *as he is*. Oh, they 'love' him, but they want him or force him or expect him to be different! Therefore he *must be unacceptable*. He himself learns to believe it and at last even takes it for granted. He has truly given himself up. No matter now whether he obeys them, whether he clings, rebels or withdraws—his behavior, his performance is all that matters. His center of gravity is in 'them,' not in himself—yet if he so much as noticed it he'd think it natural enough. And the whole thing is entirely plausible; all invisible, automatic, and anonymous!

"This is the perfect paradox. Everything looks normal; no crime was intended; there is no corpse, no guilt. All we can see is the sun rising and setting as usual. But what has happened? He has been rejected, not only by them, but by himself. (He is actually without a self.) What has he lost? Just the one true and vital part of himself: his own yes-feeling, which is his very capacity for growth, his root system. But alas, he is not dead. 'Life' goes on, and so must he. From the moment he gives himself up, and to the extent that he does so, all unknowingly he sets about to create and maintain a pseudo-self. But this is an expediency—a 'self' without wishes. This one shall be loved (or feared) where he is despised, strong where he is weak; it shall go through the motions (oh, but they are caricatures!) not for fun or joy but for survival; not simply because it wants to move but because it has to obey. This necessity is not life—not his life—it is a defense mechanism against death. It is also the machine of death. From now on he will be torn apart by compulsive (unconscious) *needs* or ground by (unconscious) conflicts into paralysis, every motion and every instant canceling out his being, his integrity; and all the while he is disguised as a normal person and expected to behave like one!

"In a word, I saw that we *become* neurotic seeking or defending a pseudo-self, a self-system; and we *are* neurotic to the extent that we are self-less" [1, p. 3].

then it becomes possible for him to work out and express all sorts of lesser delights, e.g., hostility, neurotic dependency. Once these are sufficiently catharted, he then tends spontaneously to go to other delights which outsiders perceive to be "higher" or growthward, e.g., love, creativeness, and which he himself will prefer to the previous delights, once he has experienced them both. (It often makes little difference what kind of explicit theory is held by the therapist, teacher, helper, etc. The really good therapist who may espouse a pessimistic Freudian theory, *acts* as if growth were possible. The really good teacher who espouses verbally a completely rosy and optimistic picture of human nature, will *imply* in actual teaching, a complete understanding and respect for regressive and defensive forces. It is also possible to have a wonderfully realistic and comprehensive philosophy and belie it in practice, in therapy, or teaching or parenthood. Only the one who respects fear and defense can teach; only the one who respects health can do therapy.)

Part of the paradox in this situation is that in a very real way, even the "bad" choice is "good for" the neurotic chooser, or at least understandable and even necessary in terms of his own dynamics. We know that tearing away a functional neurotic symptom by force, or by too direct a confrontation or interpretation, or by a stress situation which cracks the person's defenses against too painful an insight, can shatter the person altogether. This involves us in the question of *pace* of growth. And again the good parent, or therapist or educator *practices* as if he understood that gentleness, sweetness, respect for fear, understanding of the naturalness of defensive and regressive forces, are necessary if growth is not to look like an overwhelming danger instead of a delightful prospect. He implies that he understands that growth can emerge only from safety. He *feels* that if a person's defenses are very rigid this is for a good reason and he is willing to be patient and understanding even though knowing the path in which the child "should" go.

Seen from the dynamic point of view, ultimately *all* choices are in fact wise, if only we grant two kinds of wisdom, defensive-wisdom and growth-wisdom. . . . Defensiveness can be as wise as daring; it depends on the particular person, his particular status and the particular situation in which he has to choose. The choice of safety is wise when it avoids pain that may be more than the person can bear at the moment. If we wish to help him grow (because we know that consistent safety-choices will bring him to catastrophe in the long run, and will cut him off from possibilities that he himself would enjoy if only he could savor them), then all we can do is help him if he asks for help out of suffering, or else simultaneously allow him to feel safe and beckon him onward to *try* the new experience like the mother whose open arms invite the baby to try to walk. We can't *force* him to grow, we can only *coax* him to, make it more possible for him, in the trust that simply experiencing the new experience will make him prefer it. *Only* he can prefer it; no one can prefer it for him. If it is to become part of him, *he* must like it. If he doesn't, we must gracefully concede that it is not for him at this moment.

This means that the sick child must be respected as much as the healthy one, so far as the growth process is concerned. Only when his fears are accepted respectfully, can he dare to be bold. We must understand that the dark forces are as "normal" as the growth forces.

This is a ticklish task, for it implies simultaneously that we know what is best for him (since we *do* beckon him on in a direction we choose), and also that only he knows what is best for himself in the long run. This means that we must *offer* only, and rarely force. We must be quite ready, not only to beckon forward, but to respect retreat to lick wounds, to recover strength, to look over the situation from a safe vantage point, or even to regress to a previous mastery or a "lower" delight, so that courage for growth can be regained.

And this again is where the helper comes in. He is needed, not only for making possible growth forward in the healthy child (by being "available" as the child desires) and getting out of his way at other times, but much more urgently, by the person who is "stuck" in fixation, in rigid defenses, in safety measures which cut off the possibilities of growth. Neurosis is self-perpetuating; so is character structure. We can either wait for life to prove to such a person that his system doesn't work, i.e., by letting him eventually collapse into neurotic suffering, or else by understanding him and helping him to grow by respecting and understanding both his deficiency needs and his growth needs.

This amounts to a revision of Taoistic "let-be," which often hasn't worked because the growing child needs help. It can be formulated as "helpful let-be." It is a *loving* and *respecting* Taoism. It recognizes not only growth and the specific mechanism which makes it move in the right direction, but it also recognizes and respects the fear of growth, the slow pace of growth, the blocks, the pathology, the reasons for not growing. It recognizes the place, the necessity and the helpfulness of the outer environment without yet giving it control. It implements inner growth by knowing its mechanisms and by being willing to help *it* instead of merely being hopeful or passively optimistic about it.

All the foregoing may now be related to the general motivation theory, set forth in my *Motivation and Personality*, particularly the theory of need gratification, which seems to me to be the most important single principle underlying all healthy human development.

The single holistic principle that binds together the multiplicity of human motives is the tendency for a new and higher need to emerge as the lower need fulfills itself by being sufficiently gratified. The child who is fortunate enough to grow normally and well gets satiated and *bored* with the delights that he has savored sufficiently, and *eagerly* (without pushing) goes on to higher more complex, delights as they become available to him without danger or threat.

This principle can be seen exemplified not only in the deeper motivational dynamics of the child but also in microcosm in the development of any of his more modest activities, e.g., in learning to read, or skate, or paint, or dance. The child who masters simple words enjoys them intensely but doesn't stay there. In the proper atmosphere he spontaneously shows eagerness to go on to more and more new words, longer words, more complex sentences, etc. If he is forced to stay at the simple level he gets bored and restless with what formerly delighted him. He *wants* to go on, to move, to grow. Only if frustration, failure, disapproval, ridicule come at the next step does he fixate or regress, and we are then faced with the intricacies of pathological dynamics and of neurotic compromises, in which the impulses remain alive but unfulfilled, or even of loss of impulse and of capacity.[4]

What we wind up with then is a subjective device to add to the principle of the hierarchical arrangement of our various needs, a

[4] I think it is possible to apply this general principle to Freudian theory of the progression of libidinal stages. The infant in the oral stage, gets most of his delights through the mouth. And one in particular which has been neglected is that of mastery. We should remember that the *only* thing an infant can do well and efficiently is to suckle. In all else he is inefficient, incapable and if, as I think, this is the earliest precursor of self esteem (feeling of mastery), then this is the *only* way in which the infant can experience the delight of mastery (efficiency, control, self expression, volition).

But soon he develops other capacities for mastery and control. I mean here not only anal control which though correct, has, in my opinion, been overplayed. Motility and sensory capacities also develop enough during the so-called "anal" stage to give feelings of delight and mastery. But what is important for us here is that the oral infant tends to play out his oral mastery and to become bored with it, just as he becomes bored with milk alone. In a free choice situation, he tends to give up the breast and milk in favor of the more complex activities and tastes, or anyway, to add to the breast these other "higher" developments. Given sufficient gratification, free choice and lack of threat, he "grows" out of the oral stage and renounces it himself. He doesn't have to be "kicked upstairs," or forced onto maturity as is so often implied. He *chooses* to grow on to higher delights, to become bored with older ones. Only under the impact of danger, threat, failure, frustration, or stress does he tend to regress or fixate; only then does he prefer safety to growth. Certainly renunciation, delay in gratification and the ability to withstand frustration are also necessary for strength, and we know that unbridled gratification is dangerous. And yet it remains true that these qualifications are *subsidiary* to the principle that sufficient gratification of basic needs is *sine qua non*.

device which guides and directs the individual in the direction of "healthy" growth. The principle holds true at any age. Recovering the ability to perceive one's own delights is the best way of rediscovering the sacrificed self even in adulthood. The process of therapy helps the adult to discover that the childish (repressed) necessity for the approval of others no longer needs exist in the childish form and degree, and that the terror of losing these others with the accompanying fear of being weak, helpless and abandoned is no longer realistic and justified as it was for the child. For the adult, others can be and should be less important than for the child.

Our final formula then has the following elements:

1. The healthily spontaneous child, in his spontaneity, from within out, in response to his own inner Being, reaches out to the environment in wonder and interest, and expresses whatever skills he has,

2. To the extent that he is not crippled by fear, to the extent that he feels safe enough to dare.

3. In this process, that which gives him the delight-experience is fortuitously encountered, or is offered to him by helpers.

4. He must be safe and self-accepting enough to be able to choose and prefer these delights, instead of being frightened by them.

5. If he *can* choose these experiences which are validated by the experience of delight, then he can return to the experience, repeat it, savor it to the point of repletion, satiation or boredom.

6. At this point, he shows the tendency to go on to more complex, richer experiences and accomplishments in the same sector (again, if he feels safe enough to dare).

7. Such experiences not only mean moving on, but have a feedback effect on the Self, in the feeling of certainty ("This I like; that I don't for *sure*"); of capability, mastery, self-trust, self-esteem.

8. In this never ending series of choices of which life consists, the choice may generally be schematized as between safety (or, more broadly, defensiveness) and growth, and since only that child doesn't need safety who already has it, we may expect the growth choice to be made by the safety-need gratified child. Only he can afford to be bold.

9. In order to be able to choose in accord with his own nature and to develop it, the child must be permitted to retain the subjective experiences of delight and boredom, as *the* criteria of the correct choice for him. The alternative criterion is making the choice in terms of the wish of another person. The Self is lost when this happens. Also this constitutes restricting the choice to safety alone, since the child will give up trust in his own delight-criterion out of fear (of losing protection, love, etc.).

10. If the choice is really a free one, and if the child is not crippled, then we may expect him ordinarily to choose progression forward.[5]

11. The evidence indicates that what delights the healthy child, what tastes good for him, is also, more frequently than not, "best" for him in terms of far goals as perceivable by the spectator.

12. In this process the environment (parents, therapists, teachers) is important in various ways, even though the ultimate choice must be made by the child.

    a. it can gratify his basic needs for safety, belongingness, love and respect, so that he can feel unthreatened, autonomous, interested and spontaneous and thus dare to choose the unknown;

    b. it can help by making the growth choice positively attractive and less dangerous, and by making the regressive choice less attractive and more costly.

13. In this way the psychology of Being and the psychology of Becoming can be reconciled, and the child, simply being himself, can yet move forward and grow.

REFERENCES

1. Anonymous, Finding the real self. A letter with a foreword by Karen Horney, *Amer. J. Psychoanal.*, 1949, 9, 3.

2. CANNON, W. B. *Wisdom of the Body.* Norton, 1932.

3. WILSON, F. Human nature and esthetic growth, *in* Moustakas, C. (ed.). *The Self.* Harper, 1956.

4. YOUNG, P. T. *Motivation and Emotion.* Wiley, 1961.

5. ZUGER, B. Growth of the individuals concept of self. *A.M.A. Amer. J. Diseased Children*, 1952, 83, 719.

[5] A kind of pseudo-growth takes place very commonly when the person tries (by repression, denial, reaction-formation, etc.) to convince himself that an ungratified basic need has really been gratified, or doesn't exist. He then permits himself to grow on to higher-need-levels, which of course, forever after, rest on a very shaky foundation. I call this "pseudo-growth by bypassing the ungratified need." Such a need perseverates forever as an unconscious force (repetition compulsion).

The Little Elf

John Kendrick Bangs

This poem expresses a thought that should never be lost sight of in our concern for the child's growth: In your concern with who a child will become, don't forget that he's somebody very important right now, and that he unlike many adults, lives in the present, not in the future. So don't worry about bad habits a child might get into if she always acts the way she acts at two and a half (or three or four, etc.). Children do grow; they need less training for the future and more supportive guidance now. And, as Maslow points out in the selection on "Defense and Growth," growth proceeds slowly, in small steps, small enough that it can be freely chosen as a delight-producing experience and not feared as an unrealistic and unattainable goal. It is, in a sense, a paradox: Deal with children day by day, accepting them for who they are and guiding them gently, and they will, over time, grow forward; worry about their growth, about their forming bad habits, about training them for the future, and they will not grow.

I met a little Elfman, once
Down where the lilies blow.
I asked him why he was so small
And why he did not grow.
He slightly frowned, and with his eyes
He looked me through and through.
"I'm quite as big for me," he said,
"As you are big for you."

5

Now That I Know I Am, Who Am I?

Think of yourself as you were last year. Imagine yourself as a school-age child. Now, search your mind for your earliest memories. Notice two things: (1) no matter how you have changed, how you have grown, the inner you, the you who has watched as the years have made their alterations, has remained stable, and (2) you probably don't have any strong memories much before age three.

In the reading at the end of this chapter, Dr. Ira Gordon notes, referring to Gardner Murphy's conceptualization, "the self-picture is fairly well integrated by the third year of life. Once it has developed, it becomes the evaluator, selector, judger, and organizer of future experience, and the child's behavior may be seen as organized to enhance and maintain his view." It is this self-picture, then, that has watched you grow all these years. Who you are now is a combination of factors including your internalized self-picture, the experiences you have had, how you feel about yourself in relation to others, how you think others feel about you, and so on. As the preceding quotation indicates, however, much of who you are now is related to the development of your basic self-picture in your very early years, since you filter all your experiences through that self.

Our concern in this chapter is with the influences on children's development of a sense of self and especially with the factors that cause children to define who they are and what they can be. The ultimate goal in effective childrearing is to help children become everything that they can be; in order to meet that goal, we must be aware of what kinds of things cause children to feel good about themselves and what kinds of things have a negative effect on the self-concept.

In the last chapter, we discussed the importance of children's experiences with the significant adults in their lives in determining how they come to feel about themselves. We stressed the need for children to develop positive feelings about themselves in relation to others in order to continue growing as persons. Children must develop a sense of self-esteem as well as the expectation that others will respond positively to them. This is an essential prerequisite to their beginning lifelong striving toward self-actualization—toward becoming increasingly all that they can be. The search for self-esteem and esteem from others continues throughout life for most people. All you have to do is watch TV commercials to know that most adults are overly concerned with how they appear to others. But it doesn't have to be that way.

One of the charms of young children is their lack of self-consciousness. Part of growing is the development of enough self-consciousness that children can learn to be self-evaluative—to judge their own behavior in a realistic and thoughtful way. Too often, however, children learn an overly critical, self-deprecating self-consciousness; they learn to doubt themselves. This doubt of one's self can only be learned from someone who is important to children. For in their formative years, if they sense doubt of their competency as persons from those whom they value, children will come not to value themselves.

Self-consciousness should never be allowed to turn to self-doubt. You should never encourage children to care more for the opinions of unknown others than they do for their own opinion. Those "others" to whom so many of us find ourselves directing our behavior in order to win their approval are only with us for the moment. But we must live our entire lives with ourselves.

Never cause a child to feel humiliated over concern with others' opinions. For example, suppose you're at the grocery store and your child accidentally knocks over a display. Inside, you know that she did not mean to do it, and you can see how upset she is. But you are concerned about what kind of parent the people around will think you are. So you sharply reprimand your child. She starts crying very loudly, and you end up dragging her out of the store without doing your shopping, very embarrassed and angry, both at yourself and at your child, but you take it out on her. The message she gets is that you are more concerned about other people's opinions than about her; she thus learns, also, to be more concerned about others' judgment of her than of her own judgment, the first step in loss of self.

This is an exaggerated account of the kind of scenario that occurs frequently when children are taken on public outings where they must obey, keep quiet, look but not touch, etc. It is neither the parent nor the child's fault. Children are naturally adventurous; they want to try out everything—feel it, taste it, smell it, etc. Grocery stores are particularly interesting. But these places are adult-oriented. They are not designed with children in mind even though children may be frequent visitors there. Because most places and people are not child-oriented, it will take extra effort on your part to keep your children from being put into situations in which they are likely to be hurt or humiliated. And you can do the most for your children by always considering their feelings above the opinions of unknown others. Everybody needs to feel that there is someone they can count on to stand by them, always, even when they're wrong. You should be that for your child.

You, yourself, should also be careful that you do not say or do things that will humiliate your child (or husband, wife, or anyone else you care about, for that matter). Ridiculing children's (or any other person's) feelings, thoughts, ideas, creations, behavior, fears, desires, etc., even good-naturedly, can hurt them and make them feel that what matters to them is not important to you. Have you ever offered a suggestion to someone and had them laugh at you or tell you that your idea was stupid or silly? Have you ever shared a secret wish or fear with someone you thought you could trust and had them tell you it was ridiculous (or in some other, perhaps less obvious way, demonstrate that they did not take your thoughts very seriously)? If so, do you remember how it made you feel? For children, it is even worse because they are so dependent on and in awe of adults, especially those who are important to them.

Be careful that you do not feed a child's self-doubt, especially at those times (e.g., between five and a half and six and a half years) when many children have a tendency to become overly self-conscious and defensive. For example, never tell a child that people don't like him, or that they only like him because he does things for them, or that people like him when they first meet him but he doesn't wear well. Don't tell a child that she's making a fool of herself, that she's not very smart or attractive, that she can't do anything well, etc., either in words or through your behavior.

You do more damage than you know when you saddle children with self-doubt, no matter how subtly administered. You create a "self-fulfilling prophecy"—because you say things are a certain way, the child comes to expect it and acts in such a way as to fulfill his expectations. Think of your own self-doubt, your own insecurities about how others see you, about your ability to do things well, about how you look, etc. Does it not interfere with your ability to do the things you're worried about? Self-doubt is debilitating. It creates a fear of failure that often keeps you from even trying. And if instilled in early childhood, it is carried into adulthood like a scar on the self.

Certainly not all insecurities are caused by parents, teachers, or other people close to a child. The general tone of a competitive and discriminatory society, an advertising establishment that sells us things we don't need by creating pseudo-needs through playing on our insecurities, tendencies to define normality in terms of conformity, etc.—these are pervasive influences in our culture that make it difficult for people to believe in themselves.

But the seeds of self-doubt can be planted in early childhood, perhaps even by loving and well-meaning adults whose intention is simply to make sure children don't get too cocky or sure of themselves. *We need to be sure of ourselves.* Who else can you count on in life if not yourself? And only when you feel secure and valued can you devote your energies to productive enterprises. Too many adults expend so much energy working out their esteem needs that there is little left for growth, creative self-expression, and productive work. This world desperately needs people who have been able to develop enough beyond the confines of their own self-interest that they can devote their energies to creative problem-solving of the issues that face us. Our hope is with the children, and their hope is in establishing a secure enough self-concept in early childhood that it can withstand the future pressures and challenges that it will face.

Because children's experiences in the outside world are likely to work against their gaining a secure, unshakable sense of their own worth, you must work that much harder toward that end. The late A. S. Neill [1] said in his autobiography that he would like to be remembered as a person who was "on the side of the child." It is our hope that all those whose lives touch children will see themselves in that way. If you ever doubt the importance of belief in self, think of those areas in which you excel. Are they not also areas in which you have confidence, in which you believe in your ability to do a good job? Help the children in your care to feel that way about themselves in all areas.

Undoubtedly, some of you are reading this and thinking to yourself, "But I don't want my kid to grow up to be conceited and self-centered." We ask you only to remember what we were always told about people like that—"They really have inferiority complexes, and act that way as a defense." In fact, people who are overly impressed with their own importance, who seem to take themselves a bit too seriously, are not reflecting a high level of self-esteem. Their attitude and their behavior indicates that they're working very hard to convince people that they're worth something. If they really believed it, they wouldn't have to try so hard. Persons who really have a strong, healthy self-concept no longer put very much energy into it. People whose esteem needs have been relatively well satisfied, who believe in their own worth as persons, can go on to the highest level of growing—i.e., toward self-actualization. And one of the characteristics of self-actualizing people is

---

[1] *Neill! Neill! Orange Peel!* (New York: Hart Publishing Company, Inc., 1970), p. 20.

their feelings of a common humanity with all other human beings. Self-actualizing persons do not feel themselves to be more worthy or more important than others; rather, they put a high value on each life as unique and worthy of great respect.

Children who have had generally positive experiences in their early years, who have been consistently made to feel that they are persons of value, will come to feel that way about themselves. They will assume that people like them and approve of them instead of worrying whether they do and trying to win their approval. Such a child will be able to be concerned about other people for who they are and for what *they* might need, not for what they can do to fulfill her needs or for what they might think of her.

It has consistently been shown that children who are secure and confident, children who like themselves, are liked by others, both their peers and adults. In addition, these children seem to do well at most things that they attempt, to which they put their energies. Self-confidence and competence are close relatives. And finally, children who believe in themselves can also deal better with setbacks, failures, and pressure in general than children who lack belief-in-self. They tend to be more persistent, sticking with problems until they've been satisfactorily solved, rather than giving up easily out of conviction that they'll fail anyway.

We have dwelled on the issue of self-esteem because it seems, along with love, to be a major focus of many people's search for self; as such, its lack of fulfillment is a primary obstacle in the way of most adults becoming self-actualizing. Maslow has suggested that few people ever reach the level of self-actualization. While this is true, it does not need to be so. It is only recently that human society has evolved to the point that self-actualization was even possible, and it is only in certain cultures that it is possible now. It *is* possible for the American existing in relatively secure economic conditions (in the sense of having an assured income sufficient to meet one's needs though not necessarily all one's desires) to begin the lifelong process of self-actualizing even in early childhood. But it is difficult since most caregivers are not at that point themselves, and it is not easy to lead someone down a path that you've never traveled yourself. But, just as all of us carry our unresolved childhood needs with us into adulthood, so also can most of us find some corner of ourselves that is self-actualizing. And having identified that part of yourself that is most truly *you,* you will be more able to act as a guide to your children in doing the same for themselves.

The other aspects of developing a healthy self-concept have been dealt with in preceding chapters or will be explained in the readings that follow. A major factor in feeling good about yourself, knowing that you are a person who can do things well, comes from positive experiences with the world of things around you. The reading by White in Chapter 3 provides particular insight here; children are found to develop competency at an early age through having the opportunity to exercise their developing skills in a well-structured, supportive environment. In the first selection in this chapter, Gordon discusses the various influences on the development of a child's self-concept, and he traces that process in the child's early years. As we have repeatedly emphasized, modeling plays a large part in defining for children who they are and what they can be; they adopt and adapt to themselves behaviors that they see in those around them. This is discussed in the reading by Pogrebin in relation to sex-role identification. The excerpt from Betty Smith's book *A Tree Grows in Brooklyn* illustrates how an adult can thoughtlessly hurt a child's feelings, thus leading the child to wonder what is wrong with her that would cause someone to treat her like that.

The Beginnings of the Self: The Problem of the Nurturing Environment

Ira J. Gordon

This selection was originally part of a special issue on early childhood education done by Phi Delta Kappan *in 1969. It reviews the changes in thought over the period of recorded human history of awareness and definitions of the self-concept, and it explains what currently are believed to be important influences on the development of a child's self-concept. Dr. Gordon stresses the importance of children's early years in the establishment of a sense of self that then serves as a filter for all future life experiences, and he points to some of the characteristics of an environment that will nurture the development of a positive self-concept.*

This article provides a summation of many of the ideas central to our entire volume: that feelings about the self are influenced both by the child's active experiences with the environment (whether the feedback from those experiences is generally positive or negative) and by the at-

Ira J. Gordon, "The Beginnings of the Self: The Problem of the Nurturing Environment," *Phi Delta Kappan* (March 1969), pp. 375–78. Reprinted by permission.

titudes, treatment, and models of important people; and that those feelings, in turn, influence how the child will continue to experience life. Dr. Gordon stresses that we must make a social commitment to creating environments for children that will nurture their development of positive concepts of themselves.

The concept of the self is an old one in religion and philosophy and has been discussed endlessly as a part of man's search for identity, as he sought to answer the question, "Who am I?" For Descartes the answer was, *"Cogito ergo sum"*—I think, therefore I am. This statement marked a sharp break with medieval thought, and contributed to the age of reason. For Descartes, cognition or reason was superior to emotion. Knowing was the self's primary function. The self was active, aware, free; the senses and emotions were passive, or confused influences upon the mind. From the early seventeenth until the late nineteenth century, this view reigned.

Freud broke with this tradition by centering upon the emotions, by denying free will, and by focusing upon the influence of the child's experiences in the earliest years. Since Freud, the Descartian answer is insufficient. We now seek to define ourselves in ways which include our feelings as well as our thoughts, and look for the origins of our personality in the first dim moments of life long before cognition seemed possible. Because of Freud, our notion of self-definition has required that its origins be in early childhood and that it be developed from the experiences we have had in that most intimate of circles—our family. For modern man, this is a truism; but it also leaves unanswered a myriad of questions concerning how we got that way.

The first step in self-awareness is both affective and cognitive: the discovery of one's own body as distinct and pleasurable. When the infant puts thumb in mouth, he experiences sensation in both his thumb and his mouth and learns that the thumb is part of him. When the numerous other objects that the infant places in his mouth do not yield the double sensation, he separates self from other. This process, labeled "self-sentience" by Sullivan[1], provides the infant with his first anchorage point, his first awareness of separateness. To paraphrase Descartes, if the infant could speak, he might say, "I experience me, therefore I am."

The second marking point is the awareness of "other." The separation of "I" or "me" from "not me" requires the introduction of people and objects from outside the child. The child needs enough of them, with enough frequency and consistency, that they can be differentiated. The infant at three months engages in social smiles[2], but much has

* All bracketed superscripts refer to the references at the end of this section.

gone on before this time to enable the child to reach this major social event. It is not purely the "maturation" of an inadequate organism toward social behavior. William James, at the turn of the century, defined the world of the infant as a blooming, buzzing confusion, but current research in learning indicates that infants are able to make much more elaborate differentiations of their physical environment in terms of sight and sound and sense than James would have thought possible.

For example, Lipsitt's research at Brown[3] indicates the ways in which both operant and classical conditioning can occur in infancy. Although its approach is not psychoanalytic, current research in infant learning substantiates the psychoanalyst's view of the infant's ability to learn and thus supports the notion of the importance of this early period. But what is it the child learns, in addition to such behaviors as feeding or cooing responses, smiles, and cries? The period of infancy has been seen as the time the child learns basic trust[4]. The nature of the inputs—that is, the way he is handled and fondled, dealt with and responded to, and how his body reacts to these events—teaches the child whether or not the world is a safe or terrifying place, and whether he can trust it or not.

Since the separation of self and world is incomplete, the self-concept, the "I," is part of the world. It is both cognitive and affective, active and passive. "I" is not only in the brain but also in the viscera. It is both Cartesian and Freudian.

Specifically, what are some of the inputs in the very early years which influence the initial picture of the self? Robert Sears and his colleagues[5,6], in a series of studies which applied learning theory rigor to psychoanalytic concepts, indicated that parental attitudes and behavior (disciplinary techniques, permissiveness, severity, temperamental qualities, and aspirations) exhibited in the areas of hunger, elimination, dependency, sex, and aggression were important factors in development and in sex-role identification, a major dimension of the self-concept. But these external inputs emphasize the affective side of life. They do not adequately consider either the cognitive dimension or the role of the child himself.

Current thought emphasizes the competence of the infant and brings together both the cognitive and affective elements of the child into one system. It emphasizes the importance of not only the characteristic childrearing patterns described by Sears, and the family drama so dear to the psychoanalyst, but also the role of the infant himself as an active, striving, curious, learning organism, who makes his impact on his family. This is no *tabula rasa* child. And the child's view of himself is not simply a mirror image of the external events which surround him early in life. From the very beginning it includes his own organism as it senses, feels, learns, and assigns meaning to these external stimuli.

The child learns who he is from what happens to him, from the language that surrounds him, from the people who are dear to him, from the opportunities to deal with the objects and events in his immediate world, and from his own responses to the welter of stimuli. His self-esteem represents his unique organization of his own biological make-up, the evaluations made of him by significant adults, and his own learning from trial and manipulation and feedback from his world. Cognitive development is inseparable from personality development.

The child obviously cannot define "self" as distinct from "other" before he has a permanent frame of reference. One measure of this frame is Piaget's "object permanence," manifested by the individual's recognition that an object continues to exist even though it is no longer visible to him. He arrives at this point somewhere in the second year of life. It is a growth marker because now he can relate affectively to other individuals in some consistent fashion, and cognitively he has achieved a level where he can actively engage in searching his environment. Gaining this ability is a giant step forward and gives the child a sense of competence in relating to his world.

We can make an intuitive leap from object permanence to Erikson's basic trust. Both mean that the child has now organized at least a portion of his world so that it is orderly and predictable—and therefore manageable. With this he can structure a positive self-concept. Without a sense of object permanence, he is powerless. Psychological inputs are important here, because only on the basis of broad experience can the child discover that both people and things have external reality. With the establishment of "other," the child's own behavior can now include role-taking and role-playing[7]. This process enables him to shift from Piaget's "egocentric" stage toward "decentration." That is, he develops from seeing others as just like him toward a recognition of the fact that what one sees and believes depends upon where he stands and what he already knows. Parents not only influence opportunities for such role-playing, but also provide the basic models for imitation. Through the ways in which they teach or deny opportunities for dramatic play, they influence both the cognitive and affective dimensions of the self-concept. Smilansky[8] has described the way parents affect this phase of learning.

Piaget's theoretical exposition of cognitive development returns us to the epistemological position of Descartes, but with added knowledge from Freud and the behavioral scientists. Decarie[9]; for example, was able to investigate both Piagetian and psychoanalytic views about the process, timing, and meaning of arrival at object permanence. Generally, she found empirical support for both, and concluded that parents are the most effective agents in presenting both cognitive and affective experience to the young child. Piaget wrote in 1954:

The other person is of course an emotional object to the highest degree but at the same time is the most interesting cognitive object, the most alive, the most unexpected. . . . The other person is an object which implies a multitude of exchanges in which cognitive as well as affective factors play a role, and if this object is of paramount importance in one of these respects, it is, I think, equally important in the other[10].

How important are these early years? Gardner Murphy has indicated that the self-picture is fairly well integrated by the third year of life. Once it has developed, it becomes the evaluator, selector, judger, and organizer of future experience, and the child's behavior may be seen as organized to enhance and maintain his view. Such a picture sounds harsh and deterministic if we did not understand that possibilities for change are always present. Life is not over at age three, but the general view toward the world and toward one's self is already present.

The longitudinal data which support the importance of early childhood are fairly consistent. Bloom indicated on the basis of reviews of longitudinal research[11] that half of what accounts for the variance in adults in aggressiveness in males and dependence in females seems to be present by age four. Not only Bloom's summary but also the classical longitudinal studies conducted in California[12] and the longitudinal studies of the Fels Institute at Yellow Springs, Ohio[13], demonstrated the effects of parental behavior in the child's first six years of his behavior and attitudes in subsequent years.

One of Bayley's findings is that the mother's affectional behavior toward her son in the first three years of his life was related to his friendship, cooperation, and attentiveness when he became a school child and an adolescent. These behaviors may be inferred to be reflections of feelings of security, a fundamental dimension of self-concept.

One of Freud's contributions is the concept of identification, and, more specifically, sex-role identification. We noted earlier that Sears adopted this concept and applied general behavior methodology to its investigation. It is central also to Kagan and Moss. For them, the notion of sex-role identification is a core concept in influencing stability of behavior from childhood through adulthood. Events early in life lead not only to the child's sex-role identification but also determine his general social expectancy for all behavior. Boys are expected to behave more aggressively, more competently, and in more task-oriented fashions; girls are to be more nurturant, more person-oriented. Parent behavior in the first six years of life influences the child's identity and the standards he will set for typical sex-related behavior. Kagan and Moss conclude that the individual's own desire to make his behavior agree with the culture's definition of sex is a major factor determining the stability of his behavior over time.

Longitudinal studies indicate how very important it is to analyze data about children by sex as well as by age. They indicate the differential effects of parental behavior on boys and girls. This should not surprise us, but it often gets overlooked. In both the cognitive and affective aspects of the self, boys and girls view themselves differently, tend to use different learning styles, tend to evaluate different aspects of self and world as important. The origins lie both in biology and in differential treatment.

Unfortunately, most of the children studied in longitudinal research have been middle-class, from somewhat stable families, where conditions might generally foster the mix of intellectual and emotional inputs that lead to positive views of the self. They fit Lois Murphy's observation that "Each experience of mastery and triumph sets the stage for better efforts in the next experience. Confidence, hope, and a sense of self-worth are increased along with the increase in cognitive and motor skills, which can contribute to better use of the resources" [14]. Their world provides them with both intellectual challenge and emotional support. Both the cognitive and affective "matches"—the connection between the child's motives and cognitive level on the one hand and the experiences being offered to him on the other[15,16]—are in phase. His positive self-image receives verification from his competence in dealing with the world.

Unfortunately, not all children have the sense of triumph described by Lois Murphy, nor do their selves match the world's demands. Yarrow's studies[17] of maternal deprivation indicate the difficulties encountered by children who lack a mother figure to provide them with some stable anchorage points. In the social domain, Clark[18], Deutsch[19], Smilansky[20], Marans[21], and Wortis[22], among others, point out the devastating effects of social deprivation on building positive self-esteem. Although the child's view of himself does not mirror and is not an exact replica of his world's picture of him, for many youngsters it comes quite close. If the larger society conceives of the child as not worthwhile and demonstrates consistently to him that it so judges him, it is difficult for the child to value himself. Children in the ghetto, children classified as slow learners, children who for a variety of reasons are told even in these early years that they are not quite good enough or smart enough or handsome enough tend to devalue themselves and thus to set the stage for continuously poorer levels of performance than might otherwise be their lot. These images are already set before entry into school[23]. Children growing up in psychologically disorganized homes suffer similar fates, as Pavenstedt[24] has indicated about South Boston children.

"As the twig is bent . . ." has long been part of Western folklore. Scientific data now support this view. The origins of the self lie in the early years. How the child will see himself is influenced by the way he is treated, the opportunities provided for him, how he is evaluated as he copes with these opportunities, and how he perceives these evaluations.

If these early years are crucial in determining school performance through the mechanism of the self-concept, then society cannot shrug off its responsibility. For very young children, negative self-views may be as damaging as physical illness or actual physical handicap. We are rapidly making provision for medical help. We need to create nurturing environments early in life so that children's concepts of themselves may possibly emerge as positive. Whether the school systems as now constructed are the appropriate agencies to reach down to the younger years is open to debate. The example of Head Start programs and the present Parent and Child Center movement indicate that new social agencies consisting of and requiring the participation of those for whom the service is intended may provide effective vehicles for change. What is needed is education so designed that parents can provide children not only with an *affective* climate which tells them they are loved and worthy but also with a *cognitive* climate that allows the child to be competent as well as feel loved. Adequate self-esteem requires this combination.

A characteristic of the American society is its own self-concept that it is capable of solving the problems which afflict it, once the problems are pointed out. The issue is clear. What is required now are social engineering skills. Intervention is essential. We have some ideas of what it should be and who should render it. Now we need to develop the types of programs which provide for all children the psychological inputs which lead to positive self-steem.

REFERENCES

1. H. S. SULLIVAN, *The Interpersonal Theory of Psychiatry* (New York: W. W. Norton, 1953).

2. RENÉ SPITZ, *The First Year of Life* (New York: International Universities Press, 1965).

3. L. LIPSITT, "Learning in the Human Infant," pp. 225–28, in H. W. Stevenson, E. H. Hess, and H. L. Rheingold (eds.), *Early Behavior: Comparative and Developmental Approaches* (New York: Wiley, 1967).

4. E. ERIKSON, *Childhood and Society* (New York: Norton, 1951).

5. R. SEARS, E. MACCOBY, and H. LEVIN, *Patterns of Child Rearing* (Evanston, Ill.: Row Peterson, 1957).

6. R. SEARS et al., *Identification and Child Rearing* (Stanford, Calif.: Stanford University Press, 1965).

7. G. H. MEAD, *Mind, Self and Society* (Chicago: University of Chicago, 1940).

8. S. SMILANSKY, *The Effects of Sociodramatic Play on Disadvantaged Preschool Children* (New York: Wiley, 1968).

9. T. DECARIE, *Intelligence and Affectivity in Early Childhood* (New York: International Universities Press, 1965).

10. J. PIAGET, *Les Relations Entre l'Affectivité et l'Intelligence Dans la Developpement Mental de l'Enfant* (Paris: Centre de Documentation Universitaire, 1954).

11. B. BLOOM, *Stability and Change in Human Characteristics* (New York: Wiley, 1964).

12. N. BAYLEY, "Consistency of Maternal and Child Behaviors in the Berkeley Growth Study," *Vita Humana* (1964), pp. 73–95.

13. J. KAGAN and H. MOSS, *Birth to Maturity* (New York: Wiley, 1962).

14. L. MURPHY and associates, *The Widening World of Childhood* (New York: Basic, 1962).

15. J. McV. HUNT, *Intelligence and Experience* (New York: The Ronald Press, 1961).

16. IRA J. GORDON, *Studying the Child in School* (New York: Wiley, 1962).

17. L. YARROWS, "Separation from Parents During Early Childhood," pp. 89–136, in Martin L. Hoffman and Lois W. Hoffman (eds.), *Review of Child Development Research*, vol. 1 (New York: Russell Sage, 1964).

18. K. CLARK, *Dark Ghetto* (New York: Harper, 1965).

19. M. DEUTSCH and associates, *The Disadvantaged Child* (New York: Basic, 1967).

20. SMILANSKY, 1968.

21. A. MARANS, D. MEERS, and D. HUNTINGTON, "The Children's Hospital in Washington, D.C.," pp. 287–301, in Laura L. Dittman (ed.), *Early Child Care, the New Perspective* (New York: Atherton, 1968).

22. H. WORTIS et al., "Child-Rearing Practices in a Low Socioeconomic Group," *Pediatrics,* 32 (1963), pp. 298–307.

23. B. LONG and E. HENDERSON, "Social Schemata of School Beginners: Some Demographic Correlates," in *Proceedings, 75th Annual Convention,* American Psychological Association (1967), pp. 329–330.

24. E. PAVENSTEDT (ed.), *The Drifters* (Boston: Little, Brown, 1967).

Down with Sexist Upbringing

Letty Cottin Pogrebin

In the preceding reading, Dr. Gordon pointed out the importance of the early years in establishing a child's sex-role identity and its impact on development of the child's self-concept. A child decides what kinds of behaviors and options are possible for him/her based to a great extent on sex-role identity. In the following article, Ms. Pogrebin describes some of the processes that operate to define children's sex-role identities. In the past, in much of the child development literature, children's early learning of "appropriate" behaviors based on sex-role identification was presented as a very desirable aspect of growth and development; this remains true among some authors. However, as Ms. Pogrebin points out, this process can be detrimental and limiting to both boys and girls; strict definitions of sexual options limits broader human options.

One of the distinguishing characteristics of Maslow's self-actualizing subjects was their full humanness, their freedom from arbitrary sexual (and cultural and racial) boundaries on what they could be. In the last chapter, we talked about growth vs. safety needs, and said that if growth appeared frightening to children, they would opt for the safety of known territory. If you feel uncomfortable with the following article and our suggestion that children's alternatives should not be limited by what physical equipment they possess, then you are observing in yourself what we discussed in the preceding chapter—the prospect of growth toward full humanness, not defined arbitrarily by what has always been before, may be frightening to you; the traditionally accepted views of what a man is and what a woman is may feel more comfortable and "safer." If so, neither we nor you should expect a sudden change of feeling, any more than you expect your child to rush headlong into threatening territory; growth must be slow enough to be comfortable.

But do try to be open, whether you are male or female, to the ways in which you have been inhibited in being all that you could be because of narrowly defined sex-role identities. And try to increase the options

Letty Cottin Pogrebin, "Down with Sexist Upbringing," *Ms.*, Spring 1972, pp. 18, 20, 25–28. Reprinted by permission.

for your own children, to enable them to be fully human, to become all they can be. As Ms. Pogrebin describes, you will have a hard task ahead of you because the cultural norms, as reflected in the schools, children's books, television advertising, and children's programs, etc. stamp in very narrow sex-role definitions. Nevertheless, as the author illustrates in her opening paragraphs, the influence of modeling of your behavior on your children's development of their own sex-role definitions is very powerful. In spite of all outside influences, it is you and your mate who set the stage for how your children will view their human options.

Our twin daughters aren't into Women's Liberation. For all they know, a male chauvinist pig is the fourth little porker on the big bad wolf's menu. They've never suffered job discrimination, never been treated as sex objects and can't be characterized as bra-burners since they're still in undershirts.

But living with Abigail and Robin, age six, is an ongoing consciousness-raising session for my husband and me. In them, and in their three-year-old brother David, we see ourselves. They mirror our attitudes and mimic our relationship. They are constant reminders that lifestyles and sex roles are passed from parents to children as inexorably as blue eyes or small feet.

From empirical evidence our children have concluded that women's work is writing books and articles, having meetings, making dinner, doing puzzles with the kids, and fixing the electrical wiring. Man's work, on the other hand, is writing legal briefs, arguing cases, having meetings, making breakfast, reading stories with the kids and fixing the plumbing.

In our household, whoever can, does. Call it convenience plus ability. I make dinner because I like to and because I cook better. My husband makes breakfast because I simply cannot get up that early in the morning and the children love his pancakes.

In homes where male and female roles are rigidly defined, children would tune in a wholly different picture. If the father restricts himself to the television room, the evening paper and the "masculine" chores in the backyard, his son is not likely to feel that folding laundry is a man's lot in life. If the mother is exclusively engaged in domestic activities, her daughter may question whether women were meant to have other interests.

Home environments tend to set the stage for sex-role stereotypes. We've all seen little girls' rooms that are so organdied, pink and pippy-poo one would never dream of besmirching them with Play-Doh or cartwheels. We've seen little boys living in nautical decors or in cell-like rooms heavy on athletic equipment but lacking a cozy place to read a book. We've seen boys scolded for parading in their sisters' ballet tutus; girls enjoined from getting soiled; boys forbidden to play with dolls; girls forbidden to wrestle.

Why are parents so alert to sex-typed behavior? Why do they monitor the "masculine" or "feminine" connotations of children's clothes, games, toys, reading material and physical activity? What's the big worry?

Homosexuality is the big worry. The specter of having a son turn out gay haunts nearly every father. Mothers seem to join in the obsession—not because they have the same investment in the boys' masculinization, but because they've been made to feel women are responsible for producing Mama's boys who fall prey to homosexual temptation.

The prospect of having a Lesbian daughter doesn't seem quite as threatening. Keeping girls feminine is largely a matter of keeping them attractive, alluring and marriageable. The tomboy is said to be "going through a phase." It can be cured with a lace petticoat and a new hair ribbon. It can even be turned into an advantage: "My daughter throws a ball like a boy," or "I swear, she thinks like a man." While some find it enviable to have a daughter who knows what a gridiron is, a son who likes to iron is another dish of neuroses. Somehow, sissy is what tomboy isn't: a grave threat to the future of the child and to the stability and social status of the entire family.

Although male homosexuals are often truck-driver-tough and many heterosexuals are gentle poets, the assumption remains that superficial masculine and feminine identities and activities will prevent sexual confusion.

"There is absolutely no scientific validity to this assumption," says Dr. Robert E. Gould, Director of Adolescent Psychiatry as the Bellevue Hospital Center. "Boys become homosexual because of disturbed family relationships, not because their parents allowed them to do so-called feminine things.

"Kids must be allowed all available opportunity to develop and achieve their full potential. They should have free access to *human* toys, books, games and emotions—all of them free from sex-stereotyping."

Dr. Sirgay Sanger, a New York child psychiatrist, puts it this way: "In the child's earliest years, masculine or feminine differences are a fake issue. Until three or four years of age children have the same needs. Beyond that age, what they require most is individual differentiation, not gender differentiation. To highlight differences only denies one sex the advantages permitted to the other.

"Such gender differences can be alarming and threatening to children. Unisex clothes and relaxed dating rituals among the young indicate that there's a natural tendency to minimize sex differences and to find comfortable common areas of human communication."

Maybe the next generation of parents will be uncoerced and uncoercive. Meanwhile, those of us raising children now must face our own prejudices and society's pervasive sexism.

How do you telegraph your prejudices and preconceptions? Blue and pink is the first label. The way you handle and coo to the infant differs. Girls get cuddled and purred over. Boys get hoisted and roughhoused. The choice of toys also tells a child something without words. Do-it-yourself crib games for boys. Delicate mobiles for girls. And later —he gets baseballs, model ships, Erector sets, chemistry kits. She gets Barbie dolls, tea sets, nurse kits, mini-mops. And still later—he goes skiing, camping, skin-diving and plays football with Dad. She goes to ballet class, piano lessons, art exhibits and bakes brownies with Mom.

And they both get the signal. That they are expected to be very different from one another. That he can experiment, solve problems, compete and take risks. That she is passive, domestic, cultured and cautious.

If the profile sounds familiar, your children may need a strong dose of nonsexist upbringing. Open the options. Let your boy know the challenge of tackling a recipe; let your girl know the challenge of tackling another kid. And beware of outside pollutants. Well-meaning friends can muddy feminist waters. The following tales are typical.

During a visit to their father's office, our three children were introduced to one of his associates. The man told David that when he grew up he could be a lawyer in Daddy's firm. Turning to the twins the man said: "And we can use some new legal secretaries, too."

On a recent plane trip, a stewardess asked my husband how many and "what kind" of children he had. Then she brought back three gold pins: one Junior Pilot wings and two Junior Stewardess wings. (My husband told the kids that all the wings were pilot's.)

When David started howling after a bad fall I overheard our babysitter tell him: "Come on now, boys don't cry." ("Crying is the ultimate human reaction to pain and sadness," says Dr. Gould. "In Egypt men were wailing in the streets when Nasser died. But Americans are trapped in the mystique of the ideal man—someone like John Wayne striding emotionless through a war movie. It's unreal.")

While individual sexist acts or statements can be counteracted by sensitive parents, for most of us the problem becomes overwhelming when we examine the educational system and the media. Here's where doctrinaire "experts" legitimize sex roles. And here's where cultural brainwashing techniques are most entrenched and hardest to fight.

In opposition to censorship, Mayor Jimmy Walker once said, "No girl was ever ruined by a book." Well, maybe not by one book. But a cumulative library of negative, stultifying stories, books and poems can go a long way toward ruination of the female spirit.

We didn't really notice them coming at us. The fairy tales that show girls sleeping away their lives until the prince hacks through the underbrush to rescue them. The nursery rhymes in which we are kept in pumpkin shells or crammed into a shoe with a bunch of kids. All of us: Lazy Mary, Contrary Mary, frightened Miss Muffet, empty-headed Bo-Peep—a sorry lot, with little relief on the positive side. Even Mother Goose herself was eccentric.

In school books, the Dick and Jane syndrome reinforced our emerging attitudes. The arithmetic books posed appropriate conundrums: "Ann has three pies . . . Dan has three rockets . . ." We read the nuances between the lines: Ann keeps her eye on the oven; Dan sets his sights on the moon.

Put it all together, it spells conform. Be beautiful, feminine, alluring, passive, supportive. Subvert your energies, dear. Conceal your brains, young lady. Spunky girls finish last on the way to the prom. Tomboys must convert. Boys don't make passes at female smart-asses. We all got the message—finally. If we're fragile, vulnerable and helpless, we'll feel that pea tucked beneath 43 mattresses. The prize is a king-sized bed. And a lifetime of making it up every morning.

The boy reading the same material is victimized by the reverse effects. If she's all dainty and diaphanous, he has to be strong and assertive. If she faints with love for a fullback then he'd better try out for the team. If Mom and the kiddies are at home all day, then who but Dad must work to keep starvation from the door? The pressure is on.

But suppose he isn't up to jousting with his fellows or scaling palace walls? What if he prefers a flute to a football? Tough luck, and that's why Georgie Porgie runs away. Because there's no place for the tender, uncompetitive boy in juvenile books—or in American life.

Children's literature and texts may favor the man-child by investing him with forcefulness, creativity and active virtues. But the concomitant effect is to stunt him emotionally, to teach him that toughness is a prerequisite for manhood, to cheat him of a full and free acquaintance with all forms of culture and to burden him with the identities of soldier and sole support of dependent human beings.

These roles are not negotiable in childhood. Much later, when *The Hardy Boys* and Sports Annuals have been carted off to some charity warehouse, the self-image created by these books is opened to scrutiny—at the psychiatrist's office or in the divorce court.

To break the pattern our children need our help:

To route them to the few realistic books available within each reading category and age level.

To impose an interpretive voice upon their reading experiences.

To seek stories that offer alternate lifestyles and that show men *and* women with cosmic concerns and diverse identities.

To ferret out biographies and history books that give women their rightful place and accord respect to female opinions and perspectives.

You can buy or borrow recommended books such as those listed below.* You can pass every book under a Geiger counter for sexist overtones. But you don't have to burn the old stand-bys and the classics in a fit of feminist pique. The simple exercise of adult intelligence and advanced consciousness will do the trick.

As a parent you should become an interpreter of myths. A feminist revisionist. Analyze, discuss, question characterizations. Portions of any fairy tale or children's story can be salvanged during a critique session with your child.

For example, Dr. Sanger suggests a transformation of *Cinderella* from a tale of a hyperlanguishing female to a constructive fantasy. Look at it this way: Cinderella wasn't a victim. She was a strong young woman and a tolerant, understanding human being. She recognized the pettiness of her stepsisters. She endured her stepmother's cruelty. Because she was sympathetic rather than bitter, she gained an ally—the fairy godmother, who epitomizes our ideal of free choice. Cinderella's reward for perseverence and strength of character is entrée into the castle: in other words, a better life.

As for the bit about marriage being a woman's be-all and end-all, you'll have to deal with that inevitable dénouement as you see fit. Most of the time, I figure it's a fair ending. After all, we don't know what the prince did with the rest of his life either.

Sexism and racism, to my way of thinking, are different intensities on the same wavelength. Being barred from medical school or doing compulsory time in the typing pool are some of the ways society sends its women to the back of the bus.

It can be effective to arouse your child's sensibility by drawing a parallel. Most books have ceased portraying black people in servile positions. Elevator operators are no longer all black and research chemists are no longer all white. Flat racial generalizations (lazy, rhythmic, etc.) are no longer tolerated.

And yet—we must point out to our kids—women are still virtually one-dimensional in literature for the young. Female stereotypes are not only endured, they are applauded. Women are helpers, not doers; procreative, not creative. Mothers in ubiquitous aprons cook, clean and

---

* Editors' note: We have not included this list in our reprint. If you are interested in obtaining it, you can write to Ms. Magazine, 370 Lexington Avenue, New York, New York 10017, and request a reprint of the entire article.

beautify themselves to please men. Little girls are nubile maidens in training for Mom's self-effacing role. Rewards are vicariously enjoyed through males. Opinions are limited. Fathers are shown in multidimensional pursuits: driving the lawn mower and driving the steam shovel; in the family room and in the conference room. Women never seem to leave the home, yard and supermarket.

While the mother who does not work outside the home is in the minority for the first time, you can count on one hand the books that positively reflect the dual-occupation family. No wonder the 22 million children of working mothers feel somewhat deprived. All the printed evidence suggests that the only normal mother is a stay-at-home mother and that a woman needs only a well-frosted cake to feel fulfilled.

Once conscious of this propaganda, you can externalize your awareness. Start reading seminars for other parents through the school or community center. Inquire into the contents of your child's reading syllabus.

You'll find, as did a Princeton group called Women on Words and Images, that 72 percent of the stories about individual children are geared to boys; that the overriding conclusions to be drawn from school readers is that girls are always late, give up easily, don't excel in school (contrary to statistical fact), and need a lot of help solving problems and getting things done.

You'll discover, as did women at Pandora in Seattle, that math textbooks are full of examples that demean your daughter by inference. Such as

Mary's way: $2 + 2 + 2 + 2 = 8$

Jack's way: $2 \times 4 = 8$

You'll find more than enough reasons to support activist groups that are closing in on publishers and educators. You may even be outraged enough to join a feminist collective to prepare non-sexist reading lists and to launch honest books of your own making.

You might demand that your bookstore and library stock equalitarian literature. Complain to publishers and editors. And don't spare the Board of Education. Remember that when repressive, slanted books are adopted by an entire school system, their contents are invested with divine authority.

The National Organization for Women's Report on Sex Bias in the Public Schools provides appalling evidence of sexism in the entire system, not just in its books. Girls are barred from 85 per cent of the play areas, from several gym activities, from many field and track sports and from most school teams. They are directed instead to volleyball courts, dancing or cheerleading.

Boys get the special assignments, whether on the audio-visual squad, hall patrol or honor guard. While boys may not be welcome in cooking or sewing classes (what male would be caught dead electing them anyway?), girls are barred from shop, metalworking, mechanics and printing courses. Not all exclusions apply in all schools but it's the rare school that has no sex-segregated special classes whatsoever.

In kindergarten and primary grades boys and girls line up separately. Often boys sit with boys and girls with girls. Spelling teams and other groupings are separated by sex. Though this may appear to be a case of separate-but-equal, in reality the sex groupings take on a calcified adversary identity. The boys' group is called upon to move chairs or lug books—though at that age both sexes are found to be comparable in strength. The girls' group is chosen to pass out cookies. The division becomes palpable. Children become polarized into "Them" and "Us."

How can you raise your kids to be free when they're so systematically shackled within the schools? The answer is, you can't. Emancipation from sex-stereotypes is not possible unless all institutions affecting a child's development are brought into harmonious accord. That's why parents are resorting to legal suits to win their daughters' access to wood-working courses or entry into boys' specialty schools or a deserved place on the varsity tennis team. And that's why children's liberation is the next item on our civil rights shopping list.

It will require widespread consciousness-raising courses for teachers. We'll have to stop guidance counselors from programming female students for limited achievement. (Why should gifted girl biology students become science teachers when bright boy students are directed into medical careers?)

We'll need more male teachers at the elementary level and more females in administrative posts. Our children must know that men can be fine caretakers of the young and that women can be respected authority figures.

If the schools are often a battleground for the sexes, the television screen is an out-and-out disaster area. Our children are exposed to quiz shows where housewives vie for washing machines or game shows where they make fools of themselves under the patronizing gaze of a male M.C. Situation comedies telecast during children's prime time include such splendid inanities as *I Dream of Jeannie* (a flagrant master-slave relationship between the sexes) or *I Love Lucy* (the die-hard scatterbrain embodying the infantilized woman and the henpecking wife). It's a wasteland all right, but children consider it friendly territory because such programs are targeted at the intellectual level of a six-year-old to begin with.

Even *Sesame Street,* despite its noble educational intentions, teaches role rigidity along with the letters of the alphabet. Susan is almost always in the kitchen. Puppet families are traditional: Dad works, Mom cooks (an inaccurate portrayal of many black and poor families and of middle-class dual-professional families as well). Boy monsters are brave and gruff. Girl monsters are high-pitched and timid. Oscar turns out to be a male chauvinist as well as a grouch. When his garbage-pail home needs a spring cleaning he calls a woman to do it.

And speaking of garbage, the commercials television feeds into our children's minds add up to pure unadulterated rubbish. Often the indictment of exploitive and insulting TV ads has been filed by committed feminists objecting to the assault on women's self-image. However, while most adults have become inured to the high-pressure sales pitch, the crucial point is that children *don't* tune out. They react with interest, not annoyance. So the problem takes on a greater magnitude than that raised by the feminists' outrage. It isn't only woman *now* who is being demeaned by guilt-producing detergent ads or by "feminine hygiene" commercials that play on self-consciousness and self-hatred. It is woman *future*—our daughters, who are being fed this commercial hogwash.

Sexist commercials are an affront to parents and children, not just to feminist women. The 30- or 60-second commercial has been found so effective a sales tool that it forms the foundation of *Sesame Street*'s format for selling knowledge. Obviously, the technique is potent. According to the Boston group Action for Children's Television, your child will see 350,000 TV commercials by the age of eighteen.

Add it all together and you have a bombardment of cultural conditioning: grown-up men buy rugged cars, drink lots of beer, shave their faces and kiss girls who are pretty enough, thin enough or fragrant enough to warrant it; grown-up women diet for love and approval, serve flavorful coffee or lose their husbands to the morning paper, and use the right soap or lose their husbands to a woman with younger skin.

To defumigate TV programming and set a standard for decent commercial messages is a monumental job. A letter to a network executive has as much chance of making waves as a pebble in the ocean. The F.C.C. should care about sexism but its commissioners have licensing, antitrust and equal time on their collective minds. So the target of our wrath must be the sponsors. They must be taken to task for their pejorative view of women in commercials and their financial support of programs that disparage women's role. Consumer power is bargaining power.

It will be a long time before enough women use their dollars to protect their children from media's warped message. Until then it might be wise to monitor the TV fare for sexism as well as sex and violence. A *Flintstones* program showing how wives play dumb to build their husbands' egos can be more harmful to a small child's developing sense of values than a panel discussion of premarital sex or drug addiction. As with children's books, television frequently requires parental supervision and sermonizing. Give the commercials a taste of their own medicine: ridicule. Show children the absurdity of three or four commercials and they'll be talking back to the television set before you know it.

Clearly, the home influence can go only so far. You may renounce role rigidity and set a beautiful example of individuality and gender freedom, only to be defeated when the kid next door calls your free child a dirty name. What is needed, then, is a total eradication of sexism, not only in your house but in the house next door and in the culture as a whole.

The stakes are high. If we fail, it's more of the same. And the same is not good enough for our children. Labeled sexuality and its attendant polarization must go. Sugar and spice and snails and puppy dogs' tails aren't relevant metaphors. Cheating one sex and overburdening the other won't do anymore.

If we win, human liberation is the prize. Our daughters and sons gain the freedom to develop as persons, not roleplayers. Relationships between the sexes can flourish without farce and phoniness. And dignity can be the birthright of every child.

A Tree Grows in Brooklyn

Betty Smith

We have discussed the impact on a child's self-concept of the imposition of sex-role stereotypes. Dr. Gordon also discussed in his reading the influence on children's development of feelings about themselves in relation to cultural stereotypes. Children who are made to feel that they are less worthy because of what their racial, cultural, or economic origins are will begin to believe that to be true and to act in accordance with those expectations. This story poignantly recalls the insensitivity of two adults to a small child's feelings. It is but one incident, but the constant repetition of such incidents can cause children to feel doubt and shame about who they are; it can wound them for life.

From pp. 126–132 ("School days were . . . sighing note.") in *A Tree Grows in Brooklyn,* by Betty Smith. Copyright, 1943 by Betty Smith. By permission of Harper & Row, Publishers, Inc.

School days were eagerly anticipated by Francie. She wanted all of the things that she thought came with school. She was a lonely child and she longed for the companionship of other children. She wanted to drink from the school water fountains in the yard. The faucets were inverted and she thought that soda water came out instead of plain water. She had heard mama and papa speak of the school room. She wanted to see the map that pulled down like a shade. Most of all, she wanted "school supplies"; a notebook and tablet and a pencil box with a sliding top filled with new pencils, an eraser, a little tin pencil sharpener made in the shape of a cannon, a pen wiper, and a six-inch, soft wood, yellow ruler.

Before school, there had to be vaccination. That was the law. How it was dreaded! When the health authorities tried to explain to the poor and illiterate that vaccination was a giving of the harmless form of smallpox to work up immunity against the deadly form, the parents didn't believe it. All they got out of the explanation was that germs would be put into a healthy child's body. Some foreign-born parents refused to permit their children to be vaccinated. They were not allowed to enter school. Then the law got after them for keeping the children out of school. A free country? they asked. You should live so long. What's free about it, they reasoned when the law forces you to educate your children and then endangers their lives to get them into school? Weeping mothers brought bawling children to the health center for inoculation. They carried on as though bringing their innocents to the slaughter. The children screamed hysterically at the first sight of the needle and their mothers, waiting in the anteroom, thew their shawls over their heads and keened loudly as if wailing for the dead.

Francie was seven and Neeley six. Katie had held Francie back wishing both children to enter school together so that they could protect each other against the older children. On a dreadful Saturday in August, she stopped in the bedroom to speak to them before she went off to work. She awakened them and gave instructions.

"Now when you get up, wash yourselves good and when it gets to be eleven o'clock, go around the corner to the public health place, tell them to vaccinate you because you're going to school in September."

Francie began to tremble. Neeley burst into tears.

"You coming with us, Mama?" Francie pleaded.

"I've got to go to work. Who's going to do my work if I don't?" asked Katie covering up her conscience with indignation.

Francie said nothing more. Katie knew that she was letting them down. But she couldn't help it, she just couldn't help it. Yes, she should go with them to lend the comfort an authority of her presence but she knew she couldn't stand the ordeal. Yet, they had to be vaccinated. Her being with them or somewhere else couldn't take that fact away. So why shouldn't one of the three be spared? Besides, she said to her conscience, it's a hard and bitter world. They've got to live in it. Let them get hardened young to take care of themselves.

"Papa's going with us then," said Francie hopefully.

"Papa's at Headquarters waiting for a job. He won't be home all day. You're big enough to go alone. Besides, it won't hurt."

Neeley wailed on a higher key. Katie could hardly stand that. She loved the boy so much. Part of her reason for not going with them was that she couldn't bear to see the boy hurt . . . not even by a pin prick. Almost she decided to go with them. But no. If she went she'd lose half a day's work and she'd have to make it up on Sunday morning. Besides, she'd be sick afterwards. They'd manage somehow without her. She hurried off to her work.

Francie tried to console the terrified Neeley. Some older boys had told him that they cut your arm off when they got you in the Health Center. To take his mind off the thing, Francie took him down into the yard and they made mud pies. They quite forgot to wash as mama had told them to.

They almost forgot about eleven o'clock, the mud pie making was so beguiling. Their hands and arms got very dirty playing in the mud. At ten to eleven, Mrs. Gaddis hung out the window and yelled down that their mother had told her to remind them when it was near eleven o'clock. Neeley finished off his last mud pie, watering it with his tears. Francie took his hand and with slow dragging steps the children walked around the corner.

They took their place on a bench. Next to them sat a Jewish mama who clutched a large six-year-old boy in her arms and wept and kissed his forehead passionately from time to time. Other mothers sat there with grim suffering furrowed on their faces. Behind the frosted glass door where the terrifying business was going on, there was a steady bawling punctuated by a shrill scream, resumption of the bawling and then a pale child would come out with a strip of pure white gauze about his left arm. His mother would rush and grab him and with a foreign curse and a shaken fist at the frosted door, hurry him out of the torture chamber.

Francie went in trembling. She had never seen a doctor or a nurse in all of her small life. The whiteness of the uniforms, the shiny cruel instruments laid out on a napkin on a tray, the smell of antiseptics, and especially the cloudy sterilizer with its bloody red cross filled her with tongue-tied fright.

The nurse pulled up her sleeve and swabbed a spot clean on her left arm. Francie saw the white doctor coming towards her with the cruelly poised needle. He loomed larger and larger until he seemed to blend into a great needle. She closed her eyes waiting to die. Nothing happened, she felt nothing. She opened her eyes slowly, hardly daring to hope that it was all over. She found to her agony, that the doctor was still there, poised needle and all. He was staring at her arm in distaste. Francie looked too. She saw a small white area on a dirty dark brown arm. She heard the doctor talking to the nurse.

"Filth, filth, filth, from morning to night. I know they're poor but they could wash. Water is free and soap is cheap. Just look at that arm, nurse."

The nurse looked and clucked in horror. Francie stood there with the hot flamepoints of shame burning her face. The doctor was a Harvard man, interning at the neighborhood hospital. Once a week, he was obligated to put in a few hours at one of the free clinics. He was going into a smart practice in Boston when his internship was over. Adopting the phraseology of the neighborhood, he referred to his Brooklyn internship as going through Purgatory when he wrote to his socially prominent fiancée in Boston.

The nurse was a Williamsburg girl. You could tell that by her accent. The child of poor Polish immigrants, she had been ambitious, worked days in a sweatshop and gone to school at night. Somehow she had gotten her training. She hoped some day to marry a doctor. She didn't want anyone to know she had come from the slums.

After the doctor's outburst, Francie stood hanging her head. She was a dirty girl. That's what the doctor meant. He was talking more quietly now asking the nurse how that kind of people could survive; that it would be a better world if they were all sterilized and couldn't breed anymore. Did that mean he wanted her to die? Would he do something to make her die because her hands and arms were dirty from the mud pies?

She looked at the nurse. To Francie, all women were mamas like her own mother and Aunt Sissy and Aunt Evy. She thought the nurse might say something like:

"Maybe this little girl's mother works and didn't have time to wash her good this morning," or, "You know how it is, Doctor, children *will* play in dirt." But what the nurse actually said was, "I know. Isn't it terrible? I sympathize with you, Doctor. There is no excuse for these people living in filth."

A person who pulls himself up from a low environment via the bootstrap route has two choices. Having risen above his environment, he can forget it; or, he can rise above it and never forget it and keep compassion and understanding in his heart for those he has left behind him in the cruel up climb. The nurse had chosen the forgetting way. Yet, as she stood there, she knew that years later she would be haunted by the sorrow in the face of that starveling child and that she would wish bitterly that she had said a comforting word then and done something towards the saving of her immortal soul. She had the knowledge that she was small but she lacked the courage to be otherwise.

When the needle jabbed, Francie never felt it. The waves of hurt started by the doctor's words were racking her body and drove out all other feeling. While the nurse was expertly tying a strip of gauze around her arm and the doctor was putting his instrument in the sterilizer and taking out a fresh needle, Francie spoke up.

"My brother is next. His arm is just as dirty as mine so don't be surprised. And you don't have to tell him. You told me." They stared at this bit of humanity who had become so strangely articulate. Francie's voice went ragged with a sob. "You don't have to tell him. Besides it won't do no good. He's a boy and he don't care if he is dirty." She turned, stumbled a little and walked out of the room. As the door closed, she heard the doctor's surprised voice.

"I had no idea she'd understand what I was saying." She heard the nurse say, "Oh, well," on a sighing note.

6

Behavior and Discipline: Spare the Rod and Teach the Child

Most parents and teachers of young children share a common and persistent concern—discipline: "How do I get my child to mind?" "What can I do about the child in my room who's always bothering the other children—taking their toys, fighting, teasing, etc.?" "How can I help to make my child be more responsible?" "What do you do about a whiner?" "How can I get my child to sit still for a minute and listen to me?" "What should you do when a child has a tantrum?" and so on.

First of all, there is no one, correct, definitive answer that will meet the needs of all children and all caregivers. Children have different personalities, different styles, different motivations, and different things that are important to them; adults have different personalities, styles, attitudes toward childrearing, expectations of children, and so on. All of the individual idiosyncrasies in each child-caregiver relationship contribute to inevitable differences in the particular techniques of behavior management that will work best for them. Nevertheless, there are some general rules that can be applied to each individual situation which can help you deal more effectively with questions of discipline.

The subject of discipline is one about which most people have strong feelings even when they lack answers. Many of your attitudes toward discipline are derived from your own personal experiences as a child—that is, how your parents disciplined you. Some people react against what they experienced, going to the other extreme in their own practice. Many others, even when they may not have liked the way they were treated as a child, respond in just the same way to their children as their parents did to them. The reason for this is that we learn our models of behavior from those that we experience early in life—they become prototypes for our own behavior. This is an important fact to remember with your own children. For example,

119

if you and your spouse engage in frequent verbal battles, it is highly likely that your children will behave similarly in their own future relationships. If you yell at your children a great deal, you may expect them to yell at their children. You don't have to wait until they're adults to observe this modeling behavior: watch your children play with their dolls or stuffed animals; you will observe their perceptions of your treatment of them.

We tell you this not to make you feel that you have no control over your behavior toward children. You do; but often people act in ways that they are not conscious of. We are not suggesting that your behavior is absolutely determined by the models that you observed in your childhood. It is not; you can change your behavior. But first you need to be aware of it and its causes. We hope that, being aware of the influence of your own childhood experiences on your present behavior, you will become more attuned to those behaviors in yourself that you do not like and make an effort to change them. Further, we hope that the knowledge of the impact of your behavior toward your children on their future relationships will be good motivation for you to try to treat them in ways that you would like to see them treat others.

Finally, it is important that you examine your feelings about discipline prior to reading the rest of this chapter so that you will be aware of how they influence your reactions to what you read. (This is always a good idea, but it is particularly important with respect to discipline since it is such an emotionally charged issue for many people.) For example, if you were hit frequently when you were a child and you don't think it did you any harm, and you intend to or already have routinely hit your own children, you may react very negatively to the suggestion that physical punishment is neither a very effective nor desirable form of behavior control (in terms of its long-term effects).

We do not intend to make anyone feel defensive about their own experiences. If you feel defensive, you'll put more energy into defense of your position than into learning something of potential value to you. What we will try to do is suggest some alternative means of behavior management that have been demonstrated to be more effective in their long-term consequences on a child's development than some of those traditionally used by many parents in the past.

The title of this chapter suggests the approach to discipline that will be presented here. It is an integration of information from a variety of sources on child development and childrearing practices and is supported by research findings as well as practical experience. Essentially, what we mean by "spare the rod and teach the child" is that discipline should not be defined as punishment for misbehavior;

rather, discipline (or "behavior management," a term we prefer) should be viewed as an ongoing process of teaching children to assume increasing responsibility for their own behavior and to develop inner controls to replace the outer controls that you exert on them. Behavior management should help children to learn the consequences of their actions and to take responsibility for them.

"Well-disciplined" children, then, are disciplined from within rather than from outside themselves. They act on their own initiative, with knowledge of how their behavior will affect themselves and others and with the willingness and expectation that they will accept full responsibility for their actions. They are concerned about the impact of their behavior on others, but are primarily motivated to act by their own inner convictions rather than by outside reward or punishment. In order to learn this kind of self-direction, however, children need positive guidance, feedback, and support given consistently by responsible adults throughout their early years.

PRINCIPLES OF BEHAVIOR MANAGEMENT

Behavior management is an inseparable part of the entire child-rearing process, and thus you will find repeated here many of the same principles of childrearing that have been offered in previous sections of the book. If your purpose in childrearing is to raise an intelligent, psychologically healthy, autonomous, happy individual who is self-assured yet sensitive to the needs and feelings of others, then your philosophy and methodology of behavior management must be consistent with the general principles of childrearing that support development of these characteristics.

Specifically, behavior management should be a routine part of your practice with children, not something that waits until there is a behavior problem. For example, it is a common wish of caregivers that their children learn to take care of their own lifespace and possessions in some kind of an organized and efficient way and without constant pestering. The time for learning this is not in adolescence, and it's not even when children are four years old and physically capable of picking up after themselves. It is much earlier, around eighteen months, when children begin to be interested in helping with household chores and in putting things in their places. But parents often fail to reinforce their children's natural interest at this time, because they're not very efficient, and it's easier to do it for them than to let them do something themselves.

There are many other examples of behaviors that should be capitalized on at the time they first begin to develop in order to avoid problems associated with them later. Eating is a common source of problems for many parents. Here again, children should be allowed and encouraged to learn to feed themselves whenever they begin to be interested in doing so (usually toward the end of the first year). As with all things, children will not be good at it when they first begin; they need practice in order to become skilled and efficient. But if you interfere with their efforts when those efforts are accompanied by enthusiasm, you will find it very difficult to interest children in the task later on when you feel they're old enough to be doing it themselves.

Responsibility for one's own behavior does not simply emerge overnight. It develops in small steps as children learn how to do more things for themselves. Too often in our culture, we see children kept very dependent on others far beyond the time that they should be, and then criticized for being irresponsible as they move into young adulthood. Responsibility is learned through experience at being responsible. As soon as children communicate an interest in doing something for themselves, they should be encouraged to do so. In that way, they will become increasingly responsible to themselves for their own behavior, very naturally, as their capacity to assume responsibility emerges.

This view of responsibility leads directly into one of the foremost issues of behavior management: the amount of freedom children should be given to make their own decisions, follow their own dictates, etc. Again, this is an issue that becomes most prominent in our culture in adolescence—when adults and children lock horns on how many restrictions there should be. And again, this is an issue that has its basis in early childhood. There is a reciprocal relationship between responsibility and freedom, such that the more responsibility persons assume for their own behavior, the more free they are of outer control. Freedom is not a gift; it is the reward that comes with being self-directed rather than other-directed.

But children can never be self-directed and responsible to themselves unless they are given the freedom to test their own limits; if they are always working within the boundaries set by their caregivers, they will never learn how much freedom *they* can handle. Children can only develop inner control through being given some freedom from outer control and trust to accept the responsibility for their own actions. Translated into practice, this means that children should be allowed as much freedom as they can responsibly handle, at their own pace.

For example, when they are coordinated enough (most children are, by three years), you should let them get themselves a drink of milk, juice, or water from the refrigerator instead of doing it for them.

You might help by putting it in a small, unbreakable pitcher and giving children their own plastic glass or cup (which they should wash when they're done). If they have an accident, help them to learn from it (i.e., why it happened, so they won't do it again) and, of course, to clean it up.

You will find, when freedom and responsibility are handled in this way, that responsibilities will be approached by children with delight rather than reluctance, since they will be signs of their growing competence and maturity. And children will develop a much more functional inner sense of how much freedom is comfortable for them than they could possibly learn if they were taught to depend on outer controls. A happy consequence of this approach in later years may be seen in an adolescent who is less likely to want to do things just because everyone else is doing them. Persons with a strong inner sense of what is right for them are much less easily influenced by a need for conformity to group pressures than those who have grown up relying on others to tell them what they could and could not do.

Early controls on young children must come from the outside, since they have no concern for property rights, too little fear of potentially dangerous things, and a zest for exploration that exceeds their sense of caution. But the goal of behavior management should be the gradual transference of control to children as they become able to internalize it. This goal can be accomplished only through methods of behavior management that guide children in the development of internal controls.

GUIDELINES AND TECHNIQUES FOR BEHAVIOR MANAGEMENT

As we have said before, behavior management is an integral part of the whole childrearing process, and the way it is handled will have a significant impact on the child's development as a person. Thus, the choice of appropriate disciplinary techniques must be made with the child's total growth in mind, not simply with concern for the immediate consequence of a particular technique. It is essential to always consider the long-term effects on the child of different techniques and approaches to behavior management. Of the following pages we include suggestions of techniques for behavior management which, if used appropriately with the individual child in mind, should promote the development of inner control and thus contribute to the child's sense of esteem. In addition, we will make note of those techniques which are potentially harmful to a child's self-concept and which tend to encourage the development of extrinsic motivation and dependence on others to direct one's behavior.

Developmental discipline[1]

We began this book with a statement of a basic premise or guideline for childrearing in general: Children's needs change as they grow, and therefore your treatment of them must change accordingly. The same guideline applies to behavior management. The kind of behavior you can reasonably expect and will accept from an eighteen-month-old child differs considerably from that which you can expect and are willing to accept from a five-year-old. Similarly, your responses to children's behavior must necessarily change as they develop.

Some of the changes that occur as children grow which affect the kinds of behavior management techniques that are necessary and possible include children's memory at different ages, their understanding of and ability to use language, the level of their thinking skills and their ability to generalize from one situation to another, and the kinds of behavior that are typical or expected at different ages. For example, children under two can often be managed best by being distracted from a potential problem situation, because their memories are short and they're likely to forget what they were involved in when something new and interesting is introduced. Language is usually ineffective in behavior management of children under two, but it can be used to explain to and reason with children over three.

As children's thinking skills grow and change, they learn to generalize from one situation to similar situations; so behavior management techniques should have as a goal, in the preschool years, giving children simple rules to apply to all situations rather than simply punishing each misbehavior individually. For younger children, however, generalization from one circumstance to another cannot be assumed, so it is wise to decide on a definite list of behaviors to be changed or avoided and to train those specifically (e.g., not touching hot things, not tearing up other people's things, not running into traffic).

Understanding what behaviors are developmentally appropriate at different stages of children's lives can help in the avoidance of many potential behavior problems. For example, runabout children are typically into everything they can get their hands on. They're not being "naughty" as we've heard many parents describe their children at this stage; they're simply expressing a very natural developmental urge to explore the world around them. Unfortunately, most homes are not set up to allow this kind of exploration. As we have suggested before, the only reasonable solution is to "baby-proof" the environment until the child develops more control.

[1] See Frances L. Ilg and Louise Bates Ames, *Child Behavior* (New York: Harper & Row, Publishers, 1955), Chapter 18, for an excellent review of developmental techniques.

Very young children are likely to tear pages in books, break toys, and otherwise destroy property. They do not mean to be destructive. But their skill with their hands is not as great as their urge to explore and experiment. Don't get angry; just remove valuable things or things you don't want destroyed from places where the child could get at them. Give children in this stage substitutes, such as junk mail or old magazines, and let them tear to their heart's content.

Dumping is another developmentally predictable behavior that can be a problem if you don't understand its significance. When children begin to gain enough control of their hands to let go in addition to holding on (usually toward the end of the first year and the beginning of the second), they begin practicing their new skill by dumping the contents of wastebaskets, drawers, cabinets, etc. You can put locks on cabinets you don't want ravaged, and you can put trash barrels up high; but you should indulge children's developmental needs by giving them acceptable substitutes (such as a basket for their toys, that they can dump into and out of).

The important thing to remember in developmental discipline is that *children do grow*. If you find ways to compromise between their developmental needs and peculiarities at different stages and your own need for some semblance of order and protection of your personal possessions, you will be rewarded by having your children outgrow these trying stages. On the other hand, if you make too much of an issue out of any of these temporary "problems," you may find that they linger.

Respect the rights of others

Most children age three and older can be taught one rule of behavior that encompasses all other behaviors: a modified version of the Golden Rule—*Respect the Rights of Others* (for younger children, fairness to others may be better understood). The importance of this rule for consistent use in behavior management cannot be overemphasized. Children do understand the concept of fair play, especially in terms of others' treatment of them. Most young children are very quick to point out that another child's taking something from them was "not being fair." In a democratic home, children readily let their parents know when they don't think they're being fair. So the place to begin (as with all things) is with a child's own experience. When Angie is mean to Shelley, remind her of how she felt the other day when Tammie did the same thing to her: "She wasn't being fair to you, and now you're not being fair to Shelley." Or if you notice Tommy doing something very thoughtful for his little sister, Michelle, compliment him for thinking about her; then you can refer to that incident in the future to remind him of the kind of behavior you mean when you ask him to be concerned about the needs and rights of others.

There is hardly a behavior, positive or negative, that cannot be related to this one rule—to respect others' rights, be concerned with their needs, and be fair to them. And children who learn to evaluate their own behavior according to this rule, in time, learn a very important lesson in addition to being aware of and concerned with others as people who have needs, wishes, rights, and feelings like them—they learn, also, to think before they act, to anticipate the consequences of their actions in terms of their impact on others. Of course, the first requirement for caregivers wishing to apply this rule to their behavior management techniques is: *you must be fair yourself.* You must consistently respect your children's rights (and be ready to apologize if you fail to do so, just as you would wish them to do if the situation were reversed). Your children, also, should have the right to point out when their own rights are being violated; a part of respecting people's rights and being fair is recognizing and standing up for your own rights. We urge you to try this technique with your children. It is an organizing principle which, alone, will teach many of the other individual principles we have suggested.

For example, one of the offshoots of using this guideline as a basis for your behavior management is the use of bargaining techniques to settle disputes. Ideally, a conflict situation can be resolved by deciding whose rights are being imposed upon and remedying the situation. For example, if Anthony takes Stacy's toy, he's not respecting Stacy's rights, and this can be given as a valid reason for his giving the toy back. But in real-life situations, it is often difficult to settle so easily; there is usually need for a compromise. This is when bargaining enters the picture.

For example, if Megan wants to stay up late and be with her parents' company and this is an imposition on her parents' rights and desires, they need to work out a fair bargain to resolve the issue. They can, for example, allow her to stay up a short while in exchange for her usual nighttime story. Or they could trade staying up for her doing something for them the next day such as helping with some housework (other than her usual responsibilities for her own things). This is a good technique because it encourages democratic practices in the home (so that neither parents nor children are allowed to become tyrannical), and it helps children learn to see things from another's point of view.

Punishment and reward

There are a number of generalizable guidelines and techniques for behavior management that apply, in principle, across age levels; that is, they seem to work no matter what age the child is. These guidelines, to be presented below, should form the skeleton of your behavior management strategies based on outer control. Then, developmental information should be used to modify these techniques so that your behavior management is always individualized and child-oriented. The guidelines to be presented are based on research in what is called "social learning theory." (The techniques derived from this research will be better known to you as "behavior modification.")

The basic premise of social learning theory is that behavior is learned primarily through positive and negative reinforcement (more or less the same as reward and punishment, with some differences).[2] "Bad" behavior is learned, just as "good" behavior is, and any behavior that a child exhibits can be changed by systematic application of behavior modification techniques. Where the techniques become individualized is in considering what is rewarding and what is punishing to a particular child. There are some things that are generally rewarding to all people, but each person also has a set of positive and negative reinforcers that are peculiar to him.

Do you remember the story of Br'er Rabbit and the briar patch? For most people, being thrown into a briar patch would indeed be unpleasant (a negative reinforcer), and Br'er Rabbit was able to convince Br'er Fox that this was true for him as well: "Whatever you do, please don't throw me into the briar patch. . . ." But as it turned out, the briar patch was a very acceptable place for Br'er Rabbit (a positive reinforcer) because he grew up there. There's a lesson here for dealing effectively with children. Don't give rewards or punishment based on what would be rewarding or punishing to *you*. Rather, find out what is rewarding or punishing to the child. Part of your answer (or at least where you can start looking) is that it depends on what the child is used to.

For example, it might seem to you that yelling at a child would be a definitely negative reinforcer. But for a child whose main attention from important adults has been yelling, yelling is a positive reinforcer. What that means is that this child will be likely to repeat those behaviors for which he is yelled at. All people, including children, are highly motivated by a need for attention, and they'll take it any way

2 Positive and negative reinforcement works as follows: If you do something, and something desirable happens (not necessarily as a consequence—maybe just coincidentally), then you'll be likely to do that thing again. Anything that definitely becomes associated with desirable consequences is likely to be repeated. That's positive reinforcement. In contrast, if you do something and something undesirable occurs, you'll be likely to try to avoid doing that thing again in the future. Anything that definitely becomes associated with undesirable consequences is likely not to be repeated. That's negative reinforcement. The thing that makes it a bit complex, however, as we explain within this chapter, is that what is positively reinforcing to one person may be negatively reinforcing to someone else.

they can get it. Some people have been fortunate enough to have received most attention for positive behaviors, and they tend to repeat those kinds of behaviors in order to continue to receive attention. Others, however, have a past record of only receiving attention when they did something wrong, so they tend to repeat those kinds of behaviors in order to continue to receive attention.

The fact of the matter is that there is generally no better way to draw attention to yourself than to do something wrong. Look at the amount of attention paid by the newspapers, radio, and television to crime in contrast to the amount of attention that they pay to the hard work and good deeds that people do every day trying to make this a better world to live in. We can't do a great deal, right now, to change the whole societal structure of which the news is just one part, but we can, in our personal lives, begin to change our responses to others and especially to children; and that, like water slowly wears away stone, will eventually change the society.

At the end of each day, ask yourself whether you paid as much attention to the good things your children did as you did to the bad. If you can answer yes to that, you'll be making a real difference in your children's behavior, now and in the future.

So far, we have offered two general guidelines: (1) what is positively or negatively reinforcing to a child is, to some extent, individual to him and based on his past experience; and (2) if you want to see a behavior again, pay attention to it.

The next guideline is the partner of the second: ignore behaviors you don't want to see, and positively reinforce a behavior that is its opposite (e.g., ignore the child's whining to get something, and give her what she wants when she asks for it without whining).

Just as attention is a universal positive reinforcer (remembering that the particular brand of attention that is rewarding depends on the child), so withdrawal of attention is a universal negative reinforcer. If you consistently ignore a child when she shows a particular behavior, and if you also give positive reinforcement for a behavior that is incompatible with the behavior that you want to get rid of, it is very likely that the unwanted behavior will, over time, disappear.

The point of a negative reinforcer is just the opposite of that of a positive reinforcer. Whereas a positive reinforcer will increase the probability of a behavior occurring, a negative reinforcer will decrease the probability of a behavior occurring again.

In general, withdrawal of attention is an effective negative reinforcer. But it is mainly useful for behaviors that you can afford to spend some time getting rid of. When a child does something that must be stopped right away, ignoring is not a good idea. For example, if a child is beating another child over the head with a block, you can't ignore it.

In that case, a different approach is called for: You can remove the child from the situation, giving as little feeling as possible, either positive or negative (that is, try to be calm and neutral). Then, give him a "time-out" to think about his behavior. When *he* feels that he can change his behavior, i.e., when he has calmed down enough that he feels he can work out the conflict in a more socially acceptable way, he should be allowed to return to the group.

In cases like this, various different techniques work, depending on the child. With some children, the best thing might be to follow the advice offered by Kamii and DeVries in their reading at the end of this chapter: let the children work it out among themselves. In another case, the child may be acting out as a cry for help, and therefore what is required is to talk to her to try to find out what's bothering her. Whatever the situation, always make your management individualized and child-centered; don't unthinkingly use any particular technique without regard for the particular children involved.

People sometimes become upset at the thought of using conscious, deliberate rewards and/or punishments (that is, extrinsic motivation) to get a child to behave in a certain way. If you feel manipulative by deciding consciously which are positive and which are negative behaviors, realize that you do it all the time unconsciously. Just try to define positive behaviors in terms of what is productive for the child and negative behaviors as those which are nonproductive. The ultimate goal of this brand of behavior management should also be to help children take responsibility for their own behavior so that they become less susceptible to extrinsic rewards and punishments and more attuned to the intrinsic reward or punishment of different behaviors for them as persons.

Make the punishment fit the crime

We talked at the beginning of the chapter about the goal of behavior management being to help children become inner- rather than outer-controlled, to become increasingly more responsible for their own behavior. Some of the techniques already mentioned will support that goal (e.g., respect for the rights of others); other methods of behavior management (e.g., extrinsic rewards and punishment) may serve to change behavior on a short-term basis, but will not, *by themselves,* do anything to promote the development of inner control.

For example, a promise of a special privilege, a piece of candy, and a smile are all examples of extrinsic rewards that may be given a small child in order to positively reward a good behavior. A spanking, taking away a special privilege, making children go to their room or leave the group of children they were playing with, and getting angry with children are all examples of extrinsic punishments that may be used to make children change their behaviors. Some are more effective than others, but none of them, per se, demands any participation on the part of the child; they will not, alone, do anything to promote the development of inner control.

The reading by Kamii and DeVries gives examples of punishments that "fit the crime"—they have a direct relationship to the problem behavior, and they require some change in the child's behavior. That, then, is the key. Spanking and yelling at children may temporarily stop a particular behavior, but both of those punishments take the responsibility away from the child. Once you've been extrinsically punished, that's the end of it. On the other hand, if you require children to do something to account for their own behavior, then they will learn inner control.

When children are struck or yelled at in an attempt to "teach them better behavior"—better, in the sense that they will learn not to do something—they learn only to avoid the behavior's punishment; they do not learn inner reason and control. We remove responsibility from the "offender" when we get angry or hit him or punish him in some way that has nothing to do with his misbehavior. The incident ends (except for resentment and sadness) when the punishment occurs. Equally important, when we, as adults, physically punish (with the lofty excuse that it is a vehicle for learning), we really teach that such behavior is acceptable, that hitting is an acceptable form of expression. Also, children who have been punished in this way are more likely to become adults who always weigh an expected punishment against the desire or impulse to commit a punishable act, rather than acting on their own conscience.

Can you remember how you felt as a child when you were yelled at or hit when you did something wrong? If you were like most children, you probably didn't learn very much from the punishment. Even as adults, when we are "attacked" verbally or physically, our natural reaction is to defend ourselves, not to listen to the reason we are being punished. Too often parents completely miss the opportunity to turn a mistake or misbehavior into a valuable lesson because their means of punishment makes the child too defensive to be open to learning.

Isn't the goal of improved behavior, guided by inner control and reason, thwarted by "teaching" through aversive punishment? Hitting and otherwise punishing by removing responsibility enhances extrinsic motivation for behavior—we come to rely almost exclusively on others to "pay us" for our bad acts, rather than acting in accordance with our own intrinsic values and beliefs about ourselves. We ought to be helping children to come to want to behave in accordance with how they see themselves and how they want to be, not teaching them to avoid this. We teach them to avoid intrinsic responsibility every time we as adults take the responsibility from them with the "short-cut" way of dealing with behavior and discipline—discipline by senseless punishment, yelling, or hitting. We must always consider the long-term implications of our behavior management techniques for children's growth as persons.

Say what you mean and mean what you say

Be careful in your response to a misbehavior that you clearly differentiate for children your feelings about them from your feelings about what they did. You should feel very free to express feelings of anger or annoyance at your child's behavior if you really feel them; that's much better than trying not to show them and thus giving off strained feelings. But be sure that children never confuse your annoyance at their behavior with a loss of your love for them. You will help communicate the right message by being very straightforward and honest about your feelings. That will help the child to read your message clearly because your messages are open rather than hidden.

Think about your own experiences with people. Wouldn't you rather have a friend or mate who told you when they were upset and explained why rather than one who pretended everything was all right but acted strangely toward you? In the first case, you know what you're dealing with, so you can handle it; in the second case, you're made very uneasy and even a bit paranoid, wondering if it's just your imagination (especially if they tell you, in a "martyred" way, that there's nothing wrong). In a similar way, direct messages are much easier, less confusing, and less potentially damaging to the child's sense of esteem than hidden, unspoken messages. When you do say something, mean it. Don't make threats or promises you're not going to keep. Don't tell children not to do something and then let them do it. Don't say no when you mean maybe. Say what you mean, and mean what you say!

A SUMMATION OF THOUGHTS ON BEHAVIOR MANAGEMENT

Children learn more from the way you act, the way you treat them and others, than from what you tell them or try to teach them. You should, therefore, be aware of what things your behavior is teaching your children, especially if it's different from what you want to teach them in words. Children do not follow the directions to "do as I say, not as I do." You should not hit your children to punish them for hitting other children. By hitting them, you teach them to hit others; your behavior shows them that temper and violence are acceptable forms of expression.

Also, be aware of what behaviors you are reinforcing in your children by the way you react to their behavior. Many behavior problems are created by well-meaning adults who meant to keep the child from showing just that kind of behavior. For example, suppose you can't stand whining. So every time your child whines, you get very angry at her and/or you end up giving her what she wants to stop her from whining. Either way, and especially if you do both, you are making sure your child will whine every time she wants something, because (1) you pay attention to her when she does it; and (2) it works—she gets what she wants.

On the more positive side, and as a general rule, ignore behaviors you don't like (unless they are harmful to you, your child, or anyone else) and respond positively to behaviors you do like. Children (and adults) crave attention, positive or negative. Try to pay more attention to positive behaviors and less to negative ones. Your children generally will learn to stop the behaviors you don't like and continue the ones you do like. Remember, however, if you're trying to undo a behavior that has been around for a while, it also will take a while to get rid of it.

Another important rule is to *be consistent*. Be consistent with your love, so that your child knows that you can be counted on for support and help when they are needed. You can never, never spoil a child with love. Your children should be able to take your love for granted; they should never have to worry about it. This will make discipline easier for you too, because you can teach your children that they have done something you didn't like without also causing them to fear that you don't like them because of it. Don't threaten to stop loving your child, and don't withdraw your love as a punishment. You can withdraw positive attention, but your love should be a constant.

Be consistent with your discipline. If there are things your children are not allowed to do, they should never be allowed to do them. Do not let them get away with something one day because you're feeling good and then get mad at them another day for the same thing because you're in a bad mood. If it's not important enough to be consistent about, then it's not important enough to get angry about. Inconsistency is confusing to children; they need to know what behaviors are acceptable and which ones are not so that they know where they stand and so they can learn to predict the consequences of their behavior.

Of course, even with the best intentions, everyone loses his temper sometimes. There's no point in feeling guilty about it. One wonderful thing about young children is that you always have another chance; they're very willing to forgive. Don't be afraid to apologize for losing your temper or responding unjustly to a child. We're all human, and it's a good lesson for a child to learn to admit a mistake. Also, don't let your concern with consistency make you inflexible. Sometimes children whine for a reason. If you ignore it every time, never checking to find out why, you could hurt a child's feelings unnecessarily. Before ignoring or punishing a negative behavior, give children their "day in court"; see if they have a reason for acting as they did.

If children are going to be punished, then do it at the time they're doing something to be punished for, not later. If you see them beginning to do something wrong, stop them right away; don't wait for them to finish the deed. Don't threaten anger or punishment, and don't build up to a punishment in little steps (e.g., starting with "Don't do that," said hesitantly as if you don't really mean it, and building up to a spanking). A firm "No!" said with real conviction is much more effective than "If you don't stop that, I'm going to. . . ." Also, if you tell children you're going to do something, then carry through with it. Don't promise things you're not going to do. You'll only teach them not to believe you.

If you punish children for something, tell them why. You want them to learn from their mistakes and not repeat them any more often than necessary to remember that they're not supposed to do certain things. And give them a good reason, not just because you said so. If not used as a catch-all, it is certainly valid for you not to want them to do something because it really bothers you. But if you know that it's really your problem, let children know that too. Whenever possible, show and tell children what they can do *instead* of the problem behavior (e.g., "Ask for a turn instead of pushing").

Don't have a large list of "no's." Decide what's really important, such as not playing with matches, not running into the street, not touching a hot stove, etc. and be absolutely consistent about those things. Structure the environment so that you avoid as many potential problems as possible. For example, remove things that could be problems, such as breakables, when your child is at the stage of grabbing everything. Don't expect self-control from children when their natural developmental urges tell them to explore and investigate the environment, and don't make them think they're bad for following their own inner drives toward mastery. Just try to keep things not meant for exploration out of their reach.

Children inevitably develop habits that can be annoying to their caregivers. Many annoying behaviors, such as whining and playing with food, only stay around if you pay attention to them; consistently ignore them, and they will go away after a while. Others, of course, like thumb-sucking or constantly carrying around an old blanket, toy, or other "prized" object, may persist in spite of you because they are intrinsically satisfying to the child. Decide whether your dislike of a behavior is really as important to you as the behavior is important to the child. When it no longer serves any function for the child, she will give it up.

Nail-biting, thumb-sucking, bed-wetting, rocking back and forth, and various tics are common ways children have of expressing temporary anxieties. If they continue over a long period of time, you should examine whether you're being overly critical or evaluative of the child or too demanding (e.g., expecting children to be too controlled, mature, and responsible for their age). Ease the pressure, and many of these kinds of habits will disappear. If you find that your child is lying a great deal, especially to cover up for misbehavior, examine your relationship—are you accepting enough of him that he can feel safe to tell you the truth?

Discipline should be seen as a way of protecting children and teaching them responsibility for their own actions as they get older; it should not be viewed as punishment for misbehavior. It's like preventive medicine: If you do a good job with behavior management all the time, misbehavior will be minor, seldom, and easy to deal with. Punishment should be reserved for very important things, and it should be the kind that requires the child to learn something from it. For example, if a child hits another child, she should be given a time out from playing while she thinks about her behavior; when she can change it, she should be allowed to rejoin the group. Harsh and abusive punishment (e.g., yelling at children or hitting them) only stops bad behavior temporarily, and what it teaches best is avoidance of punishment; it does not teach the child to refrain from repeating the problem behavior.

Use problem situations and misbehavior as opportunities for teaching. For example, talk calmly to children about why their action or behavior was unacceptable. If they're over three, ask them how they would feel if someone did something like that to them. Relate their behavior, if you can, to a similar situation they have experienced—e.g., "Do you remember when Joseph took away your toy? How did you feel?" "Well, it made Vivien unhappy too when you messed up her picture." As much as possible, listen to the children's version of the story and direct your questioning to get them to talk about it rather than your telling them what you think about it. Don't turn your teaching into a moral lecture.

In a preschool setting, you can use common problem situations as a focus for occasional organized dramatic play. Have a couple of children play the roles of two children squabbling, for example, and have a few more watch. You can stop the role-playing, have the children switch roles, trade with a couple of children in the audience, and so on. Then you can talk about what happened, why, and what should be done about it. You can learn a great deal from listening to the children's responses. It's generally a good idea *not* to use children who were actually involved in a problem situation to act it out at first; it could get out of hand. Let them be in the audience. Also, if it's slow starting, you can help by playing one of the roles.

Let children settle their own disputes as much as possible without your interference. They learn important social skills through working things out among themselves.

Most important, react to problem behavior appropriately, according to the age of the child. In general, hitting children is not a good idea because it only teaches them that hitting is an acceptable form of behavior. Never hit children under two years. They won't learn anything from it, and it will make them afraid and confused. Remove them, bodily, from the problem situation without a fuss, and distract them with a toy or other activity. If problem behavior persists, ignore them until the behavior improves. Don't threaten to or actually withdraw your love, but do withdraw your attention.

Use eye control and touch control instead of yelling or hitting, especially in that period around two years when children begin to have tantrums. A firm but gentle hand on the child's shoulder or arm, or holding both her hands in yours while you look into her eyes, accompanied by soft, rhythmic talking (it doesn't matter what you say; it's the soothing quality of the sound that's important) will stop or calm down a tantrum much more effectively than yelling. Eye control for children in the runabout stage and beyond can be very effective; the child will learn to "read" the message in your look, and you won't have to yell.

Talk to children over three and explain simply what the problem is. Don't make them feel guilty. Never make them feel that they were bad, but only that you didn't like the behavior. Don't embarrass children in front of friends. Give them a chance to save face by telling them to go off, think about the behavior and come back when they think they can change it. (This is especially appropriate if the child has been hitting or taking things from others.)

Don't expect behavior from a two-year-old that you'd expect from a five-year-old, and you'll save headaches. By five, most children, given good behavior management up to that time, can be expected to have assumed a good deal of responsibility for their own behaviors; they have developed some inner controls. But the two-year-old still needs a great deal of outer control, preferably in the form of avoidance of problem situations as much as possible; actual restraint should be kept to a minimum.

Two can be a difficult time, but if handled well, those two-year-old behaviors won't carry over into later ages. Remember that two-year-olds are trying out their new independence. They're still part baby, but trying to be child. So it appears that one minute they're reasonable, the next they're angry. Their anger usually comes from frustration—not being able to do something, or having something turn out differently from what they expected. At this age children know certain things about the world; they have developed rules for the way things work. If a routine changes or something unexpected happens, it can be cause for a tantrum. You can help not by getting upset, but rather by ignoring the temper. Sometimes you will need to reassure them too, because children frighten themselves with the strength of their tempers, and often they can't control them.

It is impossible to give you all the answers to handling behavior problems, especially since each child is different. In general, if you remember that you're reinforcing any behavior you pay attention to, even yelling at a child, and if you examine your responses to the child, you can begin to handle his behavior better by being more aware of your own.

The readings that follow expand on some of the ideas that have been presented about behavior management. The first is about punishment; from interviews with a large number of mothers about their childrearing practices, Sears and his associates conclude that punishment "is ineffectual over the long term as a technique for eliminating the kind of behavior toward which it is directed." The second reading is a selection by Drs. Kamii and DeVries that offers a different concept of "punishment," derived from Piaget's work. Finally, a short piece entitled "Making Sense of Discipline" suggests that sometimes the best "discipline" is letting children experience the natural consequences of their actions.

Punishment

Robert Sears, Eleanor Maccoby, and Harry Levin

In the last chapter, the reading by Gordon mentioned several studies by Sears et al. This selection is taken from the book that reports on one of those studies. As part of a larger research study undertaken by the staff of the Laboratory of Human Development of the Graduate School of Education of Harvard University, Sears and his colleagues interviewed almost 400 American mothers. They asked them questions about their childrearing practices and encouraged them to talk about their feelings about being a parent as well as the results of their training methods.

Although the purpose of the interviews was to reveal how mothers actually bring up their children rather than how they should, valuable information was gained when all the collected data were compiled about which kinds of techniques were most or least successful. The section we have chosen on punishment is that kind of finding. From the mothers' own reports it is apparent that a punitive approach to changing a child's behavior is not generally effective. More often, the behavior that the child is being punished for is strengthened by the punishment rather than eliminated: a child punished for being dependent and clingy will become more so. A child punished for aggressive behavior will be more aggressive. This finding is consistent with the principles of social behavior we have been discussing: (1) if you want to see a behavior again, pay attention to it; punishment is a form of attention; and (2) children learn to model their behavior from ones they observe in important others; if they are hit, they learn to hit others.

In our discussion of the training process we have contrasted punishment with reward. Both are techniques used for changing the chiild's habitual ways of acting. Do they work equally well? The answer is unequivocally "no"; but to be truly unequivocal, the answer must be understood as referring to the kind of punishment we were able to measure by our interview method. We could not, as one can with laboratory experiments on white rats or pigeons, examine the effects of punishment on isolated bits of behavior. Our measures of punishment, whether of the object-oriented or love-oriented variety, referred to *levels of punitiveness* in the mothers. That is, the amount of use of punishment that we measured was essentially a measure of a personality quality of the mothers. Punitiveness, in contrast with rewardingness, was a quite ineffectual quality for a mother to inject into her child training.

The evidence for this conclusion is overwhelming. The unhappy effects of punishment have run like a dismal thread through our findings. Mothers who punished toilet accidents severely ended up with bed-wetting children. Mothers who punished dependency to get rid of it had more dependent children than mothers who did not punish. Mothers who punished aggressive behavior severely had more aggressive children than mothers who punished lightly. They also had more dependent children. Harsh physical punishment was associated with high childhood aggressiveness and with the development of feeding problems.

Our evaluation of punishment is that *it is ineffectual over the long term as a technique for eliminating the kind of behavior toward which it is directed.* This sentence must be read carefully. We are not concerned here with whether aggressiveness and dependency are good or bad, or whether a mother should or should not want to eliminate them. A good many mothers in our group *did* want their maturing children to behave unaggressively and non-dependently toward the parents, and certainly none of the mothers liked either feeding problems or chronic bed-wetting. But these attitudes are beside the point. Having decided to eliminate certain kinds of changeworthy behavior, mothers varied in the extent to which they used punishment as the *method.* By their own reports of their children's behavior, the method did not work.

As we emphasized in our earlier discussions of this matter, our present data do not permit a sure conclusion on the question of whether punishment actually increased the kinds of behavior it was designed to reduce; there is always the possibility that children who initially showed more of a particular kind of undesired behavior received more severe punishment. Whether this was the case or not, however, there is clear evidence that continuing punishment of changeworthy behavior was associated with greater intensity of such behavior than was a non-punitive method of handling the behavior.

In addition, of course, we have seen a demonstration of the side-effects of punishment, particularly physical punishment and the severe punishment of aggression toward parents. The former was associated with feeding problems, with aggression in the home, and with flight or aggressive reactions to deviant behavior—what we have called the slow development of conscience.

These findings all relate to child behavior that occurred over reasonably long periods of time. That is, the aggressiveness that we measured was a *level* of such action, a day-in-and-day-out frequency and intensity. We did not—and could not with the interview—determine the effectiveness of punishment as a device for eliminating single items of behavior, such as a single kind of aggressive act like biting. From the details as reported by a number of mothers, we are inclined to believe that punishment of specific acts not infrequently had just the effect the mother wanted. This seemed especially to be the case when she was able to explain fully what she was punishing for and what substitute behavior would be desirable. It must be remembered that punishment is not only an impelling force, but also a directive one. A slap on the hand will not only make a child jerk; it will make him jerk *away* from the forbidden object. If the punishment is of a kind that produces (directs) action of a kind the mother wants, the punishment is likely to have a salutary effect—just as an offered reward would have. Some of the mothers seemed to have discovered this principle, and thought they were able to get good results from punishment. But we report this as an impression, only; a different method of research will be required to discover what, if any, is an efficient way of using punishment for the elimination of isolated bits of changeworthy behavior.

Piaget for Early Education

Constance Kamii and Rheta DeVries

The section of Kamii and DeVries' manuscript that is presented here contains an explanation of Piaget's approach to discipline and punishment. The ideas are very much in line with the approach that we have presented in this chapter—that discipline and punishment are not practices that can be separated from the rest of the child's learning; they are intimately tied to the child's development of autonomy and moral judgment. As such, appropriate adult practices are those that (1) as much as possible, treat the child as an equal; (2) facilitate children's working out their own conflicts; (3) help children to take responsibility for their own actions; and (4) are directly related and appropriate to a child's misdemeanors.

We will discuss below the art of promoting interpersonal coordination in connection with the teacher's use of her adult power to facilitate exchange of points of view.

Practice cooperation and equality with the child insofar as this

Constance Kamii and Rheta DeVries, "Piaget for Early Education," in R. K. Parker, ed., *The Preschool in Action*, 2nd ed. (Boston: Allyn and Bacon, in press), pp. 23–27. © 1974 by Constance Kamii and Rheta DeVries and used by permission of the authors.

This chapter describes a curriculum for preschool education based on Jean Piaget's work that has been developed by the authors over the last few years. A more detailed description of this curriculum will be published by Prentice-Hall, Inc. under the same title.

is possible.* When we say that the adult should "practice equality" with children, we do not mean that we have to act in all ways on a completely equal basis with children. Every child knows that adults are not children, and there is no use trying to kid them. What Piaget advocates is treating children as the adult's equal *to the extent that it is possible.* For example, if we want children to be careful not to break certain objects, we can either establish certain rules for everyone to follow or explain that it would make us feel very bad to have these things broken. The latter approach places the child and the adult on an equal basis as human beings who have feelings which can be hurt by one another. This approach is in contrast with invoking adult authority or preaching abstract virtues. Invoking adult authority and preaching go counter to the child's moral development because they get him to abide by a rule through external control rather than through the autonomous construction of his own moral rules.

Although we advocate equality and cooperation with the child, we recognize with Piaget that coercion is unavoidable in countless instances (for example, in order to insure survival when the child is about to run out into the street). Adults are also coercive when they require children to obey their rules, such as going to bed and not eating candy before meals. Even when this is done with warmth and affection, coercion is present when the child *feels* coerced, regardless of the adult's intentions. Piaget (1932) says, "adult authority . . . perhaps . . . constitutes a necessary moment in the moral evolution of the child" (p. 319).

Thus, the educational challenge is to *maximize* the child's opportunities for constructing his moral values, his intelligence, and his personality through *autonomous choices.* Wherever possible, adults should make the child realize that choices exist. When choice is not possible and the adult must curtail the child's autonomy for whatever reason, he should try to make himself as equal to the child as possible in imposing his wishes. Examples of what we mean are given shortly.

We are *not* saying that a child will be psychologically damaged for life if an adult slaps his hand away from an electrical outlet or even if a parent consistently refuses to permit the child to play certain musical instruments in the house. What we are saying is that if the bulk of the child's *do's* and *don'ts* are determined by the adults, the child will not have enough opportunity to practice the autonomy necessary for his moral and intellectual development.

Punishment is sometimes an unavoidable and appropriate means of

* We would like to acknowledge the assistance of N. Fortin, Assistant at the University of Geneva, in putting these principles into the perspective of a classroom teacher.

helping children become conscious of the need for cooperation with others. In this connection, we have to be very clear as to why we sometimes punish children in the classroom. There are three kinds of situations: (1) when a child is in conflict with another child, (2) when the teacher and the child are in direct conflict, and (3) when a child's behavior goes counter to the welfare of the group for which the teacher is responsible.

In the first situation, as we said above in connection with peer interactions, the teacher's attempt should be to facilitate an exchange of viewpoints so that the children can come to a resolution of their own conflict. Separating them is generally a poor way to intervene because when children are separated, the problem may be "solved" for the time being, but the parties involved cannot learn anything about interpersonal regulation. The preaching of virtues, such as "We must all share," is also not educational, since it is the imposition of a ready-made rule from the outside. The timing of certain remarks such as "Who had it first?" and "What do you think you should do?" when the children are hitting each other is truly an art. The teacher's power in this situation should be consciously limited to restraining the children while trying to get them to calm down, decenter, and find a solution on their own.

The second and third situations (direct teacher-child conflict and conflict between the child and the group for which the teacher is responsible) are not always distinguishable. We will, therefore, discuss principles of teaching for both of these situations together.

Piaget distinguishes between expiatory punishment and punishment by reciprocity. Expiatory punishments are those which are arbitrary in relation to the misdeeds, with no relation between the content of the guilty act and the nature of its punishment. Depriving the child of dessert for telling a lie, or making him write 100 times "I shall never lie again," are typical examples. Such punishments go hand in hand with coercion and the external imposition of respect for the law.

In contrast, punishment by reciprocity has a natural or logical relation to the misdeed and can therefore be more easily accepted as just by the child. Piaget (1932) notes the following six types of punishment by reciprocity:

a. *Excluding the wrongdoer from the social group.* Exclusion demonstrates to him that his act has temporarily broken the social bond with others. For example, children may refuse to play a game with a child who cheats. When a particular child disrupts the group, the teacher may say, "You are bothering everybody now. I want you to go rest for a while and calm down in the doll corner until you can come back." Ideally, this suggestion should come from other children rather than the teacher. The teacher can also try to get some children to say, "You are bothering us!"

b. *Allowing the logical or natural material consequences to follow a misdeed.* For example, a certain child had the habit of knocking down other children's block constructions. One day, the victims got tired of being victimized and decided to go get a bigger boy to come and bring justice to the situation. Not without apprehension, the teacher let this situation evolve. The bigger boy "took care" of the aggressive four-year-old in combat and let him know that he would be back again if the destructiveness did not stop. The teacher wondered what would happen next. The group rejected the aggressive child for a while but, before long, they invited him back "but *only* if you don't mess things up any more." The fact that the group invited the aggressive child back was probably a reflection of the general atmosphere the teacher had already created.

c. *Depriving the child of a thing he has misused.* For example, if a child tears a book, the teacher may say, "Look, that's *my* book I put out for everybody to enjoy. If it were *your* book, you could do anything you please with it. But since it's *my* book, I will lend it only to the children who can take care of it. . . ." Note that the teacher here is being coercive but is also putting herself on the same level as the child. She is saying to him that he has the right to do whatever *he* wants with *his* belongings. She is likewise saying that she has the right to do whatever she wants with *her* belongings.

d. *Doing to the child what he has done.* For example, when a child refuses to help at clean-up time, the adult can later refuse to help the child. Piaget points out, however, that "this kind of punishment, while it is perfectly legitimate when we want to make the child understand the results of his actions, becomes irritating and absurd when it only means giving back evil for evil, and capping one irreparable destruction with another" (p. 208).

e. *Encouraging the child to make restitution.* For example, if a child knocks down somebody else's block construction, he can be asked if he wants to help rebuild it. Ideally, the victimized peer should be the one to demand restitution. When the adult forces restitution, the child's compliance is restitution in behavior only, and does not reflect cooperative reciprocity. It is far preferable for the child to make restitution out of some desire of his own. Sometimes children are more punitive than adults, and they generally do not consider a wrongdoer's intention. For example, when a child knocked down a big jar of paint one day, some children reacted with strong disapproval and condemnation. The teacher intervened at this point, casually saying, "All we have to do is clean it up. You know it was an accident. Let's all help."

f. *Censuring the child without further punishment.* Censure is often sufficient to make a child realize that he has broken the bond of mutual trust and solidarity by doing something that displeases others. If there is a strong relationship between the child and whoever expresses disapproval, this expression is usually enough to make the child want to avoid disapproval in the future.

Piaget warns us that any of the above forms of punishment can take on an expiatory character according to the spirit in which it is applied. The important element, therefore, is the adult's attitude of reciprocity. Although the above punishments can be used by an adult, they can also be used by peers. Punishment by peers particularly promotes the development of reciprocity.

The reader may wonder whether or not the above six types should be called "punishment." As usual, Piaget's terminology is slightly different from the dictionary sense. From the standpoint that there is an element of coercion in these interventions, however, we must agree that they share certain qualities with punishment. When we want to communicate our expectations to children, the principle to keep in mind at all times is to put ourselves as much as possible in a position of equality with the child. A relationship of equality is what maximizes a child's opportunity to make choices in a truly autonomous way.

REFERENCE

PIAGET, J. *The moral judgment of the child.* New York: The Free Press, 1965. (First published in French as *Le jugement moral chez l'enfant.* Paris: Alcan, 1932.)

Making Sense of Discipline

Hettie Jones

This selection is taken from "The Open Home," a short monthly pamphlet containing easy-to-read, common-sense ideas about living

Hettie Jones, "Making Sense of Discipline," *The Open Home,* Series 2, No. 1 (1973). Reprinted by permission.

and learning with children. The piece on discipline that we've chosen to include here explains another, very important perspective on discipline as a teaching process. Caregivers too often obscure the natural lesson that results from many problem situations: they either protect the child from the consequences of his actions or they punish in addition rather than directing their attention to the natural consequences (e.g., "See what happens when you're not careful with your toys. I'm sorry your doll got hurt, and we'll try to fix her. But maybe next time, you'll be more careful."). The author gives a number of practical examples of how to discipline fairly and effectively, so that the discipline makes sense to the child, and she can learn from it.

A baby bumped into a wall and hit his head. The wall wasn't punishing him for bumping against it. It had no rules. It wasn't even angry. It was only a wall. But bumping into the wall caused a consequence that told the baby something about the way the world is: Walls can't be walked through.

The baby crawled to his mommy, settled comfily in her arms, laughed, grabbed her hair and pulled with pleasure. Mommy frowned and said, "Ouch," and undid his fists from her hair. She didn't punish him. She had no rule. She wasn't even angry. But the baby learned of another cause and consequence in this complicated world: If you pull people's hair, they are unhappy with you.

This baby was being disciplined. Whether it comes as the wall's solidness or his mother's "ouch," discipline is what happens when a child bumps up against reality, takes in the consequences he causes. The trouble is that walls are self-evident; people are not. We make up a punishment for spilled milk when the real consequence is cleaning it up. We make rules, "No jumping in the house," when the real issue is complaining neighbors in the apartment below. We haul out moral regulations, "Gum chewing is vulgar," when what we could so easily say is that *we* just can't stand the way it looks. And finally we make nonsense of reason by saying, "Because I say so." It is not discipline to layer rule on rule, to hit, to yell, to give a moral lecture, to be the boss. It is discipline to be, like the wall, expressive of what you are like, what situations mean, how people feel and how it all makes sense.

A child who uses the stick he is playing with as a weapon must be stopped. There could be a sudden rule, "No playing with sticks." But sticks are good for playing—for digging in the sand, for fishing poles and golf clubs, for marshmallow skewers, drumsticks, batons. Everybody plays with sticks. There could be a punitive consequence. "I saw what you were doing with that stick. Now you'll have to sit on the bench until it's time to go home." But sitting on the bench has nothing to do with what is happening. The real issue is the child's ability to deal safely with the stick, himself and another child. That's what he needs to know about. A stick is hard, sharp and hurts. You will not allow him to hurt others. Either he can do safe things with the stick, or he can't use the stick at all for now. And you can say so; and you can take the stick away.

Discipline makes sense when it is a way of explaining what is really happening. If your child slops water all over the bathroom floor, that's not a crime; it's a nuisance. You're tired; you need his help to clean it up: "Yes, it's hard." "Yes, it takes a long time." "Yes, it puts me in a bad mood." "That's what happens when you slop water on the bathroom floor."

If your child insists on bringing a big baby doll with her on a trip to the zoo, explain the consequences—she will have to carry it the whole time you're there. If she will not wear mittens, you won't be able to help her out if her hands get cold. If she will not eat lunch, she won't be able to eat until dinner time. Stick with the consequences —she caused them. That's discipline. That's simply, sensibly, the way things are.

7

Learning Is Growing

What images come to your mind when you think of learning? Do you think of sitting in a classroom and being told something by a teacher? Do you think of memorizing names and dates for a history course, or of proving theorems in geometry? Do you imagine reading a book or watching a movie or TV show that you really enjoy and that gives you an insight you lacked? Or do you feel you are learning when something helps you in some way, in your day-to-day life? Would you consider getting to know yourself better and getting along with others a part of learning? What about sports and other forms of recreation? Do you think they involve learning?

Clearly, learning is a bit of all these things, and more. But paradoxically, the first examples, those referring to "school learning" (as a rule) actually involve less real learning than any of the others. How much can you remember of what you learned in school (or, if you're still in school, of what you "learned" last year)? If you're like most people, your answer probably is "not very much." There are many things in our lives that we "learn" and then forget; these are things that have no particular importance to us, that are in no way applicable to the real lives we lead outside the classroom. Or they may be things that were once important but are not any longer (e.g., the phone number of a former friend).

These thoughts about learning are important to keep in mind when we think about what is meant by learning in relation to young children.[1] There are many ideas and opinions about what children *should*

---

[1] Learning is a lifelong process that begins at birth (or even before). Many of the ideas we have discussed thus far in the book relate to children's learning throughout their first years; we do not feel it would be productive to repeat them all here. Therefore, we will focus primarily on the "preschool" period, the years from three to six, when many children may begin to attend nursery school, kindergarten, or day-care centers.

learn in their early years (i.e., what should be the focus of early childhood education). As a parent (present or future) or teacher of young children, you should give serious thought to what *you* think is and/or should be a major part of the learning experiences of the children in your care. We will present, in our writing and in the readings we have selected, what some people have identified as important components of children's learning in the early years. As you read what is contained in this chapter, reflect on your own reactions to what is said, especially in terms of how you have learned and what your experiences have been through the years.

WHAT DO WE MEAN BY LEARNING?

Learning is usually equated with schooling and thus is thought to consist primarily of accumulation of information. For this reason, parents and preschool teachers have occasionally misunderstood the chief focus of early childhood education to be the learning of skills such as reading, writing, and arithmetic (or the learning of the alphabet, numbers, colors, and other isolated bits of information). This is a very narrowly defined view of learning. Actually, young children are continuously learning, from exposure to different kinds of information and experiences, opportunities to practice newly developing skills, and so on, not simply when an adult is deliberately and purposefully *teaching* them.

Children's "teachers" include all their life experiences. Learning is growing; it is the main "business" of young children's existence. There are many important things for children to learn in their early years. For example, they need to learn to get about on their own, to become more competent and self-sufficient, to master basic human skills such as walking, talking, and using simple tools. They need to learn control of their own bodies, feelings, thoughts, and actions. They need to figure out how things work—what the rules are, with people and with things. And they need to learn what they can do and who they can be. They need to become functioning human beings, able to meet both the expectations and the challenges of the world in which they live in a creative, individualized manner.

Some of these things children will learn from or in relation to other people. As we have discussed earlier in various contexts, children learn a great deal from modeling: they adopt behaviors (e.g., ways of coping, ways of relating to others, interests and skills, etc.) that they see in those around them, adapting them and making them their own. For example, reports from Northern Ireland suggest that even the very young children are becoming aggressive and violent in their behavior, toward one another and toward "the enemy." [2] In addition, children are reinforced by adults around them to behave in ways that are consistent with their personal and cultural norms. For example, little boys "learn" to be aggressive and independent because those behaviors are reinforced; little girls "learn" to be nonassertive, dependent, and nurturant because *those* behaviors are reinforced.

Many of the things that young children learn as they grow are largely independent of specific action by adult caregivers—most motor abilities, for example, are learned by children through their own action. They must, of course, be given the opportunity to move about and encouragement to do so (rather than restriction); but children do not have to be taught to use their hands, walk, climb, run, and so on. Even the learning of the use of tools (such as eating utensils and writing implements), though certainly influenced by modeling, is more a function of practice with the tools than of teaching. You cannot "show" children how to use a pair of scissors and expect them then to use them competently. They must *use* the scissors in order to learn to use them well.

There are some things that children learn as a result of direct, deliberate training or through being told. Such things as table manners and other social amenities (e.g., "please" and "thank you") as well as prohibitions (e.g., not touching certain things) are learned through these means. But this is, by far, the least effective means of learning for children even though, too often, it seems to form the basis of much of their treatment by adults.

Children's real learning occurs through their own active involvement with the environment. They need stimulation and experience, but they will use it at their own pace. For example, children learn to speak the language that is spoken around them; but they learn through listening and then "making up" their own system of rules about how their language works. Their rules change in a regular pattern as they practice and get feedback (by listening to others and comparing their own productions with what they hear), and so on; until, by age five, most children have mastered most of the rules of how to speak their language. But language is not *taught,* and children do not learn to speak by copying what they hear. Children must have the stimulation of hearing other people talk and the opportunity to practice talking themselves, but they will learn to speak at their own pace. Thus, children do not learn from having adults correct their language; they are the only ones who can correct it, slowly, as they learn, try out, and revise their developing rules.

---

[2] Arturo F. Gonzalez, Jr., "Teaching in War-Torn Belfast," *Learning,* 2, No. 2 (October 1973), 72–78.

We may draw some conclusions from these descriptions of different avenues of learning for young children: The directness and deliberateness of your role in children's learning varies—in some instances, children need only opportunity, encouragement, and lack of interference; in others, they need specific guidance; in still other areas, they learn from watching you and/or from your positive and negative reinforcements of, and reaction to, their behaviors. But in all circumstances, children learn from doing—from their own active involvement and experiencing, at their own pace.

Perhaps the key to effective teaching (as well as to childrearing, in general) is the art of knowing when, how much, and in what ways to assist, suggest, direct, guide, or leave be. The role of adults in children's learning and growing is very important. But there must be a delicate balance between your involvement and lack of interference. As expressed in the reading by Maslow in Chapter IV, what is called for is a "helpful let-be." Too much adult direction prevents children from developing the autonomy of thought, feelings, and actions so necessary in order to achieve mastery in learning, now and in the future. Too little adult direction prevents children from learning to be competently functioning members of the world in which they live. We will try, in the next pages, to give you some guidelines to being an effective facilitator of children's learning in the home, in the classroom, and in any other contexts in which you interact with children.

LEARNING AND TEACHING

What factors influence the child's learning? [3]

MOTIVATION. We have discussed the influence of motivation on children's behavior throughout the book—in relation to growth in all areas, in relation to discipline and the development of inner controls, in relation to changes in children's needs as they grow, and as the underlying force influencing all behavior. What motivates a child to learn has been discussed before in the context of other, related topics. We will deal with motivation to learn more specifically in the sections following.

Children learn best when they are motivated to learn; that is, when they have a reason, desire, or need to learn. Motivation to learn may be both extrinsic and intrinsic.

[3] For readers interested in further exploration of many of the ideas contained in this section, we recommend Jerome Bruner, ed., *Learning about Learning* (Washington, D.C.: U.S. Government Printing Office, 1966), particularly the reports on attitudinal and affective skills.

Extrinsic motivation comes from outside the child. She works at a learning task in order to win the praise and recognition of people who are important to her; for the young child, at first these are parents and teachers; gradually her age-peers will also become important to her so that she will act to win their approval also.

Children may also work to avoid punishment. But they learn better when motivated by desire for reward than when motivated by threat of punishment.

Extrinsic motivation may include *tangible* rewards such as a gold star or a piece of candy, or *social* rewards such as a smile or telling a child that he did a good job.

Very young children may respond more to a tangible reward than to a social reward as reason to do a specific task. The effectiveness of a social vs. a tangible reward depends both on the value of the person rewarding the child and the relative value of the reward to the child; individual children find different things rewarding. Children, like all of us, are highly motivated by the very natural desire for attention, particularly from people who are important to them. The history of how children have been given attention by their caregivers and others in the past will predict what will be rewarding to them in the present. For example, one child may perform best when given the encouragement of a smile; another, especially if he is used to being given things when he does something his caregiver wants (or having things taken away when he does something wrong), may respond more to something tangible. It depends on what a child is used to.

You may be disturbed by the thought of using conscious, deliberate rewards and/or punishments (that is, extrinsic motivation) to get a child to learn. And, as will be discussed, intrinsic motives for learning *should* be primary. Learning should be its own reward; if the skill to be learned is important and interesting to children, they will learn it for that reason, not because someone else wants them to learn. But realistically, adults are continuously rewarding and punishing children, often without realizing it. It is important for you to be aware of how your behavior toward your children influences their behavior. By realizing what things are rewarding to a child, you can be a more effective teacher. Not only will it help you to be more conscious of the things you have been teaching the child without realizing it, but it can also help you to use your influence with children in the most thoughtful, effective ways possible to help them learn, ultimately, to direct their own learning.

Intrinsic motivation comes from within the child. She learns because learning itself is rewarding to her. The child's desire to learn comes from (1) her identification with a positive model and (2) her desire for competence and self-worth.

Children *identify* with people whom they see as having qualities which they think are important to them and other people, and whom they see as being like them in some ways. Children try to act in a way and learn things that will make them more like their identification models. Children's first identification models usually are their care-givers. This stage in intrinsic motivation is like a bridge between extrinsic motivation and the next stage of intrinsic motivation, described below.

Children who value learning because of a desire for *competence and self-worth* seek out learning tasks that (1) will increase their competency in self-chosen areas (i.e., they want to do well those things that they're interested in doing), and/or (2) enhance their good feelings about themselves as people who can be responsible for their own learning. Children who are intrinsically motivated to learn, out of a desire for competence and self-worth, are primarily self- rather than other-directed in their learning; learning, for them, is a means toward greater self-reliance and an opportunity for self-growth and self-expression.

Both extrinsic and intrinsic motives work to encourage children to learn, but by age four to five children should pursue learning tasks based to a great extent on intrinsic motivation. Even before that time children can be encouraged to engage in learning (1) if the learning activity is in itself satisfying and rewarding to them, and (2) through seeing people around them involved in learning activities.

Learning which children engage in for intrinsic motives is more meaningful, and therefore more lasting, than learning motivated by extrinsic rewards. If a learning task is interesting and personally meaningful to children, they will not need any outside motivation to engage in it.

Intrinsic motivation is the key to children's future success in the world. People who are motivated by intrinsic reasons learn new things because they themselves are interested in them and because it will give them abilities which they, themselves, consider valuable. They are motivated from within to do whatever they do; they are not dependent on other people's approval for their actions. They are autonomous, independent, and self-directed. Children who are intrinsically motivated learn because learning is consistent with how they see and understand who they are and who they are becoming.

SELF-CONCEPT. Probably the most important learning children do in their early years is about themselves. You may recall our discussion in Chapter II of infants' developing awareness of themselves as persons: When they are born, babies do not know the differences between themselves and the world around them. As they begin to realize that things and people exist apart from them and their actions, not as extensions of them, babies also begin to define for themselves who they are. Two important and related things influence a child's definition of his/her self-concept: (1) he develops feelings about himself based on the way the important people in his life react to him—what they think of him, how they treat him, etc.; (2) she clings to things which are part of her developing "me"; she *is,* to herself what she looks like, the way she talks, the clothes she wears, etc.

Children's ability to learn is influenced greatly by what they think of themselves—by their self-concept. Whether children will make an effort to learn new skills and information and what kinds of skills and information they will make an effort to learn is related to whether or not what is to be learned is consistent with their self-concept.

For example, if a child has gotten the impression from the way her teachers, parents, or other persons treat her that she is not a good or smart person, then it would be inconsistent for her to display any learning ability. Her unconscious logic is something like this: "I am stupid. Stupid people don't do things well. Therefore I can't do anything well, so there's no point in even trying." The child does not make a conscious decision about her motives to learn or not to learn; she is (like most people) usually totally unaware of their influence.

Children will resist learning things that are threatening to their self-concept. For example, children who speak a language or dialect other than standard English will resist learning to speak standard English if it is taught by correcting the way they talk. If you tell a child, "No, we don't say it that way; we say it like this, . . ." you're telling him that something that is part of him is unacceptable. For the child to reject his language is to reject himself.

Part of children's developing self-concept is the learning of appropriate role behavior—defining who they are in relation to others. This includes accepting (making their own) behaviors that are related to "what is me" and rejecting behaviors that are seen as "what is not me." Children's self-concept may be seen as a self-system, containing all their different role behaviors. Some of the different roles a child might assume include boy or girl, child, grandchild, student, brother or sister, son or daughter, caregiver to pets, and a variety of make-believe roles. Children are more likely to learn things they think are appropriate to their role, that is, fitting for them.

For example, part of a child's self-concept is related to what sex he/she is. It has been shown that little boys and little girls learn very early, from modeling behaviors they see in their caregivers and to which they are exposed through different media (e.g., children's books, television); and because of which behaviors are encouraged and discouraged for each (that there are behaviors that are for boys and not for girls and vice versa). Because girls and boys learn these "appropriate" behaviors, they will begin to choose for themselves only those behaviors that "fit" with the ideas they have of "what a girl is" and "what a boy is." And if a learning task is not consistent with his/her definition of who he/she is (i.e., boy or girl), it will be rejected. So very early, we see little girls playing with dolls while their brothers play with more "masculine" toys. This kind of stereotyping of what is appropriate is very limiting for both sexes.

A child's ability to engage and succeed in learning tasks is influenced also by others' (parents, teachers, society's) expectations of him (probably because what they expect of him unconsciously affects how they treat him). For example, children who, from the beginning of their education, are labeled disadvantaged or deprived and who are expected, because of racial and/or economic origins, to be capable of less than their "advantaged" age-peers, may fulfill those expectations. When children are not expected to be able to do certain things, they may not be required or even encouraged to do them.

Children should be thought of and treated as children, not as advantaged or disadvantaged, middle or lower class, male or female. Every human being, especially in early childhood, should be responded to as an individual, special person, not categorized and/or treated as a member of any class, race, sex, etc.

Children learn much of who they are in their early years. The foundations of their self-concept become formed before they enter school. Their cultural, racial, sexual, and personal identity is learned through the models they see and the experiences they have. A child learns many things that are not directly taught to her; she learns from watching the people around her and observing, for example, how they act, what they feel, what is important to them, how they see things, how they treat her and others, and how they are treated by others.

Children learn their first (and for many, lasting) attitudes toward life and toward other people in early childhood. Their attitudes are based on two factors: (1) things that seem to be true on the basis of their own experiences in life and (2) what they are told in words and behavior by other people, particularly by those who are important to them. They learn, for example, what is important to them, what and who they are for and against, and how they feel about things. These attitudes, in turn, act as filters for the rest of their learning, since how children feel about something will not only influence *whether* they will learn but also *what* they will learn. (This was explained in the reading by Gordon in Chapter V.)

Different children, presented with the same information, will respond to it differently depending on what associations they can make.

For example, the smell of flowers may remind one person of a funeral parlor and another of a beautiful garden. In the same way, children filter information, and thus their learning, through their own past experiences and their attitudes. Thus, a child will work harder at something that will give him success at something valued in his own subculture than he will at something that has no immediate "payoff" for him. For example, a city child may work harder at a learning task that will help him to cope on the street than at one someone says will help him do well in school.

SUCCESS, FAILURE, AND LEVEL OF ASPIRATION. Children learn best when they expect to succeed; expectation of failure by children inhibits their ability to learn. Children will learn to tolerate failure if they are used to experiencing success, and failure is thus the exception and not the rule. Then a failure will be seen as a challenge, not as proof of a child's fears that she can't do things well.

Expectation of success or of failure can be a self-fulfilling prophesy: children who believe in themselves, who expect to do well at whatever they apply their energies to, usually are confirmed in that belief. On the other hand, children who expect to fail will tend to give up easily whenever a task becomes in any way challenging (and thus threatening), thus confirming their belief that they can't do things. Some children may even give up when they are doing a good job, because their negative feelings about themselves prohibit them from feeling comfortable with success; thus, in anticipation of success, they quit rather than face the conflict between how they see themselves and how they are actually performing.

In your interactions with children, it is important to be sensitive to their feelings about their ability to succeed at what they do, and to try to keep the learning environment nonthreatening and provide experiences in which success is assured so that success and failure become less of an issue. But in addition, you must consider the child's own level of aspiration: there are some children who always feel they have failed even when, objectively, they have done well; their concept of what they *should* be able to do may be unrealistic and unreasonable. Other children may be perfectly pleased with what the former child would consider a failure. It all depends on what the child's expectations of himself are. You should help each child learn to make reasonable expectations of his own level of aspiration, based on realistic appraisals of his own interests and abilities.

Children learn best when they, themselves, decide and know when they have been successful and when they have not. They thus learn to rely on their own judgment rather than on others' judgment of them and their capabilities. They need to learn good self-evaluative abilities in order to feel free to take a few risks, to learn without being told, to resist doing things that aren't good for them and others, etc.

What do children need to learn?

When we ask what children need, we must ask another question— What are the present and future demands on them? What kind of life do they live now, and what kind of life might they live in the future? Children need to develop generalizable and adaptive skills which will enable them to function productively and happily in the environment in which they live now as well as in the one they might live in as adults.

We must also ask who children are. For while much of what children become is a function of the environment in which they grow, each child is an individual and responds to her experiences in her own unique way. Therefore you have a responsibility to consider children, in the decision of what they need and how they should be treated.

Children are people too. They have human rights like any adult and should not be treated like second-class citizens. They have a right to their own choices as to how they will act, what they are interested in, what they will spend their time doing, etc. Adults have a responsibility to care for children, protect them from harm, and guide them in becoming happy and productive people, but they do not have the right to control children's lives. Adults should present children with alternatives—many possibilities—and then allow the children to make their own choices as they are able. Children will not learn to think for themselves or to control their own behavior if all of their decisions are made by adults. Children should be treated with respect, for they are the continuous renewal of hope for the future of humankind.

Young children do not need to be taught in order to learn. But their learning can be made fuller and more effective if you provide a flexible organization of materials and experiences for them, and if you are around to answer questions and to direct learning when necessary. A prepared environment leaves children more freedom to direct their own learning, since the materials and their organization themselves suggest things that can be done with them.

Children should be allowed and encouraged to direct their own learning as much as possible. Although you may structure the materials somewhat—set them out in such a way that suggests activities —you shouldn't tell the children what to do. You might have to offer a child who is not used to directing his own learning and cannot decide what to do several choices to guide his learning. For example, "Would you like to play with the blocks, put together a puzzle, or read a story?" Your selection of alternative choices should be based on your knowledge of the child—for example, what you have seen him enjoy before, what things he needs to learn or practice, or what skills he needs to develop.

Children should be involved actively in their own learning, either through working with materials that require them to do something or through interacting with other children or adults. Children learn much more and better when actively involved than when receiving passively what another person or thing is teaching without a chance to respond to and interact with the teacher. The learning must be personally meaningful to and involving of the child in order for her to really learn anything of lasting value.

Many commercial toys for children (and quite a few of those advertised as "learning toys") discourage creative, individualized involvement on the part of the child; they often do only one thing, go only one way, or require a stereotyped response. For example, a toy that produces a molded figure from modeling dough at the turn of a crank does not contain the same potential for learning by children as the children's making whatever they want from modeling dough that they make themselves with your help. Materials such as blocks, clay, paints, paper and crayons, and so on, that allow children a great deal of freedom to experiment, imagine, and in general to structure in their own personal way, are good.

Toys and materials such as puzzles, stacking toys, some pegboard materials, many of the Montessori materials, etc., that are designed to go together in such a way that they produce the "correct" solution when the child puts them together in the right way *do* have value. They are good materials for individualized activities; children can work alone and tell for themselves whether they are right or wrong, rather than depending on someone else to evaluate their success. In addition, they learn not only from the process of doing the activity but also from the product of the activity done correctly. Process and creative combinations should be emphasized even with these kinds of materials, however; don't push children to get the "right" answer. Rather, encourage them to see how many ways they can use the same materials.

Even an ordinarily passive medium should be made active in order to get the children involved and reactive. For example, you can watch television shows such as Mr. Rogers or Sesame Street with the children and encourage them to sing along, talk back to the TV, and so on. Then, when the show is over, you can follow up on the parts that the children seemed particularly interested in, using real props and more real-life, concrete experiences in your follow-up. A story read to children should involve them; be sure to show them the pictures, and to talk about them. Encourage the children to improvise from the story and to offer ideas from their own experience or imagination. Stories that are familiar are more fun when the children act out the parts. Children learn much more from doing than from being told.

You should provide the children with a large variety of materials and types of activities from which they may choose. In making decisions about what kinds of materials and activities to include, you should refer to the children's background, culture, and interests. For example, they should have books about children like them. City children should have some materials relating to city life, to teach them more about the world they live in. Children should have play equipment and dress-up clothes which reflect their subculture.

Materials and activities should relate to what the children already know and then build from there to teach them about people, places, and things different from what they know. The same thinking skills and language skills can be taught through using many different subject areas, and for the young child it is easiest and most interesting if the subject is familiar. Teach children about themselves and where they live and what they do. Then teach about new things they may never have seen or experienced. For example, in learning classification skills (i.e., what things "go together"), the city child might group together things to ride on—a car, a bus, and a subway—whereas a child from rural areas might include a horse and a tractor.

Materials don't have to be expensive in order to be good. You can make many learning materials from things you might ordinarily discard.[4] The children will learn a great deal from making their own materials with your help, and they'll learn, from your model, to be resourceful and creative instead of relying on ready-made things. You can make furniture, puppets, props for dramatic play, climbing equipment, and so on. In addition, common household items like pots and pans, empty boxes and cans, etc. can be sources for learning activities. Use your imagination and ask the children for their ideas too.

There are many expensive "educational toys" and learning materials, some of which imply in their advertising that if you don't buy them and stimulate your child properly, he may have learning problems later. That is both unfair and inaccurate. Children who are given love, support, and responsive care by interesting and inter-

---

[4] The bibliography at the end of the book contains some good references on easy-to-make, inexpensive materials.

ested adults, with nothing more than ordinary household items to play with, will develop better than children who are given special learning materials and teaching time by their caregivers as a substitute for honest, spontaneous care. There is a danger in overly self-conscious childrearing. Children move too quickly for you to constantly be trying to remember what is "right" to do. It is important to get to know child development information well enough that it becomes a part of you. Then you can learn to respond to your child spontaneously and to trust yourself without always having to worry whether you're doing the correct thing.

Children need real-life experiences that teach them about the world they live in. Let everyday life be your curriculum. For example, children will learn more useful information if sorting laundry and putting away the groceries in an organized way (e.g., all the fruits together, all the soups together, all the vegetables together) form the basis of an activity in classification (grouping like things together) than if they sort little plastic animals into trays.

In many parts of modern America, young children live a very isolated life. They experience only through watching television or through special field trips many of the things which most children growing up in a small town a hundred years ago would have experienced naturally. For example, for children who have not been "taught" otherwise, milk comes from plastic cartons and bread comes sliced in wrapped packages. They have no idea of the sequence of events that led to the things they see at the supermarket.

Watching something on TV or reading about it in a book, though informative, is not the same as actually experiencing it. For one thing, you only get the auditory and visual parts of the experience, not the smells and feelings and tastes. There are so many things that children need to learn about the world they live in (hopefully through real-life experiences, not through being told) that it seems a misuse of their time to concentrate on teaching such abstractions as colors, numbers, and other "words" with no connection to experience. These things should be part of a child's learning, but only as they relate to real experiences, not as ends in themselves.

There are many things young children need to find out about the world. You can help them sometimes by telling them, especially by answering their questions. But many of the things they need to know they can't find out by being told; they have to experience them themselves. For example, a child can find out about how things feel and how they react to her actions on them better by herself than by being told. You can tell her that if she drops something, it will fall, but she'll have to try it out on everything to really know it. You can tell her that if it's glass it will break, but she'll learn better the first time she breaks a glass. (This doesn't mean you should happily let children throw glass around, but accidents can be a time for learning.)

Young children need to learn to organize the way they look at the world—for example, how things are alike and different; what the relationships between different things are in terms of similar properties and amounts; what things go together; how things are arranged in time and space (e.g., what things always go before or after something else); the different ways of representing the same thing (for example, the thing itself, a picture of it, a name for it, a model of it, an acting-out of it: make-believe, etc.). You can give young children experience in organizing their world—in forming concepts—by organizing things around them and pointing out the organization in different ways, such as putting things that are the same together, having different ways of representing the same thing, etc.

Children need a great deal of repetition in order to learn something fully—to make it their own. Anyone who has been around young children knows that they love repetition and even demand it—for example, asking to have the same story read again and again or repeatedly asking the same question. You should respect children's desire for repetition; they need it in order to practice what they are learning. After a period of time of doing the same thing over and over in the same way all the time, however, children begin to lose interest and then will not learn any more from that particular activity. They usually still need practice and repetition of the concept or learning skill underlying the skill, however. So you should think of different ways of changing the activity to renew children's interest, strengthen the concept, and ensure the transfer to other settings of the concept or skill learned.

For example, puzzles that show a sequence of actions (e.g., children getting up in the morning, getting dressed, eating breakfast, brushing their teeth, and going to school) are very good learning materials. However, the same puzzle done over and over no longer teaches them anything after a while and is no longer interesting. But many similar puzzles can be made with children using photographs of themselves or of things familiar to them or of experiences they have had, using pictures cut from magazines, drawings, etc. You should be careful, however, not to make the task harder for the children when varying it (until they are ready for a harder task).

Children need to learn to apply skills and information learned in one setting to other situations including new, unfamiliar ones they will meet in the future. It will help children to learn to transfer skills learned in one setting to another by having opportunities to practice using each of the skills they have or are learning in a variety of different kinds of tasks.

Teaching may be thought of as a process of retranslation. Whatever children know can be translated into different words or their skills can be put to different uses through different materials. Whatever concept or skill is ever to be taught must be translated into children's levels of understanding or ability. Retranslation refers to a sort of general rule of "what's another way of saying (or doing) something?" and should be used both to reach children and to extend their learning. Although children learn things at first from doing them over and over again, their learning is made fuller if the learning task or situation is regularly changed in response to their needs; e.g., by using a variety of related but different materials, by asking different questions, and by changing the types of responses expected.

In order to understand fully a general idea, children need to learn about it in a variety of ways. You should, therefore, arrange materials and learning experiences that will reinforce (strengthen) the concept a child is learning. For example, if a child is interested in learning about size—big and little—you could provide many examples of objects in two sizes to let the child group. You could teach him other words for the same concept such as large and small, or huge and tiny, and talk about whether these words really mean the same thing. You can look around you and take a walk to find things that are big and little. You could let the child find pictures in magazines of big and little things, and talk about things in school, at home, in the city, etc., which are big and little. And you can compare such things as a little elephant with a big dog to get across the idea that some little things are bigger than some big things, that size is relative, not absolute.

Children learn from each other; they learn from watching each other, playing by and with each other, from working on projects together, and from teaching each other. They learn social behavior, such as seeing things from another's point of view, sharing, friendship and allegiance, protecting and standing up for a friend, and leading and following behavior; they learn to use language as communication to talk to each other to share ideas and feelings; they learn motor skills by watching and imitating older children; they learn that each child is different and knows different things and has different skills. Some of these things children learn on their own, simply by being together. Some things you must help to point out. What is most important is that children be given a chance to be with other children, the same and different ages. Early childhood education should not copy a system that has not worked. Children should not be separated into contained classrooms with groupings according to age. Young children of all ages should be allowed to be together and to learn from each other.

What is your role in children's learning?

Just as there are many definitions and kinds of learning, so also are there a variety of interpretations of teaching. As we said earlier, children's "teachers" include all their life experiences. A teacher, by this definition, is anyone or anything that stimulates, provokes, or makes possible learning in the child. The emphasis, then, is on what and how the child learns rather than on what you teach. We have suggested, in the previous pages, many ways in which you can facilitate the child's learning. We will try to summarize them below.

Children are constantly learning; they learn from each other, from adults, from materials and equipment, and from the structure of the environment—the arrangement of things around them. The other side of the coin that children are always learning is that they are always being taught by the people and things around them. Young children seem to have a hunger to learn that makes a teacher out of everyone and everything they come into contact with. You should always, therefore, think about what you are teaching children, on purpose or by accident, by your behavior as well as your words.

YOU ARE A MODEL. We have stressed the impact of your behavior as a model for the children in your care. Here is a poem widely known to preschool educators that expresses this eloquently.

Children Learn What They Live

Dorothy Law Nolte

If a child lives with criticism,
  He learns to condemn.
If a child lives with hostility,
  He learns to fight.
If a child lives with ridicule,
  He learns to be shy.
If a child lives with tolerance,
  He learns to be patient.

If a child lives with encouragement,
    He learns confidence.
If a child lives with praise,
    He learns to appreciate.
If a child lives with fairness,
    He learns justice.
If a child lives with security,
    He learns to have faith.
If a child lives with approval,
    He learns to like himself.
If a child lives with acceptance and friendship,
    He learns to find love in the world.

How you act toward your children, how you treat them, will affect how they will react to others. In addition, your behavior will also act as a model to your children in less direct ways. Children identify with their caregivers (if they have a mutually rewarding relationship); they copy behaviors they've seen in people they want to be like. Thus, your children will learn to enjoy learning if they see that you enjoy and value learning. You will teach your children to read, listen to music, draw, etc. as much by the fact that you do it yourself as by deliberately trying to teach it. A child who grows up in a house where people read all the time will be more likely to want to learn to read himself than a child whose parents encourage him to read but who, themselves, seldom pick up a book.

Children model your behavior in other ways also. For example, as we explained earlier, children tend to identify with people who are like them in some way, and to adopt some of their behaviors. A little girl, for example, will identify with her mother, whereas her brother will identify with his father.[5] The roles that you play will serve as models for your children's conceptions of those roles. In the home, and in a preschool setting, there should be people of the same sex as the child to serve as identification figures. But these people, male and female, should provide flexible models, not stereotypes. They should *not*, by the models they provide, limit children's visions of what they can do and be. Children should have both men and women teachers and should see them both engage in all sorts of activities. No activity (other than those related to childbearing) is, by nature, right for men or right for women. The children should see that they do not have to be limited by whether they are male or female. Encourage boys and girls to play together at all activities rather than

---

[5] There is, of course, cross-identification also, with children adopting behaviors of the opposite-sexed parent. And children learn from other models in addition to their parents.

separating them into activities for boys and activities for girls. You should not accept rough behavior from boys any more than you would from girls. You shouldn't stop a little boy from crying or being affectionate because "boys don't do that." You shouldn't force girls to be "ladylike" or to participate in certain kinds of activities such as playing with dolls or playing house. Children should be allowed to be children and to make their own choices about what is right for them to do and be because of who they are as people, not because of what sex they are.

Through your behavior, the way you act, the things you do, the way you treat children, the experiences you plan, the guidance you offer, and so on, you play a very important role in their learning. You should try, at all times, to be aware of your impact on children, and by being aware of your own behavior, to help them to become all they can be.

YOU ARE A REINFORCER. A very important part of being a good teacher is being aware of your own behavior as it influences the children in your care. How you treat children, how and when you respond to their behavior, will influence what behaviors become a consistent part of their repertoire and which ones disappear.

In the last chapter, we discussed this at length in relation to behavior management, and we referred to it earlier in this chapter in the explanation of extrinsic motivation. It is especially important to be conscious of your behavior in the learning situation so that you can maintain your role as facilitator of the children's learning, and not let yourself fall into the role of dictator of their learning. Your approval and attention is so important to the children that you can easily become too directive. For example, you might make suggestions or offer choices that communicate a hidden bias that the children pick up because you frown or get a certain tone in your voice if they make a choice different from the one you wanted them to make.

Be aware of your behavior so that you can be honest in your responses to the children. It's better to give no choices at all and to be honest about it than to pretend to give the children autonomy and to be false about it. Examine your own thoughts and feelings about learning and teaching, and study the ways in which your behavior is causing or blocking behaviors in your children. Your behavior is a powerful influence; get to know how it is operating.

YOU ARE AN ENCOURAGER. We may conceive of education as the encouraging process—encouraging and supporting children in their attempts to master their environments in order to function effectively and comfortably in the world. You may serve, as needed, as a safe home base, a source of strength, support, and belief, a rooting gallery. Learning in early childhood should take place in a psychologically "safe" environment. Children should feel free to play around with ideas and practice new skills without the fear that their "performance" is constantly being judged. Children should feel secure that you care about them for themselves, not for what they do.

Think of your own learning experiences; remember how difficult it is to learn and function at your best when you're constantly worried about someone else's evaluation of your performance, and when there's someone (whom you're concerned about impressing) watching and directing you. Your children are concerned about your opinion; your evaluation of them will affect their learning. They will learn better if you don't push, if you are not evaluative, if you take the attitude of "helpful let-be."

Since we have begun to discover how much young children are capable of learning in their early years, there has also begun a trend toward viewing this period as a time for "making your child smarter," sort of like building a bigger and better mousetrap. It is critical that we temper our concern for increasing children's cognitive skills by a consideration of their social and emotional development.

It is felt by many of those concerned with social reform that part of the reason for many of our social ills can be traced to the fact that modern man has progressed much faster intellectually than he has socially and emotionally. We thus find ourselves having difficulty coping with many of the social and emotional pressures exerted by our modern society. Man has learned how to use his mind to make great discoveries, build a complex technology, and forge new frontiers, but he has not learned as well either how to understand himself or how to get along with others happily and productively. And this is the part of life that is with us all the time, in whatever we do. Therefore, it is essential that we prepare children socially and emotionally as well as intellectually—that we do not forget the person in our concern with the mind.

Education of the heart should accompany education of the mind. Your first step in this direction should be to provide a supportive, encouraging atmosphere in which your children can learn and grow. A secure and happy child can like herself and get along with others too.

YOU ARE A GUIDE AND RESOURCE. We have stressed the importance of children directing their own learning. If they could learn and grow completely on their own, there would be no need for adult guidance. But as adults, we can help children to learn and grow in a world with which we're already familiar. We can share with them insights and understandings, shortcuts, helpful "rules of the game," and so on.

Social learning comes only through other people, and children need your guidance in this realm in order to learn to cope.

In other types of learning, a noninterfering, sensitive kind of guidance is helpful. For example, you should not tell children if they're right or wrong about something or give them an answer that they can find out for themselves. Instead, you should direct questions to children which will help them to find the answer that is right for them. Usually the best statement to make to children is "Let's find out"; then guide their explorations to help them find out about what they want to know. Whenever possible, children should be guided to discover answers for themselves rather than being told.

Young children's thinking needs to be directed to the qualities and properties of objects: for example, their size, shape, color, texture, whether they break, bend, stretch, flatten, etc. Provide children with a variety of different kinds of objects and suggest different ways of looking at and acting on the objects to find out about them. Be sure that you point out the important, relevant attributes of a thing, not just always color, size, and shape. For example, more important than the fact that an apple is round and red (neither of which is always true) is how it tastes, smells, and feels.

You can help children with a difficult task they have chosen. It is useful first to work out with them what the goal or product of the task will be and what the processes or steps should be to reach the goal. For example, if a child wants to make a puppet, you might make one with him, then draw a picture with him of the steps he will go through in order to put his puppet together. The child then has a plan to follow (like a pattern for making a dress or a model airplane, but using simple pictures, not words). Children should always be encouraged to do as much of the planning themselves as they can and guided, through directed questioning, on the parts that they leave out. This is as much a part of the learning experience for a child as going through the steps to reach the final goal.

Choosing materials and activities

Both the reading by Kamii and DeVries and that by Hartley in this chapter suggest that many of the materials and activities which have been a traditional part of nursery school education over the years (e.g., block-building, sand and water play, sociodramatic play, arts and crafts, etc.) should still be considered valuable learning resources. What both readings offer are a rationale for the use of these materials and activities as well as suggestions for a fuller use of them, given an understanding of their potential as "teachers." In addition, Kamii and DeVries offer the use of group games and Piaget-derived activities as further stimuli for children's learning. Essentially, both readings affirm, in different ways, the value of children's self-directed play in their learning of skills and deriving much of the knowledge and understanding of the world around them that they need at this time in their lives.

For example, group games teach children such things as principles of cooperation, matching their movements to words, awareness of body position in space, and understanding and following rules. Water play can be the basis for lessons in sinking and floating (a prelude to displacement theory, something that will come later) and understanding of the properties of objects (e.g., weight, porousness, size, volume). Puzzles teach about parts and wholes, relationships (similarities and differences in terms of size, shape, color, and subject), position in space, and so on.

In the context of this kind of play, then, your role as the facilitator of children's learning has two facets: (1) you should provide materials that will spark the children's interest and involvement; and (2) you should be alert to ways in which you can enhance or extend a child's learning by asking open-ended questions ("Tell me what you think would happen if. . . ."), suggesting different ways of using materials ("Can you build something with blocks that you could use to reach the toy on that high shelf?"), or posing a problem ("How could you make the paper stay together without using glue or paste?").

We have suggested throughout the book that children, themselves, are your best guide to what they need—they tell you through their behavior (and their words, if you listen) what they need. This remains true in the realm of learning. For example, if you are trying to teach a child something and he tunes you out, gets fidgety, looks around the room, etc. or if the teaching takes too much time and energy, then you are getting a clear message from the child that you're on the wrong track. He may not be ready to learn what you're teaching; your approach may be wrong (e.g., too pushy, demanding, or impatient); the material you're presenting may be too different from what the child has experienced before; and so on. On the other hand, when children get very involved with an activity, so much so that they may be reluctant to leave it when it's time for nap or lunch, you're getting a clear message that the material and activity is developmentally right.

Children tell you what they want and need to learn by what they choose for themselves to become involved with. If you provide an imaginative assortment of materials, space in which to use them, and time for children to pursue their own interests and apply their own imaginations to the use of the materials, you will be going a long way toward facilitating their learning. An important part of your role, then, is to be very observant—to see what kinds of materials and activities the children are interested in and to find others that will similarly provoke their involvement and stimulate the development of similar skills.

CHILDREN LEARN FROM WHAT THEY KNOW. Piaget [6] has offered a very useful concept that can be applied to the choice of appropriate materials and activities for children. He has suggested that human beings, like all organisms, develop through a process of active adaptation to the environment. There are two complementary processes that are part of this: assimilation and accommodation. Children are constantly, through their interactions with the world around them, taking in information;[7] each new bit of information that is taken in is *assimilated*; i.e., filtered through and made to fit with what a child already knows. In addition, children *accommodate*; i.e., adjust what they know to allow for (fit with) the added information. Through this ongoing process of adaptation to the environment, children progress to increasingly higher levels of functioning.

Each time children assimilate new information into their structure of thinking and accommodate their structure to fit that new information, they broaden the territory covered by their structure. For example, imagine that a young child had eaten red apples before, but never yellow ones. When given a yellow apple, she *assimilates* it into her conception of "apple"—e.g., it's sweet, crunchy, shaped like an apple, has a smooth skin and a stem, etc. In addition, she must *accommodate* her concept of apple to allow for the fact that not all apples are red; this is an apple, but it is yellow. Therefore, in her new structure (or schema), apples can be both red and yellow.

The important aspects of this concept, in terms of application to teaching and learning, is that children will only assimilate information that is close to what they already know and understand; and the processes of assimilation and accommodation are *active* by definition. Children do not absorb information like sponges; they seek out new information through their own active explorations of the world around them, and they bring to bear their past information and experience in their reception of new input. Learning, seen in this context, proceeds in small steps as children gradually accommodate what they knew before to allow for differences between input that they assimilate and their structure of thinking prior to the assimilation of the new information.

Thus, as a teacher (we use teacher in the broadest sense to include anyone who exerts an influence over a child's behavior), you should

---

[6] See Jean Piaget and Barbel Inhelder, *The Psychology of the Child* (New York: Basic Books, Inc., 1969), pp. 5–6.

[7] Information is used here very broadly to mean any kind of input.

take children's leads as to what they are ready to learn: they will naturally be attracted to what they can readily assimilate. For learning to occur, there must be what Hunt[8] refers to as a "proper match" between what the child already knows or can do and stimulation from the environment. Input must contain just the right amount of novelty. Children learn best from things similar to but slightly different from what they already know. If something is just the same and the child has explored the activity or material in every possible way, then it will no longer be interesting, and he will not learn from it. In contrast, if it's too different, too new, he won't be able to relate it to something he knows, and he will not learn from it.

Related to the amount of novelty a material or activity contains for a child is the degree to which it challenges his thinking skills. To be interesting (and thus provoking of learning in the child), stimulation should be a little puzzling or challenging. Thus, when choosing things for children to play with or when thinking of good activities, try to provide just the right amount of difficulty, coupled with just the right amount of novelty. "If there are no unknowns, no mystery, the learner will ignore the task. If the situation is so unfamiliar that it is incomprehensible, and therefore frightening, the learner will do everything possible to avoid the task." [9]

The response you receive from children when your choice of materials and activities is not matched to their interests and abilities may not necessarily be fear and avoidance; it may simply be lack of attention or other signs of boredom. In order to find out what children are interested in, what is "just right" for them (not too hard but not too easy, not too new but not too familiar), watch them. See what interests them, what they pay attention to for more than a very short time. Then find other activities and materials which are similar, but a little different. If the children become involved with the new materials and activities, you've chosen well; if they're not interested or if they avoid the task, it may be too easy, hard, etc.—try again.

WATCH CLOSELY AND CARRY A NOTEBOOK. Children let you know the level of their learning skills and when they're ready to learn something new by the materials and activities they choose and what they do with them. One key to meeting children's learning needs and insuring that they develop to the fullest of their potential in a flexible child-centered and child-directed learning environment is sensitive and informed observation. You might want to keep a small notebook on the children

[8] J. McV. Hunt, *Intelligence and Experience* (New York: The Ronald Press Company, 1961), pp. 267–88.

[9] Muriel Beadle, *A Child's Mind* (Garden City, N.Y.: Anchor Books, Doubleday & Company, Inc., 1971), p. 107.

and make notes about their learning and social behavior so that you can be most effective in guiding them in becoming all that they can be. Your goal should be to help each child to become flexible in his learning style, not to make him act in a certain way. When the children are involved in self-directed activities, watch them closely and make note of answers to the following kinds of questions:

What kind of materials does each child choose? Does she always or often choose the same materials or activity, or does she go from one to another? Is he willing to try something new or hard, or does he just want to stick with things he knows he can do? How long does she spend at the same activity? Does she usually stay with an activity until she has finished what she set out to do, or does she get tired of an activity quickly? Does he usually get involved in what he's doing, or is he distracted easily? Does she always work very fast or very slow, or does it depend on the activity? Does he think before he acts or answers a question or does he act on impulse, jumping quickly into things? Does she usually play and work alone, with other children, or both, depending on the type of activity? Does he usually choose his own activities, or does he usually need your help in deciding what to do? Does she usually try to do things for herself, or does she always ask for help? Does he use adults and other children as resources to answer questions or help him with things he can't do alone? Does she know when she's done something well, or does she need constant praise and encouragement? Is he usually very quiet or very talkative, or does it depend on the activity?

There are other questions you should ask yourself as you watch the children and, of course, there are many answers. But often, writing these things down can be a very good beginning toward good child-centered teaching practice. After answering these and other questions about each child's learning style try to plan experiences based on your observations to help each child learn to learn in the most effective, efficient way possible.

For example, we have already discussed the importance of noting what kinds of materials and activities children choose as a basis for knowing what kinds to present them with in the future in order to extend and expand their learning.

Persistence—sticking with something until it's satisfactorily completed—is a very important learning skill. Try to help those children who can't seem to finish anything to find something they enjoy and feel confident enough about to work at for more than a few minutes; work with them on a one-to-one basis, showing them different, fun things to do with a material they've shown some interest in. Don't force a child to stick with a task that he really finds too difficult or objectionable. Better, just point out to him that next time he should think more about his choice before he makes it. Finally, be very careful that your responses do not discourage persistence: making a child stop an involving activity because "Now, it's time for . . ." works against the child's development of persistence. If it's absolutely necessary, then help her put her work away in such a way that she can come back to it later. Also, don't interrupt a child's work with interfering questions. The time to ask questions is when the child shows, through his behavior, that he's exhausted all the possibilities he can think of for the activity himself; then a leading, open-ended question can help redirect his energies. But know when to leave a child to her own devices.

A child should be able to work effectively both alone and as a member of a group. If a child has not learned to play cooperatively yet, don't push him into group situations; rather, find ways of including him in small group activities, and encourage the other children to be understanding and help him to learn to share and take turns. Plan a variety of experiences to give children chances to play alone and together. Encourage them to use each other, as well as you, as resources and guides in their learning.

Some children are so used to being told what to do, when to do it, and how to do it that they can't make their own decisions. Help this kind of child by offering her choices. Increase the number of choices you give her as she is able to handle them comfortably. At first you may have to choose materials and activities for her, but give her free choice in what to do with them; gradually, help her to make her own decisions. Similarly, children who are not used to doing things for themselves need to be given responsibilities for things they're expected to do. Start with things you know without doubt that they can do, such as putting on their coat and hat, and be supportive of their gradually learning to do things on their own. If a child really needs help, give it to him; don't force him into an uncomfortable situation.

If you have a good relationship with the children in your care, then they will obviously be concerned about your opinion. Thus, you should try to be very sensitive to their feelings and to give them positive reinforcement about their work and their behavior—you should let them know you care about them. However, it is also very important that children do not come to value your opinion of them more than their opinion of themselves; they need to learn good self-evaluative powers, to know when they've done a good job without looking to others for the answer or for reward. You should encourage children to be their own judges; for example, if a child asks you if you like what she did, you can ask her, in turn, how *she* feels about it. And, as a matter of course, you should ask the children to evaluate their own work: "How do you feel about what you made?" "What did you learn from that?" "Are you happy with what you did?" and so on. Remember not to undo the purpose of such questions, however, by asking them in such a tone of voice that the child knows what answer you expect. Some children are very hesitant to express their own opinions because no one has ever been interested before. Be alert to the child who tries to figure out what you want to hear, and keep emphasizing to her that you really are concerned with what *she* thinks and feels, not with what she thinks you want her to think and feel.

Use the other children to help bring out a silent child as well as to occasionally quiet a constant talker; teach them a modified form of the Golden Rule—fair play. If someone is always talking (or playing with the same toy, etc.), then nobody else gets a turn, and that isn't fair. But remember to respect each child's individual style. Don't try to "normalize" children to fit a pattern. For example, some children like to be alone; they should be allowed to do so and invited, but never forced, to join group activities.

We have already mentioned the two readings we have chosen to include in this chapter in addition to our own material. The first is further material by Drs. Kamii and DeVries, describing curriculum objectives, and selection and organization of content for their Piaget-derived early childhood curriculum. Both this material and the second selection, an article on play by Dr. Ruth Hartley, stress the importance for learning and the development of autonomy of children's self-directed play.

Piaget for Early Education

Constance Kamii and Rheta DeVries

The material that follows is another section of the manuscript from which we took the piece on discipline used in the preceding chapter. Because Piaget has had such an enormous impact on thinking about children's development in recent years (Piaget has been around a long

Constance Kamii and Rheta DeVries, "Piaget for Early Education," in R. K. Parker, ed., *The Preschool in Action,* 2nd ed. (Boston: Allyn and Bacon, in press), Part II: *Curriculum Objectives,* Part III: *Selection of Content,* Part IV: *Organization of Content,* and Part V: *Methods of Implementation—Parents' Childrearing Practices at Home.* © 1974 by C. Kamii and R. DeVries. Used by permission of the authors.

time; it's just taken this country some time to accept his theories), we thought it important to present his ideas as they relate to early childhood education. Few can do it as well as the authors of this selection. Of all the people who have adopted Piaget's ideas and adapted them to the educational setting, Dr. Kamii is one of the very few whom Piaget himself has endorsed as presenting his ideas in a context that adequately reflects his intentions. Some of the vocabulary is difficult, but we think the insights gained are worth the effort. We refer you to Dr. Kamii's other writings, included in their references, for explanations of many of the terms used.

A. Long-term objectives

We stress the importance of long-range objectives derived from Piaget's work which shows the adaptive value of attaining developmental maturity in the intellectual, moral, and socioemotional realms. These values are not arbitrary values of personal taste chosen from a bag of virtues, but are derived from research and theory which encompass the development of the species and the individual. Thus, we feel that the objectives of early education must be conceived in the context of long-range goals. These aim at the development of the entire personality, with particular emphasis on intellectual and moral autonomy.

In the intellectual realm, Piaget's views can be seen in the following quote:

> The principal goal of education is to create men who are capable of doing new things, not simply of repeating what other generations have done—men who are creative, inventive, and discoverers. The second goal of education is to form minds which can be critical, can verify, and not accept everything they are offered. The great danger today is of slogans, collective opinions, ready-made trends of thought. We have to be able to resist individually, to criticize, to distinguish between what is proven and what is not. So we need pupils who are active, who learn early to find out by themselves, partly by their own spontaneous activity and partly through material we set up for them; who learn early to tell what is verifiable and what is simply the first idea to come to them (1964, p. 5).

These objectives are obviously much broader than formal operations in the sense of ability to solve Piagetian tasks at the formal operational level. Formal operations are necessary for adults to be critical and inventive in daily living and to be able to distinguish between what is proven and what is not. Being able to criticize and resist individually also takes a lot of specific knowledge and moral courage. A conformist education, or the traditional school, according to Piaget, does not encourage critical, independent thinking. Schools must encourage autonomy from the very beginning if they are to be successful in helping individuals eventually attain the highest levels of emotional and cognitive development. We cannot expect children to conform to coercive parental and school pressures during the first ten years (or longer) and then suddenly show initiative and autonomy later.

B. Short-term objectives

1. SOCIOEMOTIONAL OBJECTIVES. Within the context of the above long-term objectives, we conceptualize the following short-term goals for early education. Socioemotional development is considered first for three reasons.* First, the development of autonomy (intellectual as well as socioemotional) requires a context of adult-child relationships characterized by mutual respect, affection, and trust. The first concern of the teacher must, therefore, be to develop an affectionate and egalitarian relationship with the child and to respect his autonomy by letting him exercise his volition as much as possible.

The second reason for placing socioemotional objectives first is that a certain emotional equilibrium is necessary for development. If a child is anxious and insecure, or emotionally upset for any reason, his general development in all spheres will be hindered to the extent that these unhappy preoccupations drain his energies. If, for example, a child is depressed because nobody in the room likes him, the teacher's main focus for this child should be on this socioemotional problem.**

A third reason for emphasizing socioemotional objectives is that learning depends largely on motivation. If motivation is high, children (as well as adults) willingly make enormous efforts to master things that are difficult. For this reason, the child's needs and intrinsic interests take priority over any other reason for his engaging in an activity.

More specifically, the following are our socioemotional objectives for the child:

a. To feel secure in an egalitarian relationship with adults

b. To respect the feelings and rights of others and begin to coordinate different points of view (decentering and cooperating)

c. To be independent, alert, and curious, to use initiative in pursuing curiosities, to have confidence in his ability to figure things out for himself, and to speak his mind with conviction. . . .

---

* It is important for the teacher to be aware of this priority because in making decisions on the spot from day to day, she has to know what goal to drop at a particular moment in favor of a broader goal.

** It should be noted that although the problem is primarily socioemotional, the solution will not be solely socioemotional. The child must mobilize his intelligence to change the objective and subjective situation.

Since "alertness" and "curiosity" are particularly prone to different interpretations, it is perhaps useful to note that what we mean stands in opposition to the empiricist approach such as that of Engelmann, despite the fact that Engelmann would agree that children should be alert and curious. The difference in our interpretations appeared when we looked at individual children taught by Engelmann. The one child we considered alert was the one Engelmann considered "lackadaisical." The children he considered alert, on the other hand, were the ones we considered "conformists" (Kamii & Derman, 1971). What Engelmann meant by "curiosity" thus referred to the child's interest in what the teacher wanted him to be curious about. Such curiosity *on the teacher's terms* is not what we mean in the third objective.

Lack of confidence can be a serious developmental handicap. We have observed children in Piagetian tasks as well as in the classroom who are so easily discouraged, or so full of fears and anxieties, that they do not even try when presented the slightest difficulty. Others are amused and challenged and laugh off things that would traumatize some children. In one Piagetian learning experiment on language, Montangero (1971) observed that spunky children who make more errors are those who end up learning faster. He found that children who do not try to figure out how to say the same thing differently do not make errors, and thus do not construct a new syntactic structure. Those who try make all kinds of errors, but they keep trying and end up learning faster. Thus, our conclusion is that we should encourage and support children's thinking, even when their ideas are "wrong."

2. COGNITIVE OBJECTIVES. Within the context of the above socioemotional objectives, we conceptualize the following cognitive objectives for the child:

   a. To come up with interesting ideas, problems, and questions
   b. To put things into relationships and notice similarities and differences.

This is a short list compared to the senior author's previous conceptualizations (Kamii, 1971, 1972a, 1972b, 1973a, 1973b, 1973c; Kamii & Radin, 1967, 1970; Sonquist & Kamii, 1967; Sonquist, Kamii, & Derman, 1970). The previous conceptualizations no longer make sense to us for two reasons. First, as discussed above, they confused the development seen on Piagetian tasks with the development of the child in the everyday world. Second, they compartmentalized the objectives into classification, seriation, numerical reasoning, spatial reasoning, etc. This juxtaposition of cognitive abilities as if they were separate mechanisms (as shown in Table 1) was an assimilation of Piaget's theory into a mechanistic notion of intelligence. One of the most central ideas in Piaget's theory is that intelligence develops as a whole. It is incorrect, therefore, to present objectives as if intelligence consisted of mechanisms by which to classify, seriate, count, spatially reason, etc. Figure 1 represents more correctly the Piagetian notion of the inseparability of all aspects of development.

Table 1. Juxtaposition of Objectives

Socioemotional objectives
a. ....
b. ....
c. ....
etc.
.
.
.

Cognitive objectives
a. Classification
b. Seriation
c. Numerical reasoning
etc.
.
.

The first cognitive objective in this recent conceptualization (coming up with interesting ideas, problems, and questions) is closely related

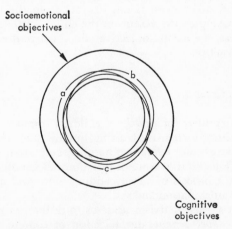

Socioemotional
objectives

Cognitive
objectives

*a, b, c, etc., stand for the various cognitive domains delineated by Piaget.

Fig. 1. Hierarchy of Objectives

to the socioemotional objectives of promoting the child's initiative and confidence in his ideas. It could have been stated more colorfully as "the having of wonderful ideas" (Duckworth, 1972). At Easter time, for example, we noticed a child doing something at the foot of the slide on the playground for the longest time. When we went to find out what he was doing, he told us that it was easy to get the egg to roll smoothly the short way; so he was trying to get it to roll smoothly the long way. The child who asked why the sun was hot or why his mother was taking a sun bath is also an example of what we mean. If there is an atmosphere conducive to learning, children will come up with questions that are so hard that adults would not dare pose them. When the problems are truly theirs, children will concentrate and work hard for an amazingly long time.

In connection with children's coming up with interesting ideas, we stress the importance of their coming up with many different answers to the same question, rather than one correct answer to each question. For example, in playing with Montessori's Pink Tower, children can be asked for one correct answer or many different ways of arranging the blocks. In the latter situation, the seriated order becomes one of the many possible ways of arranging the blocks. This emphasis on many different things to do with the same material is not simply an emphasis on creativity as a value. In Piaget's theory, creating new relationships, as well as the mobility of thought involved in looking at the same thing differently, are at the heart of cognitive development.

The second objective (putting things into relationships and noticing similarities and differences) is not distinct from the first one. While the first objective puts the accent on the child's initiative and the content of his ideas, the second objective puts the accent on the process of reflecting abstraction.

SELECTION OF CONTENT

Curriculum content for preschool children commonly includes such things as counting to ten, recognizing number and letter symbols, reciting one's address and telephone number, and naming colors, shapes, and animals. This kind of content selection reflects the empiricist view of learning as a process of simply adding more and more bits to the child's store of information and skills.

Since Piaget's constructivism leads us to define our curriculum goal as the child's *development,* our selection of content is not a list of specific items like these, but is a list of situations and activities which promote development. More specifically, we derive curriculum content from the following three sources:

1. Daily living
2. The child-development curriculum
3. Aspects of Piaget's theory which suggest other activities.

DAILY LIVING. In his research, Piaget avoids content taught in school. His findings of marked developmental differences in children's knowledge of things never taught directly demonstrates that they learn and develop simply by living. Countless situations in daily living stimulate children to learn and develop. Below are a few examples.

At the dinner table, the child tastes things that have different consistencies, textures, and other reactions, and thereby develops his physical and logico-mathematical knowledge. He quantifies objects as he puts a certain amount of everything on his plate. As he knocks his glass of milk over or pours milk, he engages in spatial reasoning and quantification. As he sets the table, he learns about number and relationships in space. He learns to make his left and right arms correspond to his coat's left and right sleeves. Getting his wet mittens to dry involves physical knowledge. When he tries to get a key hanging out of reach on a wall, he compares heights and puts objects into relationships as he thinks of standing on a chair and knocking it down with a stick. Washing hands without getting long sleeves wet, figuring out what to do when juice is spilled, playing with shadows, walking home without getting lost, arguing with another child over possession of a toy, taking a message on the phone, discovering and examining a bug, playing in the bathtub, noticing a funny hat, and figuring out how to sneak something without getting caught are among the endless activities in which the child uses his intelligence in daily living.

One of the most impressive feats of learning in daily living is language development. By the time they come to school for the first time, children know all the basic elements of language without having had any formal instruction. Learning to speak is like learning to walk in the sense that it happens naturally if there is the proper encouraging atmosphere and biological maturity.

The child's motivation to adapt to the physical and social world is both natural and strong. This is why we feel that daily living is a rich source of curriculum content. For example, snack or meal time can be turned into a gold mine of educational opportunities. Unfortunately, teachers often overlook these opportunities and think of teaching only in terms of whatever they consider "educational." In their desire to avoid accidents, too, they often work very hard to do everything *for* children, setting the table, filling each plate, pouring a tiny bit of milk in each cup, etc. We feel that such efforts on behalf of the child actually rob him of many learning opportunities. In our curriculum, the teacher tries to use every opportunity to encourage the child to anticipate, make judgments, and compare his anticipation with the outcome. Deciding how much meat, vegetables, and milk to take are acts of intelligence in which the child anticipates, makes judgments, and compares the anticipation with the outcome.

Other examples of ordinary situations the teacher can use to promote development include the following:

Figuring out how to open a can of paint (physical knowledge, i.e., using a lever)*
Putting cardboard under the leg of a wobbly table (physical knowledge and spatial reasoning)
Tying a shoelace (spatial reasoning)
Looking for a lost mitten (spatial reasoning about places where it could be and temporal sequence before the disappearance)
Polishing shoes (physical knowledge)
Mopping up spilled juice (physical knowledge and cooperation)
Settling disputes (decentering and language development)

What makes these situations particularly desirable as a source of curriculum content is that they require the use of intelligence in a personally meaningful way. Above all, it is in daily living that children learn to be inventive, resourceful, independent, proud of their accomplishments, and morally autonomous.

THE CHILD-DEVELOPMENT CURRICULUM IN THE CONTEXT OF PIAGET'S THEORY

The curriculum we derive from Piaget's theory has much in common with the child-development curriculum exemplified by the Bank Street Model (Biber, Shapiro, and Wickens, 1971) and Read's (1971) classic text. Child-development teachers have long believed in the value of play, and their experience with children has led them to identify many activities as being intrinsically interesting to young children. These activities include block building, painting and other art activities, sociodramatic play, raising animals and plants, singing and playing musical instruments, movement, cooking, sand and water play, stories, and puzzles. Since Piaget's theory, too, emphasizes the importance of children's play, we incorporate the child-development curriculum and build upon it.

Table 2 is an analysis of child-development curriculum activities from the point of view of Piaget's theory. First, let us briefly review the

---

* We focus on the predominant aspect of cognitive development promoted by each situation, and omit the many possibilities for socioemotional development.

cognitive aspects of Piaget's theory listed across the top of the chart. (Since we generally agree with the child-development curriculum with regard to socioemotional aspects, these were omitted from this table.) We have already discussed the basic distinction among logico-mathematical knowledge, physical knowledge, and social knowledge. However, some further remarks are in order on logico-mathematical and spatio-temporal knowledge, and representation.

Table 2.
Analysis of the Child-Development Curriculum
in Terms of Piaget's Framework

Child-development curriculum activities	Logico-mathematical knowledge			Physical knowledge	Spatio-temporal knowledge		Social knowledge	Representation		
	Classification	Seriation	Number	Physical knowledge	Spatial reasoning	Temporal reasoning	Social knowledge	Index	Symbol	Sign
Block building				X	X				X	
Painting				X					X	
Other art activities				X	X				X	
Sociodramatic play					X	X			X	X
Listening to stories					X	X				X
Raising animals and plants				X						
Singing and playing musical instruments				X		X				X
Movement					X				X	
Cooking				X		X				
Sand and water play				X						
Playing with playground equipment				X	X					
Table games (such as puzzles)										

When we speak of classification, seriation, and number in relation to preoperational children, we can only refer to processes that lead to classification, seriation, and number concepts.* When we say "classification," therefore, we are referring to the process of *noticing similarities and differences* and *grouping* things that are similar. For example, upon noticing that large blocks make more stable constructions than

---

* The criterion of "classification" in a strict concrete-operational sense is class inclusion, and the criterion of "seriation" is transitivity.

small ones, the child may systematically look for large blocks as he builds with them. When we say "seriation," we are referring to the process of *comparing* and *coordinating differences.* For example, the child may look for a block that would be long enough to bridge a certain space, and, having found one that is too long and one that is too short, he may look for a middle-sized one. When we say, "number," we are referring to the process of *establishing equivalence.* For example, the child in sociodramatic play may decide to get just enough chairs for all the dolls and himself.

Spatio-temporal knowledge is similar to physical knowledge in some ways, and to logico-mathematical knowledge in other ways. Space and time are like physical knowledge in that they have an existence "out there" in reality. For example, the child who sees three beads, ABC, sees them "out there" in time and space. On the other hand, if we put the three beads on a pipe-cleaner and into a tube that hides them, and then rotate the tube 180°, the reasoning involved in predicting that the order has changed to CBA requires the creation of spatial relationships just like in logico-mathematical knowledge. The order ABC can be constructed only by reflecting abstraction, and the order CBA can be predicted only by deduction from this construction.

Representation includes three types that Piaget distinguished: the index, the symbol, and the sign. The index is either part of the object or is causally related to it. For example, the sound we hear from a jet and the trace it leaves behind are indices of a jet. When we hear the sound, we know that there is a jet even if we cannot see it.

In contrast to indices, symbols and signs are not part of the object but exist apart from it. The difference between symbols and signs is that symbols bear a resemblance to the real object, and signs do not. Below are five types of symbols delineated by Piaget:

1. *Imitation* (the use of the body to represent an object, e.g., zooming around stretching one's arms out like the wings of a jet)
2. *Make-believe* (the use of an object to represent another object, e.g., nailing two boards together in the form of an airplane and calling it a "jet")
3. *Onomatopoeia* (e.g., making a roaring sound of a jet)
4. *Three-dimensional models* (e.g., making or recognizing the model of a jet)
5. *Pictures* (e.g., making or recognizing a pictured jet)

Signs, such as words, do not resemble the object at all. The word "jet," for example, does not resemble a jet. Other examples of signs are the Morse code, traffic signs, and mathematical signs.

For purposes of teaching, it is important to recognize that it is not the index, symbol, or sign *itself* which represents an object. Representing is what the person does by giving meaning to indices, symbols, and signs. Words, for example, are only as meaningful as the knowledge of the individual who uses them. Thus, teaching of representation does not consist of presenting a list of words to learn, but, rather, it focuses on developing the ability to represent knowledge already constructed on the practical level.

We now turn to an analysis of each of the child-development curriculum activities in Table 2, in relation to the above discussion. The X's in the table indicate the aspects of cognition predominantly promoted by each activity. Some activities received more than one "X". Since, in reality, all aspects of knowledge are present in all activities simultaneously, we could have put an "X" in almost every box of the matrix. However, we feel it is useful for the teacher to know the predominant aspects of knowledge stimulated by each activity. In the logico-mathematical realm, we did not put any "X" because a logico-mathematical framework is always involved in all activities.

Block-building first of all involves physical knowledge. For example, the child tries to balance a tall tower so that it does not fall over. Block-building also involves the structuring of space when the child tries to make walls and roofs. When he builds a hospital, garage, or road, he represents his knowledge symbolically.

Painting involves physical knowledge as the child mixes paint, drips it, smears it on paper, and waits for it to dry. When first beginning to paint, the activity involves mostly physical knowledge, since the child is primarily fascinated with simply using the brush and paint to see the result. Later, when such actions hold no more mystery and this physical knowledge is well mastered, representation becomes the fascination.

Other art activities also involve physical knowledge. The child gets different reactions from different objects when he uses paste, crayons, felt pens, tissue paper, bits of tile, macaroni, or aluminum foil. Spatial reasoning is promoted when he is surprised at what happens when he tries, for example, to paste a picture cut-out by putting paste on the side he wants to show! Playdough is a good material to stimulate representation, as well as physical knowledge.

In sociodramatic play, children are the symbols as well as the symbolizers. They symbolize their ideals of "mommy," "daddy," and "doggy," and at the same time use themselves as symbols. They symbolize a great deal of social knowledge and every other aspect of knowledge. Stories likewise involve all aspects of knowledge. Both sociodramatic play and stories are particularly good for promoting representation with language and for dealing with temporal sequences.

Plants and animals are much more complicated than the physics which Piaget specifically has in mind when he speaks of physical knowledge. In a large sense, however, much of biological information is the construction of knowledge about objects in reality and can thus be considered part of physical knowledge.

Playing musical instruments involves physical knowledge. Both singing and playing instruments involve the comparison of pitches, durations, intensities, and melodies, and encourage the sequencing of temporal patterns. Singing and chanting are obviously good for language development.

Movement activities require spatial reasoning, for example, when the child imitates a posture. When he has to think how to move in one way to the wall (e.g., skipping), and back in another way (e.g., hopping), he has to coordinate similarities (moving in a straight line) with differences (different actions). Movement also involves representation when the child pretends to be a tree, a horse, a cloud, or a flashlight.

Cooking involves physical knowledge, quantification, and temporal sequences. Sand and water play likewise involve physical knowledge and quantification as the child fills and refills various containers, wets and sifts sand, and drains the water table. Sand play also leads to the representation of mountains, rivers, castles, and cakes.

Outdoor playground time is usually considered in terms of the child's gross motor development. It is, in addition, a rich terrain for the development of physical knowledge and spatial reasoning. Sliding down an incline, swinging on a swing, and playing on a see-saw are obvious examples. Steering a wagon, riding a tricycle, and kicking a ball also involve spatial reasoning and physical knowledge.

Puzzles are probably the most popular of all table games. They require a great deal of analysis and spatial reasoning.

All the above activities have passed the test of appealing to children's intrinsic interests. Most of them also pass the test of allowing for progressive elaboration and development. The block-building, painting, sociodramatic-play, movement, and puzzle-solving abilities of four-year-olds can develop considerably over a year. Piaget's theory helps us to understand that these activities do not merely promote block-building, painting, and singing competencies but are the vehicles through which the child develops his basic cognitive framework.

DIFFERENCES BETWEEN THE CHILD-DEVELOPMENT AND PIAGET-DERIVED CURRICULA

Although our curriculum incorporates much of the child-development curriculum, we do not simply import it and put a Piaget label on it. Behind the similarity in materials and activities lie theoretical differences which often result in different ways of teaching and different experiences for the child. The characteristics of the child-development curriculum which are in contrast to our curriculum can be sum-marized in the following three points which are discussed below:

1. The child-development curriculum is based mostly on empiricist assumptions about how the child learns.
2. The child-development curriculum methods are largely intuitive.
3. The child-development curriculum does not reflect an adequate appreciation for the nature of preoperational intelligence.

Regarding the first point, Read (1971), for example, reflects an empiricist view when she says:

> As a learner, the child of this age is still taking in and storing sensori-motor impressions that form the bases for learning (p. 189).

> . . . the intellect must *receive* stimulation if it is to grow (pp. 189–90, italics ours).

> The child learns about the world around him through his senses, seeing, hearing, feeling, tasting, and smelling, and through his kinesthetic sense. The greater the input of sensory impressions, the more material he has out of which to build concepts of what the world is like. He improves his tools for understanding the world as he improves the keenness of his sensory perception (p. 197).

These empiricist views state that knowledge comes from outside the individual through the senses. The discussion in the theoretical introduction of this chapter on empiricism, rationalism, and Piaget's relativism, as well as his constructivism, was presented in part to explain the differences between the child-development curriculum and ours. We do not believe that the child learns by "taking in and storing sensori-motor impressions" or by passively "receiving" stimulation. Rather than multiplying "the input of sensory impressions" or improving "the keenness of his (the child's) sensory perception," we feel that the most important educational principle is to encourage the child to *use his initiative to act on objects* and know them in a physical and logico-mathematical sense. In other words, we believe in encouraging mental actions that entail simple and reflecting abstraction. Sensory information is important only in the context of these types of abstractions.

Having assumed that knowledge comes through the senses, the child-development curriculum typically approaches curriculum in terms of traditional disciplines (such as motor skills, language and literature, mathematics, physical and biological sciences, social studies, music and dance, and art). In other words, the child-development curriculum is conceptualized in terms of specific disciplines without an explicit theory that relates these subject matters to the development of intelligence. As a result, if we ask a child-development teacher, for example, in what way dramatic play contributes to the development of intelligence, we never get a satisfactory answer.

Our second point concerning the difference between our curriculum and the child-development curriculum is that their methods are largely intuitive. In our opinion, the child-development curriculum is generally good and often even excellent, but only because a teacher's intuition is well developed. However, since the child-development curriculum is not derived from a coherent theory, teachers with different intuitions sometimes teach in drastically different ways. For example, we recently visited a well-known child-development teacher-training program in order to find out to what extent our curriculum is similar to theirs. We spent three mornings in the classroom of an outstanding teacher in whom we found almost nothing to criticize. However, we were shocked to see an entirely different kind of teaching in a videotape which was widely disseminated as model teaching. In this videotape, the teacher completely disrupted a child's block-building to ask him many questions about the way he faced the "open" sign on his gas station door. She literally poured a sea of words over him which reduced him to inactive staring at his clasped hands. When we inquired about these very different teaching styles, we found that both were considered acceptable and simply reflected different personalities. Therefore, we concluded that what is missing from the child-development curriculum is a theoretical rationale which prevents such contradictions. The absence of this theoretical rationale often leaves the child-development teacher to make decisions according to what *feels* right. When asked to explain decisions, she cannot give a rationale that matches the theoretical rigor of a Distar Teacher.* Knowing the distinction among physical, logico-mathematical, and social knowledge, as well as the relationship between operativity and representation, would help the child-development teacher to make and defend decisions based on an explicit theory.

Our third point concerning our difference with the child-development curriculum is that it does not reflect an adequate appreciation for the nature of preoperational intelligence. One of the unique aspects of Piaget's theory is the discovery of preoperational intelligence. It is true that the child-development teacher intuitively knows a great deal about what is going on in the child's head, but she does not suspect that the child's logic might be as different as it is from that of adults. As a result, the child-development teacher often interacts with the child completely above his head or beside the point (from *his* point of view). Taylor (1969), for example, reports the following science activity:

---

* We do not at all imply that we approve of Distar. In fact, Distar methods are contrary to ours in almost every way. We simply want to point out that without a strong theoretical rationale, the child-development curriculum cannot withstand the challenge of behavioristic programs such as Distar, which sounds "scientific."

A preschool teacher had planned her day around the weather. She wanted the children to become more familiar with rain. She readied her equipment and then gathered the children around her. She put a pan of water on a hot plate and waited for it to boil. Then she took a small pyrex custard cup and placed some ice in it and held it over the steam from the pan. Moisture began to collect on the outside of the bowl and soon drops of water fell from it. She told the children about the principle of rain. The children sat very attentively until after the demonstration and then without question or comment they went outside to play. It was assumed the experiment was a success. The next morning when a mother brought her mature four-year-old to nursery school, she said, "Would you be interested in the comments Mala Ree made about the science experience you had yesterday?" Of course, the teacher wanted to hear what the mother had to relate. The mother continued, "Mala Ree reported 'Mother, Heavenly Father doesn't make the rain, I learned how to make it at school.'" Without this vital feedback, the teacher would have assumed that the children had gained correct concepts for the experience. It was necessary for her to go back and help this child, and others, to get their thinking straightened out (pp. 76–77).

Piaget's theory leads us to react to the above report by saying, first of all, that the origin of rain is completely beyond the ability of four-year-olds to understand. Yet, this activity appears in many child-development curricula. Second, this particular teacher is said to have gone back to help this child and others "to get their thinking straightened out." It is not clear what the teacher considered "straight thinking," but it is clear that the child was in one world, and the teacher in another, without any awareness of the nature of preoperational intelligence.

OTHER CONTENT DERIVED FROM PIAGET'S THEORY

In addition to the content derived from daily living and the child-development curriculum, we find certain ideas in Piaget's theory which suggest three additional types of activities. The distinction among the three kinds of knowledge leads us to develop physical knowledge activities which we consider an extremely important component of our curriculum. Second, his research on moral development and interpersonal cooperation lead us to put major emphasis on group games. Finally, activities can occasionally be taken from Piaget's tasks, provided they do not become the core of the curriculum.

1. Activities based on physical knowledge

Science education in nursery school has generally focused on content such as the production of rain as seen above and the growth of seeds into plants. We have also already noted that preschool education has overmagnified the role of sensory experience. Piaget's view is different from this empiricist view in that he emphasizes the role of the child's physical and mental actions on objects. By pushing things, rolling them, throwing them, pulling them, swinging them, blowing on them, and balancing them, the child can observe how objects react to his own actions. Piaget thus does not deny the role of the senses, but says that sensory information is a small part of the child's coming to know objects. Based on the different actions of the child, we have developed activities such as the following:

a. SHUFFLEBOARD (pushing). The teacher puts out a half-dozen unit blocks, and a half-dozen long blocks, and encourages children to try to use the longer block to push a unit block to some target.

b. TARGET BALL (rolling). The teacher puts out marbles and balls of various sizes and weights, and eventually introduces a rubber doll for the children to try to knock down.

c. INCLINE (rolling). The teacher sets up two or three inclines on tables (triangular hollow blocks work well) and puts out balls and containers of various sizes. She encourages children to roll balls down the incline and catch them with a container at the end of the incline. Later, she asks them to set the container on the floor so the ball will fall into it.

d. THROWING BALLS. The teacher puts out a few large balls near a wall and encourages children to throw them against the wall. The children can study the ball's bouncing back by catching it or aiming it at a target.

e. DRIVING A TRUCK WITH ROPES (pulling). The teacher ties a laundry cord to the back of a toy truck and gives the free end to a child to pull the truck backward. She ties a second, longer rope to the front of the truck, passes it behind the leg of a table as shown in Figure 2, and gives that free end to the child. The general procedure is for the child to "drive" the truck by pulling the ropes, and mentally coordinate the fact that the same action produces opposite results (pulling one rope makes the truck go *backward,* while pulling the other one makes the truck go *forward*). Incidentally, words such as "backward" and "forward" can easily be taught in the context of activities based on physical knowledge.

f. PENDULUM (swinging). The teacher suspends a rope from the ceiling and ties a unit block to the free end of the rope, very close to the floor to make a pendulum. She introduces a rubber doll for the children to try to knock down.

g. BLOWING. The teacher encourages children to bring to the table things that they want to try to blow off the table (e.g., paint brush, crayon). Cylindrical objects are more likely to move when they are in a certain position that enables them to roll off the table. After children get tired of blowing, she can vary the activity by asking whether it is possible to get wind on things without their actually blowing on them (i.e., by fanning, by using an electric fan, and by exposing things to the wind).

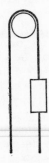

Fig. 2

In the child's construction of knowledge of the physical world, a certain continuum can be envisaged with regard to the relative roles of action and observation. The above examples are at one extreme of the continuum, where the child's action is predominant. When he pushes an object, for example, this action produces a simple, directly observable effect. At the other extreme of the continuum are activities in which observation predominates, and the role of the child's action recedes in the background. When the child goes around touching everything with a magnet, for example, the effects of this action are not possible for him to understand in the same way that he understands the effect of pushing an object. Nevertheless, the irregularity of the effects is fascinating to the child and helps him to develop his knowledge and, more importantly, his curiosity. Other examples of this type of activity are playing with a magnifying glass, cooking, raising plants and animals, and playing with reflections of mirrors.

Between the above two extremes are other activities which involve interactions among objects as a function of the child's actions. Below are two examples.

a. POURING, SIFTING, AND DRAINING. The teacher puts out water, sand, salt, rice, corn, and/or pebbles with various containers, funnels, and/or sifters for the children to play with. In this play, children quantify things, mix them up, and separate them.

b. PUTTING THINGS IN WATER. The teacher encourages children to put various things in water and see what happens, e.g., salt, sand, crayon, marble, candy, rice, ice cubes, Ping-pong ball, and a block. Some objects dissolve quickly, others dissolve slowly, and some do not dissolve at all. Some sink and some float.

2. Group games

Group games are not included in the child-development curriculum as educational activities. When they are used, they are considered important only for physical development, energy release, or entertainment. However, Piaget's (1932) study of the developmental changes in the game of marbles, as well as our own research (DeVries, 1970), suggests to us that group games can be used to promote cognitive and social-moral development. Games are uniquely suited to promote the development of cooperation because children are motivated by the fun of the game to cooperate voluntarily (autonomously) with others in following rules. Games require a great deal of decentering and inter-individual coordination, and children are motivated to use their intelligence to figure out how to play the game well. We classified games in the following way, and note below some of their cognitive advantages:

a. *Games without strategies*

(1) *Imitating* (for example, "Going on a Bear Hunt") in which children imitate the leader in representing ideas such as "running," "climbing," "swinging," etc.

(2) *Doing rituals* (for example, "Mulberry Bush") in which children do a ritual prescribed in every detail.

(3) *Collaborating* (for example, "Wheelbarrow" in which one child walks on his hands while another child holds his ankles and walks behind).

b. *Games of strategy*

(1) *Racing.* In a plain running race, children learn notions of "getting started at the same time" and arriving at the finish line "first," "second," and "third." Thus, there is a lot of *comparing* involved in this game. Races can be combined with physical knowledge activities. For example, if children have to run while balancing a tennis ball on a spoon, they have to figure out to what extent they have to slow down so as not to drop the ball. "Musical Chairs" is a particular form of race. Children learn number concepts in addition to figuring out strategies for getting a chair.

(2) *Hiding-finding.* In "Hide and Seek," for example, children need to decenter (to see themselves from the point of view of another person) and to reason spatially (think about possible places to hide or seek).

(3) *Guessing.* Piaget's idea about physical knowledge can be devel-

oped into a guessing game in which everybody closes his eyes and guesses which two objects "It" clinked together to produce a sound. A spoon clinked against a glass sounds different from two blocks, two sticks, or two spoons clinked together.

(4) *Chasing-keeping away.* "Duck, Duck, Goose" . . . is a well-known nursery school game. When we observe the mistakes made by many four-year-olds in playing this game, it is clear that ordering and spatial reasoning are involved (knowing in which direction to run, as well as the point where the chase ends).

(5) *Imitating.* "Simon Says" is a game of strategy when "It" tries to catch the other children making a mistake. (A child who follows a command such as "Stand up!" when it is not preceded by "Simon says" is out).

(6) *Remembering.* "What Is Gone?" in which "It" hides one (or more) of an array of objects while the children close their eyes is an example of a memory game which is popular with older children. Children use strategies to remember the objects, and these strategies involve a process of sorting and structuring the characteristics of a group of objects.

(7) *Inventing.* Piaget's idea of "make-believe" (Table 2) can be used to make up a game of invention. For example, the teacher can give a cylindrical block to each child sitting around a table and ask each child, when his turn comes, to show what the block can be. In a particular session, the children came up with ideas such as corn on the cob, a cigar, a pop bottle, a whistle, a rolling pin, lipstick, and a telescope.

3. Piagetian tasks

Upon becoming impressed with Piaget's theory, the newcomer almost invariably thinks of teaching Piaget's tasks in order to promote intellectual development. However, as already stated in the section on objectives, such an educational application of Piaget's work is a *mis*-application.

Although it is generally inappropriate to teach Piaget's tasks, and their use should never become a large part of the curriculum, we do not rule them out completely. Certainly, they are useful for diagnostic purposes. In addition, some of the tasks do seem useful in promoting certain processes of reasoning.* Below are two examples of tasks, or modified tasks, which we would recommend for use with children individually or in a small group.

* Other tasks make no sense to teach. We have already discussed why we do not teach seriation. In the case of conservation, the effects of teaching may be not only useless, but actually harmful. For example, if a child *believes* that eight objects spread in a long row are "more" than eight that are pushed into a shorter row, an explanation that the two rows are the "same" only confuses him and forces him to conform to the adult's "right" answer.

a. *Copying shapes with sticks.* For example, the teacher arranges four sticks into a square, or six sticks into a "house" (a square to which a roof has been added), and asks the child whether he wants to make a copy of the model. This activity helps children to structure space without being distracted by the motor coordination required in drawing the shape. Besides, sticks are unique in that they can be manipulated for successive approximation. Drawing, in contrast, has to be erased, and the child cannot correct the wrong line just by pushing it. This structuring of space is obviously an important foundation for the child's ability to read and write later.

b. *Classification by touch alone.* The teacher cuts two holes on the side of a small box so that the child can put his hands in it and feel objects inside, without seeing them. She puts an array of objects into the box and asks the child to sort them. (The use of a divider is helpful.) This activity seems good for many reasons. First, the child has to construct a mental image of each object by acting on it with his hands. Second, mobility of thought is stimulated by having to establish relationships among objects without looking at them. (By being allowed to look at the objects, the child can see many objects at the same time. When he can only touch the objects, on the other hand, he can "see" only one or two things at a time. Therefore, he has to think back and remember why he puts certain objects in each group, and how he should make decisions about where to put every subsequent object.)

Third, the child has an intrinsic reason for using language when the teacher asks what he put in each group inside the box. We had observed that some children sort objects, but remain speechless when we ask why they put these objects together. We felt that one of the reasons why the children did not talk in this situation (where everything was visible) was that they knew that the teacher saw everything that took place. Therefore, they must have felt, "Why tell the teacher what she already knows?" If, on the other hand, the child knows that the teacher did not see how he sorted things inside the box, he would have a reason for using language. Surely enough, many children started to justify their sorting when we used the box.

ORGANIZATION OF CONTENT

In general, we derive from Piaget's theory the moral that it is fruitless to try specifically to organize content for children. Whatever we tell children or show to them is bound to be assimilated in ways that are different from our adult notions. Fortunately, young children organize things for themselves because they constantly try to make sense out of their world. If they are encouraged to be alert and curious, they will even ask questions all day long until we get tired of them. These questions come from *them* and are rooted in *their* way of thinking. The specific information we give to them at these moments has very different meaning from what we might impose on them through our adult initiative.

Specific learning consists for the most part of superficial bits that are comparatively easy to teach. The names of colors, shapes, and sizes, terms such as "over" and "under," "smooth" and "rough," the alphabet, and counting are typical examples of specific learnings. We have nothing against these bits of knowledge, except that when the curriculum developer's preoccupation becomes limited to such specific bits, the result is a well-organized list of dull trivia. Our energies are better spent trying to figure out how to encourage children to be alert and curious. Duckworth's (1972) "having of wonderful ideas" should be the sharp focal point of our curriculum development. Specific knowledge can always be fitted into the context of wonderful ideas, but no list of organized content will add up to making connections among ideas and constructing a coherent, interesting system of ideas.

In other words, Piaget's theory enables us to make a theoretical distinction between two different ways of learning the same thing. Let us take as an example learning the names of colors. A child may eagerly ask for blue and yellow paint to make a painting. The words "blue" and "yellow" in this context do not have the same emotional and cognitive meaning as the same words in a question-and-answer session conducted by the teacher. Therefore, the depth of what the child learns is not the same in the two situations. Likewise, the teacher may teach words like "long-short" and "heavy-light" to a small group of children sitting around her with a variety of objects. These exercises tend to focus merely on discrimination and giving the correct descriptive word. We think that the same words can be taught much more effectively, for example, with a rubber band toy on which children hang various objects, trying to find something heavy enough to make the rubber band reach the floor or break. From the long-range developmental point of view, children who constantly use their initiative to figure out wonderful things to do are more likely to learn more deeply and go on creating new ideas than those who dutifully sat in a group in front of the teacher, waiting for her to ask a question.

• • •

PARENTS' CHILD-REARING PRACTICES AT HOME

While most parents readily accept our philosophy and entrust the education of their children to us at school, only some practice childrearing in ways that are consistent with this philosophy. Some even have a completely contrary philosophy deeply rooted in the conviction that what is good for the child has to be "taught," drilled in, or even beaten into him. Such child-rearing by parents at home attenuates the effectiveness of a Piagetian curriculum.

If the adults at home relate to the child in a coercive, authoritarian manner (giving the child little choice in matters which concern him), and have little appreciation for the unique quality of the child's thinking (and thus little patience with "messy" play, "silly" stuff, or "pestering" questions), the child may become constricted and unable to initiate his own activities or assert himself at school. Such a situation of conflicting expectations may put the child in a bind and make him anxious. After all, a four-year-old has deep emotions about what is acceptable and not acceptable at home, and these are the emotions he brings to school.

For example, we have seen children afraid of touching and breaking objects in physical knowledge activities. Instead of actively manipulating objects, these children refuse to touch them. Other children feel free to touch objects but not to express their ideas verbally. They have learned at home that the less they say, the better off they are. These children are seriously handicapped not only socioemotionally, but also cognitively because the possibility of acting on objects and exchanging views with others is blocked. Consequently, the possibility of developing an inner world of ideas is reduced. Some children, in fact, are such "nice" passive conformists that the teacher's overriding concern becomes that of developing autonomy and assertiveness. Other children who are constantly coerced at home explode into uncontrolled aggressiveness when the lid is removed at school, thus creating survival problems for the group.

Most children are amazingly tough, and they have a capacity for adapting eventually to two different sets of expectations at home and school. Nevertheless, they will always be in conflict to some extent if the home remains repressive or otherwise uncompatible with school. Parent education* is therefore important for the implementation of a Piagetian curriculum.

* We realize that it may be presumptuous to speak of "educating" parents because we cannot assume that the teacher's values and cultural background are superior to those of parents, or that teachers know more about the child than parents. However, we take the liberty of saying "parent education" because we believe that understanding the importance af autonomy is an issue which belongs to the realm of education. We also realize that there is a lot more to child-rearing than the child's autonomy. However, we limit ourselves to this one issue because it is central to Piaget's theory and because child-rearing in the broader sense is beyond the scope of this paper.

While it is relatively easy to convince parents that we know what we are doing at school, getting them to change their child-rearing patterns at home is quite another problem. Parents have had twenty years or more in which to develop strong habits, beliefs, and ways of relating to people. Even four-year-olds have already learned many habits that are hard to unlearn. Moreover, the momentum of well-established ways of relating to one another after four years of living together is not easily redirected.

We have tried various ways of working with parents. The details of these attempts are beyond the scope of this chapter, but we would like to mention that the parents who changed as a result of our work tended to be the ones who already had some appreciation for the child's autonomy.

Parenthetically, we would like to add that adolescence (before parenthood) may be the time when parent education may be most effective. Since the adolescent is not burdened with the responsibility of providing for a child, he can consider child-rearing issues without the pressure of practical concerns which often drain the young parent's energies. It is true that the adolescent may not have the motivation initially to think seriously about how to raise his own children in the future. However, he is vitally concerned with how his parents are rearing *him*. Since the adolescent is usually still under adult domination in one way or another, the issue of autonomy is one that is of vital concern to him, and he can easily empathize with the effects of coercion. Moreover, Piaget's work has shown that the adolescent's cognitive development enables him to envision a new world of the possible, rather than being limited to the social-political world as it is. It is this emerging ability which is often expressed in adolescent idealism. Since most adolescents are naturally interested in questions of human nature and morality, and are able to think about them in new ways that were not possible before, adolescence seems a fruitful time to educate toward parenthood.*

REFERENCES

BIBER, B., SHAPIRO, E., and WICKENS, D. *Promoting cognitive growth: A developmental-interaction point of view.* Washington, D.C.: National Association for the Education of Young Children, 1971.

* Experimentation in high schools, in conjunction with practical work in kindergarten classrooms (for example, Erickson, 1966), looks very promising. What happens when these adolescents become parents is a longitudinal study that seems worth undertaking.

DeVries, R. The development of role-taking as reflected by behavior of bright, average, and retarded children in a social guessing game. *Child Development*, 1970, *41*, 759–770.

Kamii, C. Evaluation of learning in preschool education: Socio-emotional, perceptual-motor, cognitive development. In B. Bloom, J. Hastings, and G. Madaus (Eds.), *Handbook on formative and summative evaluation of student learning*. New York: McGraw-Hill, 1971.

Kamii, C. An application of Piaget's theory to the conceptualization of a pre-school curriculum. In R. Parker (Ed.), *The preschool in action*. Boston: Allyn and Bacon, 1972a.

Kamii, C. A sketch of the Piaget-derived preschool curriculum developed by the Ypsilanti early education program. In S. Braun and E. Edwards. *History and theory of early childhood education*. Worthington, Ohio: Jones, 1972b.

Kamii, C. A. sketch of the Piaget-derived preschool curriculum developed by the Ypsilanti early education program. In J. Frost (Ed.), *Revisiting early childhood education*: Readings. New York: Holt, Rinehart and Winston, 1973a.

Kamii, C. A sketch of the Piaget-derived preschool curriculum developed by the Ypsilanti early education program. In B. Spodek (Ed.), *Early childhood education*. Englewood Cliffs, New Jersey: Prentice-Hall, 1973b.

Kamii, C. A sketch of the Piaget-derived preschool curriculum developed by the Ypsilanti early education program. In J. Torney (Ed.), *The prepared teacher*. Glenview, Illinois: Scott, Foresman, 1973c.

Kamii, C. and Derman, L. Comments on Engelmann's paper: The Engelmann approach in teaching logical thinking: Findings from the administration of some Piagetian tasks. In D. Green, M. Ford, and G. Flamer (Eds.), *Measurement and Piaget*. New York: McGraw-Hill, 1971.

Kamii, C. and Radin, N. A framework for a preschool curriculum based on some Piagetian concepts, *Journal of Creative Behavior*, 1967, *1*, 314–324.

Kamii, C. and Radin, N. A framework for a preschool curriculum based on some Piagetian concepts. In I. Athey and D. Rubadeau (Eds.), *Educational implications of Piaget's theory*. Waltham, Massachusetts: Ginn-Blaisdell, 1970.

Mantangero, J. Apprentissage de la voix passive. *Archives de Psychologie*, 1971, *41*, 53–61.

Piaget, J. *The moral judgment of the child*. New York: The Free Press, 1965. (First published in French as *Le Jugement moral chez l'enfant*. Paris: Alcan, 1932.)

Read, K. *The nursery school: A human relationships laboratory* (Fifth edition). Philadelphia: W. B. Saunders, 1971.

Sonquist, H. and Kamii, C. Applying some Piagetian concepts in the classroom for the disadvantaged. *Young children*, 1967, *22*, 231–246. (Reprinted in J. Frost (Ed.), *Early childhood education rediscovered.* New York: Holt, Rinehart and Winston, 1968.)

SONQUIST, H., KAMII, C., and DERMAN, L. A Piaget-derived preschool curriculum. In I. Athey and D. Rubadeau (Eds.), *Educational implications of Piaget's theory.* Waltham, Massachusetts: Ginn-Blaisdell, 1970.

TAYLOR, B. *A child goes forth.* Provo, Utah: Brigham Young University Press, 1964.

Play, the Essential Ingredient

Ruth Hartley

In recent years, as an awareness has grown of the importance of early childhood years for learning, some people have interpreted this to mean that they must take advantage of these years by systematically "teaching" children the things they need to learn. But, as Dr. Lawrence Frank is quoted as saying, "Play is the way a child learns what no one can teach him." In this article, Dr. Hartley examines the importance of play, explaining how each different type of "child's play" helps to further the growth of the child's thinking and coping skills. The importance of play is that it is child-directed, not teacher-directed, and as we have stressed throughout this volume, it is children who are the best judges of what they need to grow.

The voice of the hurrier is being heard in the land. We have not come unscathed through the crippling attacks of the developmentally ignorant who so recently sought to set early childhood education back into the dark ages of the Dame schools and the horn book. Many of us, including parents, teachers and psychologists, are still anxious and uncertain about the values of child-oriented, rounded basic early education, of which the child's own eager play is the chief tool.

"Play," said Lawrence Frank, "is the way a child learns what no one can teach him." More than ever before, we need to deepen our understanding of the power of this spontaneous, absorbed activity. We need to see what enormous and necessary contributions play and creative activities can make toward the learning and thinking abilities of chil-

Ruth E. Hartley, "Play, the Essential Ingredient," *Childhood Education,* 48, No. 2 (November 1971), 80–84. Reprinted by permission.

dren—toward the desired cognitive growth that is currently being emphasized almost to the exclusion of all other facets of development.

COGNITION—PROCESSES AND CONCEPTS

First, perhaps we need to review briefly what cognition is and how it develops. During the child's early years we can identify a number of *processes*, through which learning takes place, and key *concepts*, the tools that are needed for thinking.

The processes make up a fairly long list: identifying, differentiating, generalizing, classifying, grouping, ordering or seriating, abstracting, symbolizing, combining, reasoning. They involve a number of activities and abilities: attending, perceiving, remembering, recognizing, focusing.

The concepts needed for dealing with ideas are even more numerous. The simplest are concepts of objects, object-qualities, and characteristics of substances: form, color, texture, consistency, elasticity, permeability, solidity—the "thingness" of things.

Children also need to acquire many sorts of *relational* concepts—relationships of object to object, of part to whole, of part to part. Within these relational concepts are included quantitative relationships of number, ordination, cardination, equivalence, size, volume and conservation. These are based on such simple learnings as: what is more and what is less; what is larger and what is smaller, heavier and lighter; that a group is more than one; that a group of many is different from a group of few; that two small entities can equal one larger one; that objects can be arranged in an orderly progression; that a given amount remains the same no matter into how many parts it is divided or what shape it takes.

Young children need to learn about the qualities of space, which include *topological* aspects of proximity, order, continuity and enclosure, as well as the simpler relationships of objects in space: up-down, in-out, far-near. They must acquire concepts of time (today-yesterday, now-later, before-after), which depend on understanding sequences, beginnings and endings; and concepts of velocity, which depend on realizing the relationships between movement and space.

They need to know about the functioning of natural forces: gravity, electricity, magnetism, air, fire and water. They need to comprehend natural processes: growth, birth, decay, death. Finally, they must begin to comprehend the relationships of event to event—causation, which forms the substratum of all logical thinking.

To acquire all these understandings, a child needs, first and most basically, a wide variety of *repeated, concrete* experiences. Both the variety and the chance for repetition are essential. Only in this way can a child master the quality of objects—through his own relationship to them. He has to taste, feel, smell, hear and manipulate as well as see them—and he has to do this over and over again until he knows the objects so well he no longer needs to have them physically present to know what they are like and how they will behave in a wide range of circumstances.

By giving the child access to many different kinds of materials (blocks, paints, sand, water, toys of different sizes and colors, objects of the same size and shape but differing in color, objects of the same color but differing in size and shape) and freedom to explore them in his own way, we make possible the first cognitive layer—his ability to recognize objects and actions, to distinguish them from each other, to become aware of similarities and differences, and finally to abstract, to classify and to symbolize. All this comes naturally and zestfully from a rich, active play life.

SOME PLAY ACTIVITIES

A most important step in the development of thinking lies in the direction of problem-solving. Skill in problem-solving involves attitudes as well as information—a willingness to ask questions, to experiment, to explore different ways of doing things, to try out alternatives. For the development of these attitudes the free give-and-take of the play world is the best of all contexts and the structured tasks of rote learning the worst. Let us look at some specific play materials to see how play serves these functions.

Fingerpainting and mindbuilding

Few people consider fingerpainting a mindbuilding activity. But notice what is happening while a child fingerpaints. First he learns what the fingerpaint "feels" like—part of the multisensory input considered so important for getting children ready to learn in more abstract fashion. Then he notices that *he* is producing an effect, which has a visible form. At the same time he gets muscle-sensations from the movements he is making, so that the form he sees and the movement sensations he feels are connected; and he gets to know the forms he is producing in the most basic fashion, from the inside out. He then goes on to learn color differences and color-blending, how to create more subtle effects with colors and more complex and rhythmic designs than he can with any other means. His own intimate body rhythms and natural motoric responses become externalized as aspects of the outside world, which he has produced. When the child can so easily create welcome impressions on the world, he is encouraged to keep on doing, trying, experimenting—all activities that go into making creative learners.

Playing with water

Now let us look at waterplay, another too frequently disregarded form of play that packs a powerful intellectual punch if made available correctly. What can children learn from waterplay? What can they not learn?

First, of course, there is the lovely *feel* of the stuff—the sheer *pleasure* of playing with water. This pleasure is extremely important to learning because it encourages the child to explore, to try out different ways of handling it. Here at once we have two essentials of intellectual growth—*interest and experimentation.* This stuff we call water—probably the best thing we can find for lengthening the interest span of jumpy, short-spanned children—leads to spontaneous exercises in control and in estimating quantity. Waterplay offers, too, the kinds of experiences of reversibility that are essential to developing an understanding of conservation.

Blocks and spaces

Wise teachers know that in manipulating objects and themselves in play children are laying the groundwork for mathematics, physics, geography. Blockplay, for example, offers opportunities for discovering equivalences (leading to understanding fractions); concepts of size, form, quantity, directionality, gravity (balance); and the whole gamut of spatial relationships. But always we must remember it is the child's spontaneous interest that furnishes the steam. And the teacher's knowledge gives focus and form, by varying the materials made available and letting the child take them over in his own way.

While "playing" with blocks children are practicing seriation, gaining skills in the dynamics of balance, learning cause and effect in physical relationships. The properties of size and spatial relations are reinforced as they fit cylinders into each other, as they pile graduated blocks into towers and pyramids. The properties of space are most intimately learned as they climb jungle gyms, nets, ropes and ladders; as they guide wagons, platforms and tricycles around obstacles; as they swing their bodies through arcs, try to cram themselves into crannies too small for them, create spirals and serpentines as they twist and weave around the playground.

The world's a stage

Dramatic play, perhaps the most prevalent type of play, is rarely appreciated for its mindbuilding functions. Yet we must realize that the child uses dramatic play to master the meaning of adult behavior. To this end he plays imitative sequences of family life over and over. He is mastering the ways of the adult world in the same way he earlier mastered the skills of walking and climbing and throwing—by sheer repetitive practice.

Another step in mental development, one we might call mental digestion, is taken when a child is able to express his perception of an object through action. The infant uses his body constantly to learn about the world: objects become meaningful to him only through sensory and manipulative experience of them. As part of his learning, he imitates them. Trying to open a box, he opens his own mouth. Getting to know a dog, he walks on all fours; if it licks him, he licks it back. He does not know that "a hole is to dig" until he has dug one. So he must complete his perception of mothers and fathers, teachers and postmen by enacting them; and this often precedes being able to talk about them. Giving the child enough uninterrupted time for his spontaneous dramatic play may do more for his language development than any number of structured lessons.

Another aspect of dramatic play related to intellectual development is its service in helping the child maintain a sense of identity and of continuity in life. Events are fleeting and discontinuous. They are like hit-and-run drivers, with children the passive targets or victims. Without the power to foresee, an incident is over before they can fully realize what has happened. Only by reproducing and repeating an experience can the child build it into his life. Through dramatic play the child transforms himself from a passive target into an active participant and *integrates* into his life what was itself only an *intrusion*.

VALUES AND PLAY

Cognitive growth is only one kind of development play facilitates. When we consider *values*, we find play filling another extremely important role. The values we see emerging in children's play relate to courage and curiosity, commitment without reserve, self-acceptance, optimism, gaiety, cooperation and emotional maturity.

We do not always approve all the values play behavior expresses, but even those we disapprove are worth thinking about. Two spring to mind immediately: sex play and aggression. These are types of play that cause parents and teachers the greatest amount of discomfort. Yet, when we consider them calmly, what do they mean?

Sex play

The little boy who explains to the male observer, "Now we show our pee-pees," in the same tone he might use to say, "Now we play with clay," is proposing neither a seduction nor a rape. He may be expressing self-acceptance, curiosity, growing fellowship with others of his own sex, trust in adults. He may also be asking for reassurance about his own adequacy or for more information about sex differences and attributes. So, too, the common games of "doctor," the toilet-room "peeking," the naptime masturbation reflect wholly reasonable urges to know and to experience, that in later guises are approved and are sought as positive values.

Aggression

Acts of aggression in play often cause real dismay. But they can be instrumental in building courage and cooperation. The toddler who strikes out in defense of a toy is showing a blessed self-confidence we would all like to see preserved. Even the unregimented snatcher, whose means we cannot condone, sometimes compels our admiration for his boldness, lack of fear, directness in approaching challenges. Every child who bounds up to a new piece of equipment to try it out, or who squeezes a handful of clay for the first time, is manifesting a flexibility and an affirmative spirit that call for cherishing. The tenderness with which a little girl puts her doll to bed, her devotion to the care of her "house" and the "daddy" bespeak a deep willingness to provide nurturance, to create order, to know joy in serving. No, it is not difficult to discover the basis for values in children's play. Our challenge is to *maintain* these so that they may find fruition in adulthood.

Finally, let me remind you that the utility of play does not end when academic learning begins. The core of play, the child's own intrinsic absorption in mastery, continues to provide energy for the learning enterprise. The ability of the teacher to prepare an evocative environment and to utilize the teachable moment gives guidance and form.

Research of D. E. M. Gardner

Research data and models are available for the teacher with courage to pursue a "play-centered" or "child-centered" program for systematic academic learning. Perhaps the most compelling research is that of

Dorothy E. M. Gardner, who has received the Order of the British Empire for her contributions to education. She compared children who had spent their school lives in child-centered schools, where *their* interests largely served as drive and directive, with a carefully matched group of others from good traditional schools. She evaluated mathematical skills, language usage, science knowledge and creative abilities. She found that in none of the traditional subject matters were the pupils from the child-centered schools inferior, while they were clearly superior in activities calling for invention and originality. The relevance of this research is undeniable. Few will disagree that, of all things we need now and in the future, original thinkers and problem-solvers head the list.

The Play Way

Why, then, is play being derogated and opportunities for play destroyed, even by well-meaning teachers? Unfortunately, many who deal with children have not received the training to enable them to understand the kind of organic learning that proceeds from knowledgeable use of play and wise provision of play opportunities, including enough uninterrupted *time* for play. It is triply unfortunate that many persons who make policy in schools and centers and many who evaluate programs know even less about this aspect of child growth than those in direct contact with children. The ability to promote the optimal development of children through the "play way" requires deep understanding and sensitivity to the unique pattern of each child's abilities and interests at any given moment of contact. It is built by mastering the vast repertoire of materials that can help a child achieve more and more complex integrations of concepts while feeding his self-initiated enthusiasm. It demands true respect for the individual, with flexibility and patience to adapt to *his* rhythms and *his* idiosyncratic patterning of sequences.

Admittedly, preparing oneself for this service is not easy. Ignorance cannot, however, be accepted as justification for giving the child less than the best obtainable. If we accept responsibility for serving children, we also accept the moral imperative to prepare ourselves to serve them well. It is no accident that OMEP (World Organization for Early Childhood Education) sees need for play opportunities for young children as primary in every country in the world. Let us go a step further—to demand that all who voluntarily undertake to guide children acquire the knowledge needed to guard and to enlarge the precious right and necessity of childhood—the right to play richly, joyously and freely.

Resources

On the following pages, we have included a number of resources. The list includes books that will give you more in-depth information about how children develop and learn as well as books that suggest ideas for activities, equipment, and materials for young children in a learning environment. Occasionally, a resource may be marked with an asterisk. This is to indicate those books that are especially valuable sources of information or that you might want to go to first to get a simple introduction to the area of child development or early childhood education.

There are many more books dealing with children than we have listed here. We have included some of the foremost "classics" in the field. In addition, we have tried to select a small number of resources that consistently have been useful to and enjoyed by those to whom we have recommended them. We suggest to readers who are interested in pursuing further some of the ideas presented in *Growing With Children* that you also consult the bibliographies at the ends of the reading selections. In addition, as you may recall, we included in footnotes within the text, reference to books and articles related to topics being discussed. Don't forget to recheck those since many of them have not been repeated in the list of resources.

A much more extensive list of resources, including newsletters, journals, and books in various areas related to children and their care can be found in our first book, *Child Development and Early Childhood Education,* which is included in the resource list that follows. In particular, on pages 103–121 are contained appendices including: listings of appropriate toys and materials for different age levels (useful for selecting gifts for your own and others' children); sources of materials, toys, furniture, etc.; resources for selection of books, movies, and other media materials for children; resources about children's development and education; resources about day care; resources about learning problems; resources about testing and evaluation; lists of free and inexpensive newsletters; and listing of some interesting and helpful magazines.

* ANDERSON, R., and H. SHANE, *As The Twig Is Bent: Readings in Early Childhood Education.* New York: Houghton Mifflin Co., 1971.

Appalachian Regional Commission, *Programs for Young Children*: Part I— *Education and Day Care,* Part II—*Nutrition,* Part III—*Health,* Part IV— *Equipment and Facilities,* Part V—*Funding for Young Children.* Washington, D.C.: Appalachian Regional Commission, 1666 Connecticut Ave., N.W. Washington, D.C. 20235, 1970.

AUSUBEL, D., and E. SULLIVAN, *Theory and Problems of Child Development,* 2nd ed. New York: Grune and Stratton, 1970.

BLOOM, B., *Stability and Change in Human Characteristics.* New York: John Wiley & Sons, 1964.

BRACKBILL, Y., ed., *Infancy and Early Childhood.* New York: Free Press, Macmillan Co., 1967.

* BRAGA, J., and L. BRAGA, *Child Development and Early Childhood Education: A Guide for Parents and Teachers.* Chicago: Office of the Mayor and Model Cities—CCUO, 1973. Available for $5.00 from Model Cities, Public Information Service, 640 N. LaSalle, Chicago, 60610.

* BRECKENRIDGE, M., and M. MURPHY, *Growth and Development of the Young Child,* 8th ed. Philadelphia: W. B. Saunders Co., 1969.

BUTLER, A., ed., *Current Research in Early Childhood Education.* Available for $5.00 from: EKNE/National Education Assn., 1201 Sixteenth St. N.W., Washington, D.C. 20036, 1970.

CANEY, S., *Toy Book.* New York: Workman Publishing Company, 1972.

CHUKOVSKY, K., *From Two to Five.* Berkeley, Calif.: University of California Press, 1966.

* CROFT, D., and R. HESS, *An Activities Handbook for Teachers of Young Children.* New York: Houghton Mifflin, 1972.

CRATTY, B., *Active Learning.* Englewood Cliffs, N.J.: Prentice-Hall, Inc., 1971.

EPIE Institute, *Early Childhood Education: How to Select and Evaluate Materials.* New York: Educational Products Information Exchange Institute 1972. Available for $4.25 from EPIE Institute, 386 Park Avenue South, New York, N.Y. 10010.

* EVANS, E., *Current Influences in Early Childhood Education.* New York: Holt, Rinehart and Winston, 1971.

FRAIBERG, S., *The Magic Years.* New York: Scribners, 1959.

GERHARDT, L., *Moving and Knowing.* Englewood Cliffs, N.J.: Prentice-Hall, Inc., 1973.

* GESELL, A., and F. ILG, *Infant and Child in the Culture of Today.* New York: Harper and Row, 1943.

GINSBURG, H., and S. OPPER, *Piaget's Theory of Intellectual Development: An Introduction.* Englewood Cliffs, N.J.: Prentice-Hall, Inc., 1969.

GORDON, I., *Human Development: From Birth through Adolescence,* 2nd ed. New York: Harper and Row, 1969.

GORDON, I., *Baby Learning through Baby Play.* New York: St. Martin's Press, 1970.

GORDON, I., ed., *Early Childhood Education: Part II, 71st Yearbook of the National Society for the Study of Education.* Chicago: University of Chicago Press, 1972.

GROTBERG, E., ed., *Day Care: Resources for Decisions.* Available for $4.50 from DCCECA, 1401 K Street, N.W., Washington, D.C. 20005, 1971.

* HARTLEY, R., and R. GOLDENSON, *The Complete Book of Children's Play.* New York: Thomas Crowell Co. (Doubleday/Apollo Books), 1963.

HENDERSON, J., *Emergency Medical Guide,* 3rd ed. New York: McGraw-Hill Book Company, 1973.

* HESS, R., and D. CROFT, *Teachers of Young Children.* New York: Houghton Mifflin, 1972.

HURLOCK, E., *Child Growth and Development.* New York: McGraw-Hill Book Company, 1970.

* JERSILD, A., *Child Psychology,* 6th ed. Englewood Cliffs, N.J.: Prentice-Hall, Inc., 1968.

KING, E., *Educating Young Children . . . Sociological Interpretations.* Dubuque, Iowa: Wm. C. Brown Company Publishers, 1973.

* LANDAU, E., S. EPSTEIN, and A. STONE, eds., *Child Development Through Literature.* Englewood Cliffs, N.J.: Prentice-Hall, Inc., 1972.

LANDRETH, C., *Early Childhood,* 2nd ed. New York: Alfred A. Knopf, 1967.

LORTON, M., *Workjobs: Activity-Centered Learning for Early Childhood Education.* Menlo Park, Calif.: Addison-Wesley Publishing Company, 1972.

* MALOTT, R., *Contingency Management:* Kalamazoo, Mich.: Behaviordelia, 1972. (This book presents the principles of behavior modification in a comic book format.) Available from Behaviordelia, P.O. Box 1044, Kalamazoo, Mich. 49001.

* MONTESSORI, M., *The Absorbent Mind,* 2nd ed. New York: Holt, Rinehart and Winston (Dell Paperback), 1967.

MURPHY, L. and E. LEEPER, *Caring for Children*—No. 1: *The Ways Children Learn,* No. 2: *More Than a Teacher,* No. 3: *Preparing for Change,* No. 4: *Away from Bedlam,* No. 5: *The Vulnerable Child.* Washington, D.C.: U.S. Dept. of Health, Education, and Welfare, 1970. Available for 45¢ each from the Superintendent of Documents, U.S. Government Printing Office, Washington, D.C. 20402.

MUSSEN, P., ed., *Carmichael's Manual of Child Psychology, vols. I and II,* 3rd ed. New York: John Wiley & Sons, 1970.

MUSSEN, P., *The Psychological Development of the Child,* 2nd ed. Englewood Cliffs, N.J.: Prentice-Hall, Inc., 1973.

* RASMUSSEN, M., ed., *Creating with Materials for Work and Play.* ACEI Bulletin No. 5, Washington, D.C.: Association for Childhood Education In-

ternational, 1957. Available for 75¢ from ACEI, 3615 Wisconsin Avenue N.W., Washington, D.C. 20016.

* Roe, R., ed., *Developmental Psychology Today*. Del Mar, Calif.: C.R.M. Books, 1971.

Smart, M., and R. Smart, *Children*, 2nd ed. New York: The Macmillan Co., 1972.

Spodek, B., *Teaching in the Early Years*. Englewood Cliffs, N.J.: Prentice-Hall, Inc., 1972.

* Stant, M., *The Young Child: His Activities and Materials*. Englewood Cliffs, N.J.: Prentice-Hall, Inc., 1972.

* Stone, L., and J. Church, *Childhood and Adolescence*, 3rd ed. New York: Random House, 1973.

Tilton, J., D. Liska, and J. Bourland, ed., *Guide to Early Developmental Training*. Lafayette, Indiana: Wabash Center for the Mentally Retarded, Inc., 1972. (Although intended for use with the mentally retarded, this document contains developmental sequences and related activities which are useful for all children. It is available for $7.95 from the Wabash Center, 2000 Greenbush Rd., Lafayette, Indiana.)

Weiner, I., and D. Elkind, *Child Development: A Core Approach*. New York: John Wiley & Sons, 1971.

Yamamoto, K., ed., *The Child and His Image: Self-Concept in the Early Years*. New York: Houghton Mifflin, 1972.